TYPING SIMPLIFIED

TWO YEAR COURSE

LOUIS A. LESLIE

PHILIP S. PEPE

AMERICAN BOOK COMPANY

New York   Cincinnati   Chicago   Boston   Atlanta   Dallas   San Francisco

TYPING SIMPLIFIED, LESLIE AND PEPE
Two Year Course
Made in U. S. A.   E. P. 1

FOREWORD

In the course of teaching 4,000 typing students, the authors have developed and tested a number of new and revolutionary teaching techniques. During this extensive experimentation and research, they have also put to use successfully, for the first time, other important and effective techniques. These are incorporated in *Typing Simplified*, which was specifically designed to be simple, to achieve higher accurate speeds, to provide practical office typing.

Here are a few of the many important techniques that have been written into this typing book:*

1. *First successful use of the sentence method.* No longer does the student have to learn to type by drilling on isolated words or nonsense syllables. He types sentences from the very first lesson. He types connected material throughout the book.

2. *First use of grouped letter patterns.* A new and revolutionary technique that permits beginners to attain a high rate of stroking from the very first lesson—through sentences scientifically constructed of grouped letters.

3. *Automatic reviews of entire keyboard.* Beginning with Lesson 6, the student automatically reviews the entire alphabet in every lesson in the book, in context. He automatically reviews in 20 per cent of the lessons all the numbers, special characters, and ten important points of typing style.

4. *Speed and accuracy building throughout course.* Intensive speed forcing and accuracy practice extended throughout entire course to build maximum typing skill.

5. *Elimination of score figuring on all timings.* For the first time students do not have to waste their speed-building time in figuring speed scores. Speeds have been prefigured on all timed writings whether short or sustained.

6. *Realistic letter production.* Intensive, office-type practice employing production forcing methods, intuitive letter placement, letter styles actually used in business.

7. *Provision for individual differences.* For the first time, lessons planned with "flexible" jobs so that the slow typist "completes" jobs as well as the fast typist.

8. *Simplified centering and tabulation.* For the first time, simplified centering without confusing double instructions for both elite and pica typewriters. For the first time, simplified tabulation without complicated arithmetic.

9. *Elimination of end-of-line hyphens.* Constant practice throughout the book in obtaining good right-hand margins without need for hyphenating.

Authors represent classroom and business. The experience of the authors includes not only extensive teaching and office work over a long period of years but also national experience as a business typing consultant.

---

* For other techniques, see also *Methods of Teaching Typing Simplified.*

TABLE OF CONTENTS

Showing Teaching Plan

NOTE: *Reference Section and Index on pages vii and xxxix.*

161 Typing Style Recall — Alphabetic Speed Drill for 5-Minute Timed Writing	162 Perfect Speed Drill — Alphabetic Speed Drills	163 Addressing Drill — Alphabetic Speed Drill (With each below)	164 Tabulation — Alphabetic Speed Drill (With each below)	165 Perfect Speed Drill — Alphabetic Production Letter (short)
166 "	167 "	168 Title Page	169 Manuscript	170 " (short)
171 "	172 "	173 Addressing	174 Tabulation	175 " (medium)
176 "	177 "	178 Contents	179 Telegrams	180 " (interoffice)
181 "	182 "	183 Addressing	184 Billing	185 " (short)
186 "	187 "	188 Announcement	189 Manuscript	190 " (short)
191 "	192 "	193 Addressing	194 Tabulation	195 " (long)
196 "	197 "	198 Invitation	199 Billing	200 " (2 pp.)
201 "	202 "	203 Addressing	204 Tabulation	205 " (short)
206 "	207 "	208 Program	209 Telegrams	210 " (short)
211 "	212 "	213 Addressing	214 Billing	215 " (medium)
216 "	217 "	218 Title Page	219 Manuscript	220 " (interoffice)
221 "	222 "	223 Addressing	224 Tabulation	225 " (short)
226 "	227 "	228 Directory	229 Telegrams	230 " (short)
231 "	232 "	233 Addressing	234 Tabulation	235 " (long)
236 "	237 "	238 Announcement	239 Manuscript	240 " (2 pp.)
241 "	242 "	243 Addressing	244 Tabulation	245 " (short)
246 "	247 "	248 Title Page	249 Manuscript	250 " (short)
251 "	252 "	253 Addressing	254 Tabulation	255 " (medium)
256 "	257 "	258 Contents	259 Telegrams	260 " (interoffice)
261 "	262 "	263 Addressing	264 Billing	265 " (short)
266 "	267 "	268 Announcement	269 Manuscript	270 " (short)
271 "	272 "	273 Addressing	274 Tabulation	275 " (long)
276 "	277 "	278 Invitation	279 Billing	280 " (2 pp.)
281 "	282 "	283 Addressing	284 Tabulation	285 " (short)
286 "	287 "	288 Program	289 Telegrams	290 " (short)
291 "	292 "	293 Addressing	294 Billing	295 " (medium)
296 "	297 "	298 Title Page	299 Manuscript	300 " (interoffice)
301 "	302 "	303 Addressing	304 Tabulation	305 " (long)
306 "	307 "	308 Announcement	309 Telegrams	310 " (short)
311 "	312 "	313 Addressing	314 Tabulation	315 " (long)

R E V I E W

316 Typing Style Recall — Alphabetic 5-Minute Timed Writing	317 Billing / Telegrams / Tabulation	318 Title Page / Contents / Manuscript	319 Invitation / Program / Announcement	320 Alphabetic Production Letter (2 pp.) / Addressing

BEFORE BEGINNING TO TYPE

1. The paper guide should be set at 0 on elite (small) type machines, or 7 on pica (large) type machines.

2. The machine should be set for single spacing.

3. The margin stops should be set at 20 and 80 on both elite and pica machines.

Illustrations of these operations are given in the Reference Section, R-66 to R-70.

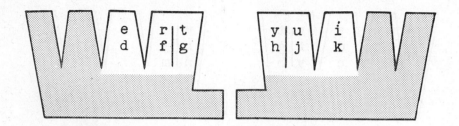

1. With the help of the teacher, learn the letters shown on the chart above. Type 10 to 20 copies of Grouped Letter Sentence 2, as instructed by the teacher, with the help of the chart if necessary. Then type 10 to 20 copies of Grouped Letter Sentences 3 and 4 *without* the help of the chart. The figure at the end of each line of practice material represents the number of 5-stroke words in that material.

2.

the three did feed the deer   6

3.

the judge did greet the jury   6

4.

the key freed the three deer   6

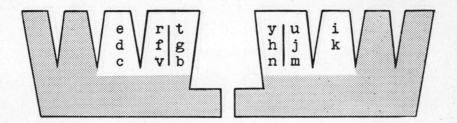

5. Recall Drill. Type 3 copies.

```
the key freed the three deer          6
the judge did greet the jury          6
```

6. With the help of the teacher, learn the letters shown on the chart. Type 10 to 20 copies of Grouped Letter Sentences 7, 8, 9 as instructed by the teacher.

7.

```
the men met them in the big inn          6
```

8.

```
meet the civic men in the inn          6
```

9.

```
the civic men meet by the inn          6
```

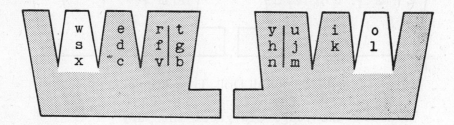

10. Recall Drill. Type 3 copies.

```
the judge did greet the jury        6
the men met them in the big inn     6
meet the civic men in the inn       6
```

11. With the help of the teacher, learn the letters shown on the chart. Type 10 to 20 copies of Grouped Letter Sentences 12, 13, 14 as instructed by the teacher.

12.

```
we will weed the good seeded sod        6
```

13.

```
we will sell the text next week         6
```

14.

```
we will fill the sill with sod          6
```

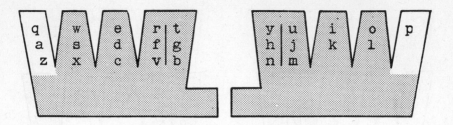

15. Recall Drill. Type 3 copies.

```
the judge did greet the jury          6
meet the civic men in the inn         6
we will weed the good seeded sod      6
we will sell the text next week       6
```

16. With the help of the teacher, learn the letters shown on the chart. Type 10 to 20 copies of Grouped Letter Sentences 17, 18, 19 as instructed by the teacher.

17.

```
all the tall trees shall fall         6
```

18.

```
the happy pet quit the happy zoo      6
```

19.

```
the queer deer passed the zoo         6
```

LESSON 5

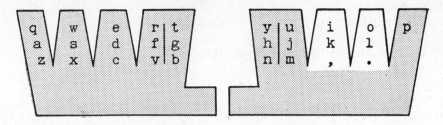

20. Capitalization. To capitalize a right-hand letter, depress the shift key with the little finger of the left hand; with the little finger of the right hand for a left-hand letter. Hold the shift key down until after the desired key has been struck, or the result will be raised letters.

21. Punctuation. With the help of the teacher, learn the punctuation shown on the right hand above. Space once after a comma, twice after a period.

22. Recall Drill. Type 3 copies.

```
The judge did greet the jury.  We will sell the text next       11
week.  Meet the civic men in the inn.  The happy pet quit        22
the happy zoo.  All the tall trees shall fall.                   31
```

23. Type 10 to 20 copies of Grouped Letter Sentences 24, 25, 26 as instructed by the teacher.

24.

```
The three free, fleet deer fled.                  6
```

25.

```
The cool, cool pool looked good.                  6
```

26.

```
We men were winning, in nine innings.             7
```

LESSON 6

27. Alphabetic Recall Drill. Type 3 copies.

```
The quick brown fox just came over to greet the lazy poodle.   12
The three free, fleet deer fled.   The cool, cool pool looked   24
good.   We men were winning, in nine innings.                  32
```

28. Grouped Letter Sentence. Type 10 to 20 copies.

```
The three shall shear the three pet sheep that were here.      11
```

29. Grouped Letter Sentence. Type 10 to 20 copies.

```
Little lilies will fill the sill by the little lily pool.      11
```

30. Grouped Letter Sentence. Type 10 to 20 copies.

```
The three steeds were fleet of foot to look for the pool.      11
```

LESSON 7

31. Alphabetic Recall Drill. Type 3 copies.

```
The quick brown fox just came over to greet the lazy poodle.   12
The three shall shear the three pet sheep that were here.      24
Little lilies will fill the sill by the little lily pool.      36
The three steeds were fleet of foot to look for the pool.      47
```

32. Grouped Letter Sentence. Type 10 to 20 copies.

```
That man may name a tall lad who was to assess the assets.     12
```

33. Grouped Letter Sentence. Type 10 to 20 copies.

```
There were nine singing in the inn as bells were ringing.      12
```

34. Grouped Letter Sentence. Type 10 to 20 copies.

```
He took the moose from zoo to zoo to look for good food.       11
```

LESSON 8

35. Alphabetic Recall Drill. Type 3 copies.

```
The quick brown fox just came over to greet the lazy poodle.   12
That man may name a tall lad who was to assess the assets.     24
There were nine singing in the inn as bells were ringing.      35
He took the moose from zoo to zoo to look for good food.       46
```

36. Grouped Letter Sentence. Type 10 to 20 copies.

```
He sees men who succeeded in winning access to success.       11
```

37. Grouped Letter Sentence. Type 10 to 20 copies.

```
It is useless for he sees these issues as useless issues.     11
```

38. Grouped Letter Sentence. Type 10 to 20 copies.

```
The five saved the very valve for the very vivid flivver.     11
```

LESSON 9

39. Alphabetic Recall Drill. Type 3 copies.

```
The quick brown fox just came over to greet the lazy poodle.   12
He sees men who succeeded in winning access to success.        23
It is useless for he sees these issues as useless issues.      35
The five saved the very valve for the very vivid flivver.      47
```

40. Grouped Letter Sentence. Type 10 to 20 copies.

```
She took a look at a good cook book to cook good odd food.    12
```

41. Grouped Letter Sentence. Type 10 to 20 copies.

```
The lass was as tall as a lady as she walked to the lake.     11
```

42. Grouped Letter Sentence. Type 10 to 20 copies.

```
We expect to ship the next new text next week by express.     11
```

LESSON 10

43. Alphabetic Recall Drill. Type 3 copies.

```
The quick brown fox just came over to greet the lazy poodle.   12
She took a look at a good cook book to cook good odd food.     24
We expect to ship the next new text next week by express.      35
The lass was as tall as a lady as she walked to the lake.      46
```

44. Grouped Letter Sentence. Type 10 to 20 copies.

```
The sea queen quit the quay quietly and sailed quickly.        11
```

45. Grouped Letter Sentence. Type 10 to 20 copies.

```
The just judge looked at the jolly youth and at the jury.      11
```

46. Grouped Letter Sentence. Type 10 to 20 copies.

```
The batted ball buzzed in the breeze like a buzzing bee.       11
```

LESSON 11

47. Alphabetic Recall Drill. Type 3 copies.

```
The quick brown fox just came over to greet the lazy poodle.   12
The sea queen quit the quay quietly and sailed quickly.        23
The just judge looked at the jolly youth and at the jury.      34
The batted ball buzzed in the breeze like a buzzing bee.       45
```

48. Balanced Hand Sentence. Type 10 to 20 copies.

```
The duty of the man is to do a good turn and he shall do so.   12
```

49. Balanced Hand Sentence. Type 10 to 20 copies.

```
He is due to do us all a good turn when he is fit for work.    12
```

50. Balanced Hand Sentence. Type 10 to 20 copies.

```
It is due to turn down a bit and then it is due to land.       11
```

LESSON 12

51. Alphabetic Recall Drill. Type 3 copies.

```
The quick brown fox just came over to greet the lazy poodle.   12
The duty of the man is to do a good turn and he shall do so.   24
He is due to do us all a good turn when he is fit for work.   36
It is due to turn down a bit and then it is due to land.   47
```

52. Balanced Hand Sentence. Type 10 to 20 copies.

```
It is right to turn down the work when it pays so little.     11
```

53. Balanced Hand Sentence. Type 10 to 20 copies.

```
A bit of the fog is due to go right down to the busy city.    11
```

54. Balanced Hand Sentence. Type 10 to 20 copies.

```
He and they shall name the town when it is due for a name.    11
```

LESSON 13

55. Alphabetic Recall Drill. Type 3 copies.

```
The quick brown fox just came over to greet the lazy poodle.   12
It is right to turn down the work when it pays so little.   23
A bit of the fog is due to go right down to the busy city.   35
He and they shall name the town when it is due for a name.   47
```

56. Balanced Hand Sentence. Type 10 to 20 copies.

```
They wish to work for the city or town for the right pay.     11
```

57. Balanced Hand Sentence. Type 10 to 20 copies.

```
The busy firm shall cut the big oak and fix the eight signs.  12
```

58. Balanced Hand Sentence. Type 10 to 20 copies.

```
It is their duty to do the work and then the town shall pay.  12
```

LESSON 14

59. Alphabetic Recall Drill. Type 3 copies.

```
The quick brown fox just came over to greet the lazy poodle.   12
They wish to work for the city or town for the right pay.      23
The busy firm shall cut the big oak and fix the eight signs.   35
It is their duty to do the work and then the town shall pay.   47
```

60. Balanced Hand Sentence. Type 10 to 20 copies.

```
It is the wish of the firm to do the work for the busy man.    12
```

61. Balanced Hand Sentence. Type 10 to 20 copies.

```
The firm is to do all the work for the town when they wish.    12
```

62. Balanced Hand Sentence. Type 10 to 20 copies.

```
The firm shall keep the good bus when it pays for the bus.     12
```

LESSON 15

63. Alphabetic Recall Drill. Type 3 copies.

```
The quick brown fox just came over to greet the lazy poodle.   12
It is the wish of the firm to do the work for the busy man.    24
The firm is to do all the work for the town when they wish.    36
The firm shall keep the good bus when it pays for the bus.     48
```

64. Balanced Hand Sentence. Type 10 to 20 copies.

```
She works for a big city firm and he works for the big town.   12
```

65. Balanced Hand Sentence. Type 10 to 20 copies.

```
The firm is due to spend it all for the title to the land.     12
```

66. Balanced Hand Sentence. Type 10 to 20 copies.

```
The men work for the town with vigor for it is their duty.     12
```

LESSON 16

67. Speed Recall Drill. Type 10 copies.

She works for a big city firm and he works for the big town.   12

68. Alphabetic Speed Drill. Type 5 to 10 copies.

It is with one goal in mind that we desire to send you the   12
next new idea and that is for you to make it easy for all of   24
us to get to the big store when we are in that zone and wish   36
to shop just after we have quit work.   43

69. Alphabetic Speed Drill. Type 5 to 10 copies.

The five men began the hike to the woods and just when all   12
seemed to be going well it was found that the man who was to   24
fix the quart size jar of food had left most of the food   35
back in town where the hike had begun many hours ago.   46

LESSON 17

70. Speed Recall Drill. Type 10 copies.

The firm is due to spend it all for the title to the land.   12

71. Alphabetic Speed Drill. Type 5 to 10 copies.

The aim of an ad is to get the word from one person to   11
another, but if the ad does not get the word across quickly   23
and clearly and just leaves the reader in a muddle, then   35
the text is bad and the ad has failed to realize its goal.   46

72. Alphabetic Speed Drill. Type 5 to 10 copies.

We felt this was the most unusual place we had ever seen, for   12
right here at the base of the mountain one could just fish   24
or swim quietly in the lake, and if one had a mind to he   35
could next go to the top of the mountain and ski down its   46
snowy, lazy slopes.   50

LESSON 18

73. Speed Recall Drill. Type 10 copies.

The men work for the town with vigor for it is their duty.   12

74. Alphabetic Speed Drill. Type 5 to 10 copies.

He was chosen to go to the home office on the word of the   11
head of the firm who had put quite a bit of value upon his   23
work in the field and next in the office, and we can now   34
judge the wisdom of the move that was made by the sudden   45
rise in sales in all zones.   50

75. Alphabetic Speed Drill. Type 5 to 10 copies.

Many notes have just come to us in the mail from our good   11
friends, in reply to which we are going to choose the ten   23
best stories from the many that have been read during the   34
past two years, and we will quickly put them together in our   46
next prize book for all to read and to keep.   54

LESSON 19

76. Speed Recall Drill. Type 10 copies.

The firm shall fit the men so they will do the work right.   12

77. Alphabetic Speed Drill. Type 5 to 10 copies.

We found that the most successful ads were those in which we   12
presented a product and then offered to aid the customer   23
solve some of his prize problems, and because of the success   35
of that type of ad we are just now making plans to offer   46
quite a number of such services next year.   54

78. Alphabetic Speed Drill. Type 5 to 10 copies.

The three of us went by train, and as we got farther and   11
farther up the next valley it seemed to me the hills grew   22
taller and taller as well as greener and greener, but soon   34
after we got to the lake the hills became quite level and we   46
found ourselves in the middle of a sizeable plain.   56

LESSON 20

79. Speed Recall Drill. Type 10 copies.

The man turns and signs the form when he pays for the land.   12

80. Alphabetic Speed Drill. Type 5 to 10 copies.

The plan was to have all of us in that office make the next   12
trip to the meeting on our own, and then for most of us to   24
share the space in one or two planes of the size which   35
would be hired for the purpose of getting those men back to   47
the office who had to be back on the job quickly.   57

81. Alphabetic Speed Drill. Type 5 to 10 copies.

Mostly for the sake of helping to plan the future of those   12
who should wish to come into the club during the present   23
year, we have just put into our prize text the ideals that   34
are to inspire us all quietly in our dealings with each   45
other and in our dealings with those who do not plan to   56
enroll.   58

LESSON 21

82. Speed Recall Drill. Type 10 copies.

To do the work and also do it right he is to do it then.   11

83. Alphabetic Speed Drill. Type 5 to 10 copies.

We have just quoted in writing about the will to make dreams   12
come true and we have said that life holds nothing finer   23
than realizing by will and brain some vision that we have   35
had, and now we are glad to find more proof in a text that   46
this is one of the things that makes life truly worth while.   58

84. Alphabetic Speed Drill. Type 5 to 10 copies.

Day after day we realize that our work is bringing about the   12
desired effect, for those who come to our place of business   23
tell us that they can feel the spirit of this business just   35
as soon as they are in touch with us, which may be through   47
a personal visit or even through the text of a letter.   57

LESSON 22

85. Speed Recall Drill. Type 10 copies.

He is also to rush right down to the city for the signs. 12

86. Alphabetic Speed Drill. Type 5 to 10 copies.

No type of job we do is worth while if in doing that work 11
we have a lazy aim to do as little as possible to get by 23
until quitting time. The person with an eye to success will 35
make it his business to get into the type of work in which 46
he expects to put his entire effort and as much time as he 58
can. 59

87. Alphabetic Speed Drill. Type 5 to 10 copies.

We often receive letters of this type and in the past we 11
have found it quite feasible just to fill orders from our 23
limited stock, but in the last six months the volume of 34
letters has increased to the point where we can no longer 45
fill sizeable orders without interfering with our regular 56
and more important work. 61

LESSON 23

88. Speed Recall Drill. Type 10 copies.

The firm shall turn down the land when the man signs for it. 12

89. Alphabetic Speed Drill. Type 5 to 10 copies.

The job of building up a de luxe store that needs the work of 12
many men and women and the finest quota of goods that can be 24
made or found in all parts of the world, and also the very 36
best that can be found in the way of a building in which to 48
show those goods to the public, is indeed a sizeable and 57
noble undertaking. 61

90. Alphabetic Speed Drill. Type 5 to 10 copies.

Times may be easy or they may not be easy, but things have 11
been so fixed that this great firm moves toward the goal 23
that has been chosen by all of us and that is good, for all 35
of us like to feel that even if we slow down for just a 46
moment the quiet wheels of a firm this size will still go 57
round and speed it on its way. 63

14

LESSON 24

91. Speed Recall Drill. Type 10 copies.

They did own eight firms and the title for the right land.   12

92. Alphabetic Speed Drill. Type 5 to 10 copies.

From the edge of the high bluff we could see below us one of   12
the most dazzling sights we had ever enjoyed, taking in a   23
vast, quiet plain a mile below us that extended almost as far   35
as the eye could see in every direction and that was almost   47
completely enclosed by the hills that stood around the very   59
rim of the plains.   63

93. Alphabetic Speed Drill. Type 5 to 10 copies.

Our plan is to reward our staff by giving higher pay to   11
those people who justly deserve higher pay whether they be   23
new or old with the company, for no matter how long a person   35
has worked with us we cannot consider a request for increase   47
in pay unless he has shown that the size of his output for   58
the company has increased.   63

LESSON 25

94. Speed Recall Drill. Type 10 copies.

It is the right of the civic body to amend the pay forms.   12

95. Alphabetic Speed Drill. Type 5 to 10 copies.

The matter of the budget for the new year will be coming up   12
in just two months, so it may be wise for you to begin to   23
think about what the needs for your zone will be for next   35
year and in about thirty days to send me a quick draft of   46
the budget for your office in order that I may go over it   58
and suggest changes for the final draft.   66

96. Alphabetic Speed Drill. Type 5 to 10 copies.

The type of spirit we try to realize in our firm is the type   12
of spirit we heard about the other day from a friend of ours   24
who related that in calling upon a certain famous store he   36
came next to one clerk who was so happy with her work she   47
said she would have requested to do it without pay if she   58
just could have afforded to do so.   65

LESSON 26

97. Speed Recall Drill. Type 10 copies.

When it is due they shall rush the form to the town body.   11

98. Alphabetic Speed Drill. Type 5 to 10 copies.

There have been those who have just added the work of one   11
day to that of another without realizing where their hard   23
work would lead them and next found themselves a success,   34
and many of those had simply dreamed of their fine goal and   46
quietly set out with nothing but the force of their own will   58
and brain and made their dream come true.   66

99. Alphabetic Speed Drill. Type 5 to 10 copies.

Let us think for a moment just how many people benefit from   12
the work that goes on in this firm, and then also let us add   23
quickly to that number the number of people who exact benefit   35
from the work that goes on in all other firms of this kind,   47
and before long we will realize the part our type of firm   58
plays in the business life of our land.   66

LESSON 27

100. Speed Recall Drill. Type 10 copies.

It is their turn and pride to name a title for the theme.   11

101. Alphabetic Speed Drill. Type 5 to 10 copies.

In the future all mail received for this zone will come to   12
our new office girl, who will open and sort it and then route   24
it to the various offices on the floor, and who will at the   36
same time pick up all letters to be filed from those offices   48
except during the last mail delivery when it is not quite   59
feasible to pick up such late filing.   66

102. Alphabetic Speed Drill. Type 5 to 10 copies.

We might consider putting a new man to work in that zone to   12
sell the whole line of goods provided the volume of sales   24
will continue to go up during the next year, but should   35
sales go down or just remain at the same level, we feel it   47
would be quite a poor move to add another man and thereby   58
cut down the income of the present field staff.   67

LESSON 28

103. Speed Recall Drill. Type 10 copies.

It is their right to turn down that title for this theme.   12

104. Alphabetic Speed Drill. Type 5 to 10 copies.

While we were passing through this zone, we made it a point   12
to stop over and visit the branch office and to make quite   24
a study of the amount of space they can devote to a display   36
room, but we did not have to go into the matter too deeply   47
to note that this is a very crowded office that just cannot   59
possibly be expected to give up any space.   67

105. Alphabetic Speed Drill. Type 5 to 10 copies.

A man just cannot expect to make many friends among the   11
public by his first quick offer of good value nor by offers   23
of good value now and then, but if he begins with good value   35
and keeps offering it without letup day in and day out, he   46
is going to realize the number of friends among the public   58
that he will need to spell success in his business.   68

LESSON 29

106. Speed Recall Drill. Type 10 copies.

The town slept when the town civic body did the good work.   12

107. Alphabetic Speed Drill. Type 5 to 10 copies.

Nearly every good manager knows that a required part of his   12
job is that of producing new ideas which may come out of   23
his own head or out of the heads of those who work next to   35
him, but an even more important part of his work is to be   46
able to recognize the good idea from the bad and to put it   58
to work after giving its owner due credit for it.   68

108. Alphabetic Speed Drill. Type 5 to 10 copies.

A firm that manages through good planning and good work to   12
get to the top of its field gains a certain prestige in the   24
eyes of the public, and everything it does or produces in the   36
future is just expected to measure up to the standard that   48
is required by a firm of that recognized position or size, or   60
the crown of leadership will fall from its head.   69

LESSON 30

109. Speed Recall Drill. Type 10 copies.

The auditor and the panel of eight shall sign the forms.   12

110. Alphabetic Speed Drill. Type 5 to 10 copies.

We hiked through the hills in every direction and it began   12
to look as though we would not find a suitable place to   23
build a fire to cook dinner, let alone to put up a tent for   35
the night, but then just before the sun went down we came   46
upon a quiet clearing next to a lake and we realized it was   58
just the perfect spot for us to put up for the night.   68

111. Alphabetic Speed Drill. The semicolon is the guide key under the right little finger. Space once after a semicolon. Type 5 to 10 copies.

One of the party insisted we were going to do things the   11
great outdoor way, which meant he was going to try his hand   23
fishing in the big lake for our dinner while the six of us   34
waited and thought wistfully of the tasty food we had taken   46
along and could be enjoying quickly; but it was not long   57
before he realized starvation would arrive before the fish.   69

LESSON 31

112. Speed Recall Drill. Type 10 copies.

The panel of eight did sign the usual forms for the work.   12

113. Alphabetic Speed Drill. Type 5 to 10 copies.

Those of us who have done a great deal of traveling around   12
the country know it is quite possible to travel a thousand   24
miles and get to a town that looks but little different from   36
the town we have left, and that in some parts of the country   48
it is possible to travel to just the next town and come   59
upon an amazing change of scenery or climate or both.   70

114. Alphabetic Speed Drill. Type 5 to 10 copies.

I have a friend who likes to tell how he considers it one   11
of the most enjoyable forms of sport to walk quietly along   23
a country road after a heavy rain has brought out the mixed   35
perfumes of the surrounding foliage, and I agree with him,   46
provided one does not have to fight his way through muddy   58
roads in order to realize the benefit of the scented air.   69

LESSON 32

115. Speed Recall Drill. Type 10 copies.

If the men mend the chair the girl shall pay for the work.   12

116. Alphabetic Speed Drill. Type 5 to 10 copies.

Most of us have seen the ability of a person grow by quick   12
leaps and bounds when an important member of a firm has   23
suddenly turned over to him an exacting job that will make   35
him realize the firm has confidence in his ability, and that   47
person will bring to light latent abilities that might never   59
have been put to use by the firm to the benefit of the firm.   71

117. Alphabetic Speed Drill. Type 5 to 10 copies.

Many of us when watching a skilled person do an exacting job   12
smoothly and quickly have had the feeling that almost anyone   24
using the same tools could do the job just as smoothly and   36
swiftly, but what we do not realize at the moment is that it   48
probably took that person many years of doing to make a   59
hard job like that look as simple as he now makes it seem.   71

LESSON 33

118. Speed Recall Drill. Type 10 copies.

The giant oak did bow to the vigor of the men who cut it.   12

119. Alphabetic Speed Drill. Type 5 to 10 copies.

We think it is a good thing to mix in a bit of competition   12
among the various departments of our business, for we feel   23
that we can quietly build pride and team spirit within each   36
group and these in the long run will not only make people want   47
to produce more but will help them realize a bit of fun   59
out of doing a good job for the firm and for themselves.   70

120. Alphabetic Speed Drill. Type 5 to 10 copies.

We are convinced that the only way to mix into our business   12
a quiet spirit that will inspire every one of us in every   23
one of our jobs is for each of us to show in our work the   35
interest that will make the public want to come to our   46
store day after day and make our friends want to tell   57
others with zeal how fine a store we all help run.   67

LESSON 34

121. Speed Recall Drill. Type 10 copies.

Eight of the men shall rush the foe and may make the goal.   12

122. Alphabetic Speed Drill. Type 5 to 10 copies.

When we arrive we can talk to the field staff in your zone   12
on the services we have just made available to customers   23
and how these services can aid the field man in his selling, 35
and after the meeting we may be able to make quite a few   46
calls on key accounts, so if you wish to line up some of   57
these accounts now it will probably save time next week.   69

123. Alphabetic Speed Drill. Type 5 to 10 copies.

My suggestion would be that you complete the rest of your   11
trip by air or by rail before coming to this office, but   23
in the meantime send in a quick report on the stops you   35
have just made so that we can analyze the results of the   46
trip in detail and let you know whether we feel it is wise   58
to plan future trips of this type in that same region.   69

LESSON 35

124. Speed Recall Drill. Type 10 copies.

The man who works with such pride is due to do good work.   12

125. Alphabetic Speed Drill. Type 5 to 10 copies.

Although we would not wish our view on the product to be   11
considered official, we would say it is quite safe to   22
assume that if you have just received a sizeable order the   34
item has probably been accepted and you can expect it to be   46
added to our regular line of goods; if you have not received 58
a first order it is likely the matter has not been decided.   70

126. Alphabetic Speed Drill. Type 5 to 10 copies.

We can just make the changes in the book that you suggested, 12
but this would put the book in quite a different class for   24
mailing and we would first have to clear the matter with   35
the local post office to be sure there would be no delays   46
in mailing next year and also to get an idea what it would   58
cost to ship the revised book to the various postal zones.   70

LESSON 36

127. Speed Recall Drill. Type 10 copies.

Both of them wish to work with us and the busy title firm.   12

128. Alphabetic Speed Drill. Type 5 to 10 copies.

Each day the quiet little boy from the next lane would go   11
racing just past our house with a little hunting dog and   23
every day the little boy played at hunting large bears and   35
the little dog at chasing large bears, but I have always   46
thought that if even a large hare had crossed their paths   58
both would have left their prize and raced the other way.   69

129. Alphabetic Speed Drill. Type 5 to 10 copies.

A boss is not meant to be busy tending to details that can   12
and should be tended to by those who work for him, and if he   24
does take up his time mixing in small matters he is doing a   36
rather bad job of being boss. One can fill up his day with   48
minor matters and never get to those sizeable matters that   60
will mean success or failure for his business.   69

LESSON 37

130. Speed Recall Drill. Type 10 copies.

Both of them own the bus but he is apt to turn us down.   11

131. Alphabetic Speed Drill. Type 5 to 10 copies.

There was a time when an office head had to make just twenty   12
decisions a day instead of ninety and therefore had a few   24
quiet minutes now and then to size up the larger problems   35
of his business, but it seems that modern speed has fixed   46
things to deprive him of such free moments and force him to   58
set aside a special hour or so for such planning.   68

132. Alphabetic Speed Drill. Type 5 to 10 copies.

It is not just practice that makes perfect but practice with   12
a purpose. We know of six people who have worked at a thing   24
for years and have not made a bit of progress toward gaining   36
perfection; on the other hand we know of some who have made   48
quick strides toward this prize goal because their practice   60
was just a matter of repetition with a purpose.   70

21

LESSON 38

133. Speed Recall Drill. Type 10 copies.

She may do half a theme and then turn the work down to us.   12

134. Alphabetic Speed Drill. Type 5 to 10 copies.

In our organization we choose carefully among those who   11
apply in order that we may find those most likely to make   22
a success of a business career, those who have the exact   34
traits required for the job and the ability that will make   46
them valuable members of our business, not just those who   58
would like to enter business thinking they are fitted for it.   70

135. Alphabetic Speed Drill. Type 5 to 10 copies.

We think one of the next important jobs that business can do   12
is to find a quicker way of getting goods to people, for we   24
are all just realizing that this function is more important   36
than that of producing the goods, and we also believe that   48
it will be the business run along the lines of ours that   59
will help meet this need for improved methods of marketing.   71

LESSON 39

136. Speed Recall Drill. Type 10 copies.

The sight of the ancient gown is apt to make a man laugh.   11

137. Alphabetic Speed Drill. Type 5 to 10 copies.

If we could just tie up certain funds at this time we would   12
be quick to place an order for the goods we will need during   24
the entire year, for we feel it will be a long time before   35
anyone in our line of work will next have the chance to buy   47
goods at such a low price in sizeable lots; but it would   59
not be wise for us to make the move during the present year.   71

138. Alphabetic Speed Drill. Type 5 to 10 copies.

It looks as though the most important move we can make next   12
year is to call a quick meeting of all the branch managers   24
to talk about the many selling problems that have come up   35
during the past five years, and we feel it would be best to   47
hold such a meeting right in this city, not just because it   59
is near most of our branches but because of its size.   70

139. Speed Recall Drill. Type 10 copies.

If he is to go to town for the coal he is to go with a bus.   12

140. Alphabetic Speed Drill. Type 5 to 10 copies.

When we first enter business many of us may have the painful   12
feeling that all about us are people who are of much more   24
worth to our company than we are and because of that feeling   36
we may fail to realize all our job has to offer, but if we   47
steadily add to our knowledge, our confidence will quickly   58
grow firmer and firmer and soon we will feel that we have   70
earned the right to move up to the next step on the ladder.   82

141. Alphabetic Speed Drill. Type 5 to 10 copies.

For some reason when we first enter business we seem to have   12
two left hands and two left feet, for everything we do just   24
seems to lack the smoothness of the person who has been in   36
and around an office for some period of time; but it is an   48
amazing thing how in the next few months we seem to orient   60
ourselves and acquire the air that marks the old hand from   72
the person just coming into an office for the first time.   83

AVOIDANCE OF END-OF-LINE HYPHENS

In the first forty lessons the material to be practiced was presented in typewritten form, line for line. Beginning with Lesson 41, all practice material is presented in type so that the typist is compelled to decide how to break the material up into lines. It is not necessary to divide words at the ends of lines in order to maintain a good right-hand margin. With a little practice it is possible to save time and avoid possible errors of syllabication by refraining from dividing words at the ends of lines.

142. Perfect Speed Drill. Type at your best speed, striving for errorless typing.

It is the duty of all good men to have to work for jury pay.   12

143. Paragraph Indention. Throw the carriage, depress the space bar 5 times, press the tab "Set" key. To indent at paragraph beginnings, as in Number Drill 144, simply press down the tabulator key or bar (these are illustrated in the Reference Section, R-66 to R-70).

144. Number Drill. Use the small *l* for the figure 1. Use the shift key to type the special character given on the number key. Type 1 copy.

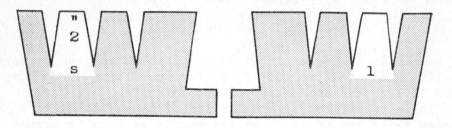

The 122 "charter" members formed the "122" Club and used the byword "122" at meetings, but after 111 meetings the members grew from 122 to 221 so 212 of the 221 decided to increase the membership to 222 and change the name to "222" Club.

145. Alphabetic Speed Drill. Type 5 to 10 copies.

Every week you will receive this letter full of amazing ideas and   13
information not available anywhere else at any price. If this   25
vital information were to be gathered by you or your company, not   38
only would the job have to be done at quite a cost but you would   51
not be able to get as complete a picture of what is new in this field.   65
Remember that you cannot get these exclusive data anywhere else.   78

146. Alphabetic Speed Drill. Type 5 to 10 copies.

If you would care to have one of our men call on you to talk over the   14
matter, just let us know when it will be convenient for you to see him   28
by returning the enclosed coupon to us. You will also receive   40
without charge a booklet that will give you details of our offer, will   54
suggest ways in which you can realize a plan to meet your express   67
needs, and will also answer questions that have no doubt been in   79
your mind.   81

147. Perfect Speed Drill. Type at your best speed, striving for errorless typing.

It is the duty of all good men to have to work for jury pay.   12

148. Number Drill. Type 1 copy.

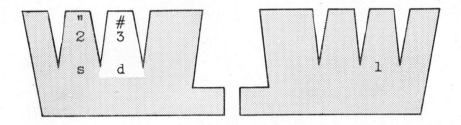

The 222 "life" members of the "222" club met at 111 West 111 Street. They decided to send 222 copies of Booklet #333 entitled "Good Planning" to the 222 readers who had received #331 and #332, and on May 3 to send 222 more copies of #333 to 222 more readers in Area #111, Area #222, and Area #333.

149. Alphabetic Speed Drill. Type 5 to 10 copies.

The remaining machines will just be replaced in such a way that   13
there will be no delays in our service. This gradual change in our   26
plant may take as long as two years, but we are quite certain you   39
realize that in the long run you will gain by this action, as we shall   52
continue to offer extra fine service and very low prices but to a   65
greater extent than ever before. We hope that we shall continue   78
to merit your business.   82

150. Alphabetic Speed Drill. Type 5 to 10 copies.

Some of the important things to remember in sowing a prize lawn   13
are to put the seeds in quickly when the birds are not watching, then   26
to hope for some rain, though not too much rain, or you can expect   39
the seeds to float away, in which case the birds might just as well   52
have had them. These are just a few of the many things to be kept in   66
mind and there are many others, like not sowing seeds at all if it is   80
too windy.   82

151. Perfect Speed Drill. Type at your best speed, striving for errorless typing.

It is the duty of all good men to have to work for jury pay.   12

152. Number Drill. Type 1 copy.

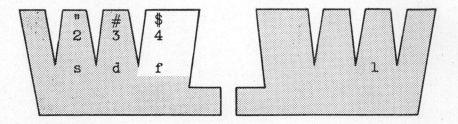

The 222 "life" members of the "222" club met at 111 West 111 Street. They decided to send Booklet #333 to 123 members in Area #333. The 123 members in Area #333 were glad to pay $4 for it, but the "222" club paid only $3, leaving $1 for the club fund, which now totaled $444, with $44 in cash.

153. Alphabetic Speed Drill. Type 5 to 10 copies.

We hope you will not think that we have just been lax in our reply   13
to your letter regarding your son, for we have analyzed it carefully   27
and have given the whole matter quite a lot of thought. The main   39
reason for the delay in answering your letter is that we wrote to the   51
dean and told him we should like to have his opinion and also what-   64
ever information and help he could give us, and to this letter he has   77
not replied.   79

154. Alphabetic Speed Drill. Type 5 to 10 copies.

We are writing you for we feel that a man in your job is in an ex-   13
cellent position to size up the type of man who would measure up to   26
the standards of a good salesman in our type of business, and also   40
because with your contacts you may know of men who might be   51
looking for this work. We take quite a pride in selecting our men, and   65
once they have been put to work they are assured of positions for   77
many years.   79

LESSON 44

155. Perfect Speed Drill. Type at your best speed, striving for errorless typing.

It is the duty of all good men to have to work for jury pay.   12

156. Number Drill. Type 1 copy.

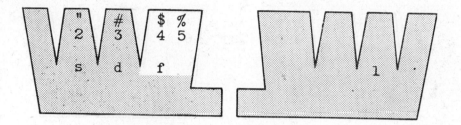

The 222 "life" members of the "222" club met at 111 West 111 Street. They sent Booklet #333 to 123 members in Area #333. The club fund of $444 rose $44 when $3 booklets sold for $4. The fund had increased 55% since they raised the dues 55%, and again 5% within 55 days at 555 West 55 Street.

157. Alphabetic Speed Drill. Type 5 to 10 copies.

If you have any friends who might be interested in membership,   12
we should like to have their names so that we may send them news   25
about the club. If you will quickly send us the names and addresses 37
of five persons, we will show our appreciation by presenting you with 51
a prize leather edition of our next travel book. We are sure you will 65
want to own a copy of the book, so start now and get your friends to 79
join the club.   82

158. Alphabetic Speed Drill. Type 5 to 10 copies.

Armed with a saw and other allied tools we next climbed the tree,   13
aiming to make short work of the job of cutting it down. After quite 27
a few hours of painfully hard work, we were ready to give up, having 40
by that time succeeded in cutting away a short length of one small 53
limb. One look at the remaining huge limbs and at the tree, which   66
still looked amazingly untouched, and we were happy to concede the 77
tree was master.   80

159. Perfect Speed Drill. Type at your best speed, striving for errorless typing.

It is the duty of all good men to have to work for jury pay.   12

160. Number Drill. Type 1 copy.

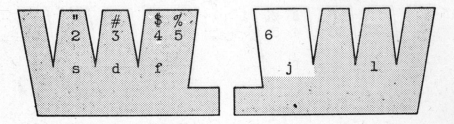

The 222 "life" members of the "222" club met at 111 West 111 Street. They sent Booklet #333 to 123 members in Area #333. The fund of $444 rose $44 when $3 booklets sold for $4. The funds rose 55% since dues rose 55% and 5%. The printing was done at 666 East 666 Road for $666, plus $44 for binding.

161. Alphabetic Speed Drill. Type 5 to 10 copies.

If you feel that the pen would not be suitable, you may be interested   13
in the long list of other items that you can purchase at amazingly   26
low prices. The items are given with exact prices in the enclosed   39
price list, but we must tell you that our supply of some of the items   53
is not very large and we will not be able to assure complete delivery   67
of your order unless it is placed quickly, before our regular supply is   80
depleted.   82

162. Alphabetic Speed Drill. Type 5 to 10 copies.

When our board finally decided to move, it also decided that we must   13
keep the plant in a zone where it will be within easy reach of our   26
many customers and that the location must provide ample space for   39
increased business. Also, it must be in a section where we can get just   53
the kind of labor we need to do a good job. After a long search, we   66
found six buildings with about four acres of floor space that are quite   80
ideal for us.   83

163. Perfect Speed Drill. Type at your best speed, striving for errorless typing.

It is the duty of all good men to have to work for jury pay.   12

164. Number Drill. Type 1 copy.

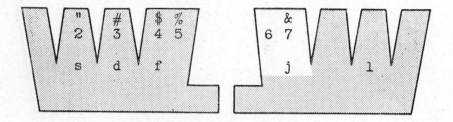

The "222" club met at 111 West 111 Street. They sold 123 copies of Booklet #333 to raise the fund to $444, a rise of 55% since dues rose 55%. Lee & Perkins, at 666 East 666 Street, did the printing. Reed & Low, of 777 West 777 Road, did the mailing for $777, plus $77 for postage.

165. Alphabetic Speed Drill. Type 5 to 10 copies.

Our company has been in this business for a great many years and   13
has a fine record with millions of people who recognize the very best   27
in quality. But a little slip on the part of a lax clerk may sometimes   40
offset the good features of our goods and may turn a customer away,   53
and for that reason I personally have made it a policy for the past   67
fifteen years to seek out and adjust these errors wherever they may   80
have been made.   83

166. Alphabetic Speed Drill. Type 5 to 10 copies.

We put in a quick call for the local tree man, and when he arrived he   14
had a crew of agile fellows with him who sprang up the tree and   27
swarmed over it in all directions, some with tools we had never seen   41
before. To our amazement, the tree just seemed to fall apart within   54
minutes, limbs and pieces of limbs falling all over the lawn; and the   68
next thing we knew two men were sawing away the little stump that   81
was once the trunk.   85

167. Perfect Speed Drill. Type at your best speed, striving for errorless typing.

It is the duty of all good men to have to work for jury pay.   12

168. Number Drill. Type 1 copy.

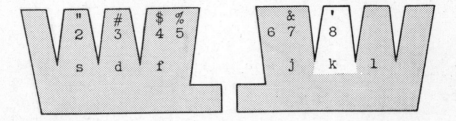

The "222" club met at 111 West 111 Street. They sold 123 copies of Booklet #333 to raise the fund to $444, a rise of 55% since dues rose 55%. Lee & Perkins, at 666 Road, did the printing. Reed & Low, of 777 Avenue, did the mailing. Low's staff of 888 used envelopes called "88's" for 8 areas.

169. Alphabetic Speed Drill. Type 5 to 10 copies.

Recently we asked one of our letter writers to compose a letter to our   13
friends who have not purchased any shoes from us during the last   25
year, and we asked him to write exactly as if he were making a   37
personal call on you. He wrote with zeal but no letter quite hit   50
the mark, for each one gave the impression that our firm could make   63
no mistakes, that our shoes were perfect, and that our service just   76
could not be improved.   80

170. Alphabetic Speed Drill. Type 5 to 10 copies.

Our friend is worried and he has good reason to be, for it seems that   14
there was a sizeable fire in his office and before it was finally put out,   28
it had destroyed most of his personal papers. He had made the mis-   41
take of keeping his tax papers in one drawer of his desk so that his   53
important papers will now have to be replaced; that will involve   66
quite a bit of trouble, and we are afraid some of the papers he will   80
just never replace.   84

171. Perfect Speed Drill. Type at your best speed, striving for errorless typing.

It is the duty of all good men to have to work for jury pay.   12

172. Number Drill. Type 1 copy.

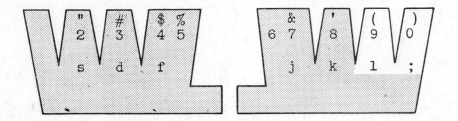

The "222" club met at 111 West 111 Street. They sold 123 copies of Book #333 to raise the fund to $444, a rise of 55%. Lee & Perkins, at 666 Road, and Reed & Low, of 777 Avenue did the job, Low's staff of 888 using "88's" for the mailing (only 999 went out in "99's" and 100 went out in "100's").

173. Alphabetic Speed Drill. Type 5 to 10 copies.

A manual of this size should set down facts that will make the em-   13
ployee feel he is part of your firm, and it should give him the answers 27
to questions about his job. In the first part there should be a good   41
deal of space devoted to the history of the company, and if your in-   54
formation is not ready in time to be included in your present edition, 68
put it out in a separate section at first; then include it in the manual 81
in the next edition.   85

174. Alphabetic Speed Drill. Type 5 to 10 copies.

The second day on the job found me delivering for the local food   13
market, and on the occasion in question I was just on my way up a   26
flight of steps with a bushel basket of food when at the top of the   39
steps there was this huge dog, which had not come to my notice until   52
we met nose to nose. All I can now remember is his big white teeth   66
and the next thing I knew my feet had covered a great distance and   79
were going with great zeal.   85

175. Perfect Speed Drill. Type at your best speed, striving for errorless typing.

It is the duty of all good men to have to work for jury pay.   12

176. Number Drill. Type 1 copy.

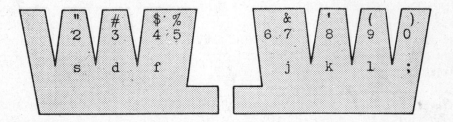

The "222" club met at 111 West 111 Street. They sold 123 copies of Booklet #333 to raise the fund to $444, a rise of 55%. Lee & Perkins, at 666 Road, and Reed & Low, of 777 Avenue, did the job, Low's staff of 888 using "88's" for the mailing (and completing 999 areas in 100 days, by May 9, 1954).

177. Alphabetic Speed Drill. Type 5 to 10 copies.

If an extra income would help you in the event you meet with an   13
accident or become ill, then play safe and provide for that income   26
now. The lowest cost way to insure that income is to share your risk   40
with more than one million members who carry our insurance,   52
written especially for people on the type of job in which you are now   65
engaged. You will quickly realize that our plan puts insurance in   78
your hands under the easiest terms.   85

178. Alphabetic Speed Drill. Type 5 to 10 copies.

You may not realize that you can read well for a few dollars a   12
year, and that it will cost you nothing to find out how. You can enjoy   26
current best selling books in brief form at quite a saving of time and   39
money, and you can become familiar with the substance of new   52
books in all fields even though you do not have time to read the   65
longer and more or less complete volumes. All this can be done   78
through our expertly planned program.   85

LESSON 50

179. Perfect Speed Drill. Type at your best speed, striving for errorless typing.

It is the duty of all good men to have to work for jury pay.   12

180. Typing Style Recalls. Given in this lesson and at regular intervals throughout the remainder of the course is a series of recall drills on typing style. Each of these Typing Style Recalls contains 10 numbers, 10 special characters, an illustration of 10 important points of typing style explained in the Reference Section, R-43. It also provides practice in tabulating for indentions. So that they may be learned gradually, one point of typing style is explained in each of the first 10 Recalls.

181. Typing Style Recall. Typing Style Point 1: The comma is always written inside the quotation mark. Type 1 copy. (The colon is the other character on the semicolon key. The hyphen is struck with the right little finger.)

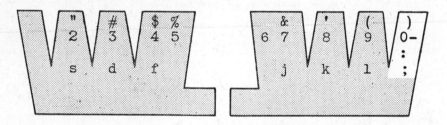

The dinner was held at 48 North 13 Street (Jones & Jones Building, Entrance #2), on June 6, 1954, at 8 p.m. Fifty of the 192 people left at 5:15 p.m. and caught the 6:04 train. Dinner tickets were $7.50, train tickets $2, and 20% or 40 cents for tax. "This meeting," the speaker said, "may be described as a 'self-inspired' meeting."

182. Alphabetic Speed Drill. Type 5 to 10 copies.

Start to enjoy our planned reading club at a saving over the regular   14
annual rate by taking the special offer at the rate that is now being   28
given to our new members only. Just as soon as you send the   41
enclosed form to us, with no money, the next magazine will be sent   54
to you quickly. Read it from cover to cover and if you are pleased   66
with that very first issue, pay only for seven months and you will   79
receive the issues for one complete year.   87

General Products Company
100 GRAND CENTRAL AVENUE
NEW YORK 10, N.Y.

July 6, 1954

Mr. D. W. Taylor
438 West 76 Street
Newark 20, New Jersey

Dear Mr Taylor:

During the past few months we have had so many calls
for our current price list that at the present time
we find that our stock is completely out of that
item, even though our order this year was for twice
as many booklets as we ordered last year.

We realize your urgent need for the material and
have asked our printer to send you a supply of them
by express just as quickly as the first copies are
off the press, and to follow that with a second
shipment later if the entire supply is not sent in
the first shipment.

                         Very truly yours,

                         John A. Student

JAS:J

LESSON 51. BLOCK STYLE LETTER (ELITE TYPE)

183. Keyboard Recall Letter. Type 3 copies of the following letter in block style. The elite model shows a 50-space line, the pica model, a 40-space line. Each Keyboard Recall Letter uses every letter and number.

(Date) Mr. D. W. Taylor 438 West 76th Street Newark 20, New Jersey Dear Mr. Taylor: During the past few months we have had so many calls for our current price list that at the present time we find that our

July 6, 1954

Mr. D. W. Taylor
438 West 76 Street
Newark 20, New Jersey

Dear Mr. Taylor:

During the past few months we have had so
many calls for our current price list that
at the present time we find that our stock
is completely out of that item, even though
our order this year was for twice as many
booklets as we ordered last year.

We realize your urgent need for the material
and have asked our printer to send you a
supply of them by express just as quickly
as the first copies are off the press, and
to follow that with a second shipment later
if the entire supply is not sent in the
first shipment.

Very truly yours,

John A. Student

JAS:J

BLOCK STYLE LETTER (PICA TYPE)

stock is completely out of that item, even though our order this year was
for twice as many booklets as we ordered last year. ¶ We realize your urgent
need for the material and have asked our printer to send you a supply of
them by express just as quickly as the first copies are off the press, and to
follow that with a second shipment later if the entire supply is not sent in
the first shipment. Very truly yours, John A. Student

LESSON 52

184. Typing Style Recall. Typing Style Point 2: The period is always written inside the quotation mark. Type 1 copy.

Lee & Brown's annual sale will be held at 22 South 14 Street (Level #3), on July 16, 1954, beginning at 9 a.m. and closing at 5:30 p.m. Ninety-five of the 180 items will go for less than $2, many at 70 cents, none for more than $3.50. "These prices," say the ads, "are really 'rock-bottom prices,' many being 50% of normal."

185. Alphabetic Speed Drill. Type 5 to 10 copies.

A new idea has been developed to help you provide an income for	12
life, far from the old idea of the old days when the only one way to	25
retire was to be rich. To get a life income you had to have a lot of	39
extra money invested in such a way as to yield a good return, which	52
surely was out of the question for most of us. Today you can realize	66
an income for yourself when you retire without touching your	78
present savings, by just taking advantage of our plan.	89

186. Alphabetic Speed Drill. Type 5 to 10 copies.

This business was organized more than thirty years ago, at which	13
time we had just a small plant and office; but in the next ten years	25
our business grew so fast we found it wise to move three times, each	38
time to bigger and more improved space. Our present plant has	51
served us well during these years, but once again we find it is	64
necessary to acquire more space and to achieve further our aim of	77
making ours the most modern plant of its kind in the world.	89

187. Perfect Speed Drill. Type at your best speed, striving for errorless typing.

It is the duty of all good men to have to work for jury pay.　　　12

188. Keyboard Recall Letter. Type 2 copies in block style, as shown in Lesson 51. See Reference Section R-1 for help in arranging letters.

May 2, 1954
Miss J. A. Grant
460 West 78 Street
Baltimore 23, Maryland

Dear Miss Grant:

The delay in printing and releasing your book was due to the fact　13
that when we checked with the local post office, it was found that　27
some material in the front pages of the book had to be classified　40
as advertising. ¶ While the post office will accept the book for　53
mailing, the material just mentioned would put the book into a　66
more expensive class for mailing to the various postal zones and, as　80
a result, the book would cease to be a profitable item. We have just　93
made several quick changes in the front pages, and the book can　105
now be released within a month.　111

Very truly yours,
John A. Student

189. Alphabetic Speed Drill. Type 5 to 10 copies of the body of the letter, as instructed by the teacher.

LESSON 54

190. Typing Style Recall. Typing Style Point 3: A quotation within a quotation is set off by single quotation marks. Type 1 copy.

Write me at Weaver & Smith, 123 South 14 Avenue (Room #121), before April 6, 1954, stating whether 7 p.m. or 8:30 p.m. will be the better time. Five of us will take 50% of the time to talk to your 625 salesmen and explain the $2 and $3.50 memberships and that for young members, which is 50 cents. "Our goal," says Mr. Lee, "is to sell the profitable 'full-privilege' membership."

191. Alphabetic Speed Drill. Type 5 to 10 copies.

We are looking for men who can be trained to represent our firm in	14
your zone, as we have a number of permanent jobs open there that	27
offer fine opportunities for men who are willing to work to get ahead.	41
We require men over thirty years of age who have had at least four	54
years of selling to business firms. Because in the next few years	68
there will be a great demand for services of this type, there is a	81
bright future for those men who stay with our firm.	91

192. Alphabetic Speed Drill. Type 5 to 10 copies.

We have made great strides in the way we go about living and	12
making a living these days, such as shorter working days and	25
shorter working weeks; but it seems to me future changes will be	39
made to make present gains look like just a good start. A prize gain	51
may come if we question the time of day we work, for it should be	64
exactly the reverse, so that we work under a roof in the evening and	78
not while the sun is shining and the beauties of nature beckon.	91

LESSON 55

193. Perfect Speed Drill. Type at your best speed, striving for errorless typing.

It is the duty of all good men to have to work for jury pay.   12

194. Keyboard Recall Letter. Type 2 copies in block style, as shown in Lesson 51.

June 14, 1954
Mr. L. V. Crane
Fayette Radio Company
678 North 30 Avenue
San Francisco 24, California

Dear Mr. Crane:

In reviewing our purchase orders for the month, we have just   12
realized that there were mailed to you two purchase orders for the   26
same model radio which, while it is a good seller, is not quite so   38
much in demand that it would be wise for us to accept both.   50
¶ The extra order was, of course, an oversight, and we hope you   62
can stop one of the shipments in time and make the adjustment   75
we have noted on the attached copies of both purchase order forms,   89
which show the purchase order to be cancelled as well as the one   103
to be filled.   106

Yours very truly,
John A. Student

195. Alphabetic Speed Drill. Type 5 to 10 copies of the body of the letter, as instructed by the teacher.

196. Perfect Speed Drill. Type at your best speed, striving for errorless typing.

It is the duty of all good men to have to work for jury pay.   12

197. Keyboard Recall Letter. Type 2 copies in block style, as shown in Lesson 51.

August 27, 1954
Mr. C. V. Walker
Ames Fabrics, Inc.
708 South 64 Avenue
Chicago 32, Illinois

Dear Mr. Walker:

Just two weeks ago today you wrote and stated that a new book   12
of ribbon samples would reach us by today. The book did reach us   25
today, just a few minutes ago in fact, and we are glad to say it was   39
worth waiting for. ¶ When we received our sample book last year,   51
we thought, and I believe we wrote you to this effect, that it was   65
quite a fine sample book and that it would be a factor in increasing   79
sales. But this edition is really a prize and we can wish for nothing   91
more except to have a second copy. If that is possible, you know   105
it will be put to good use.   111

Sincerely yours,
John A. Student

198. Alphabetic Speed Drill. Type 5 to 10 copies of the body of the letter, as instructed by the teacher.

LESSON 57

199. Typing Style Recall. Typing Style Point 4: Spell out numbers starting a sentence. Type 1 copy.

From 10 a.m. to 4:30 p.m. I can be reached at 508 West 17 Street. Thirty, or 20% of our well-trained staff of 150, will be here (with Smith & Company, Room #421) until August 6, 1954. "After that date," says Mr. Brown, "we can also dispense with this 'skeleton' staff." Most of our products will be reduced $1 to $2.50, and some items 50 cents.

200. Alphabetic Speed Drill. Type 5 to 10 copies.

We prefer a man who has not quite reached his maximum earning 12
power and who will be able and willing to realize a profit from our 25
training program. If you know of such a man, please be good enough 38
to show him this letter; or, if it is more convenient for you, just send 52
us his name and address and we will arrange an interview for him 65
with one of our managers. We hope you will feel free to call on us 79
any time in the future when we can render you any service of 92
similar nature. 95

201. Alphabetic Speed Drill. Type 5 to 10 copies.

I wonder if you are familiar with the many advantages that will be 14
yours when you join our travel club, if you know that you will be 27
given special reduced rates in the finest hotels and shops all over the 41
country. If you travel abroad you will be supplied with a list of de 54
luxe hotels in which your membership card will entitle you to special 68
rates. By joining now, you will receive a magazine that will bring 81
you quickly a lot of news that will help you make your travel fun. 94

202. Perfect Speed Drill. Type at your best speed, striving for errorless typing.

It is the duty of all good men to have to work for jury pay.   12

203. Keyboard Recall Letter. Type 2 copies in block style, as shown in Lesson 51.

September 18, 1954
Mr. T. T. Baker
Brooks Sales Company
760 West 38 Place
Denver 24, Colorado

Dear Mr. Baker:

I have just received a summons for jury duty, and while it would be   13
quite possible for me to ask for a change of date, a postponement   27
may mean receiving my next summons when I would be even less   39
free to serve, so I have decided to serve at this time. ¶ Of course,   52
this means that the trip I had planned through your part of the   66
country is cancelled for the time being, but I will write again   79
shortly after the end of my jury duty and will at that time inform   92
you of the new date for my trip in your zone.   101

Yours truly,
John A. Student

204. Alphabetic Speed Drill. Type 5 to 10 copies of the body of the letter, as instructed by the teacher.

LESSON 59

205. Typing Style Recall. Typing Style Point 5: Write clock time in figures, using a colon between hour and minutes; write a.m. and p.m. Type 1 copy.

Monthly dues of $4 to $5.50 must be increased 80 cents, a minimum of 14%, except those received before May 1, 1954, during the hours of 9 a.m. to 5:30 p.m. Twelve new magazines have been added to the present 167 at our Plant #4 library (11 North 14 Avenue) by Brill & Company. "This well-planned library," writes Mr. White, "is just 'bursting at the seams' with good reading."

206. Alphabetic Speed Drill. Type 5 to 10 copies.

We have just returned from your city, where we attended a meeting   12
with several people for the purpose of discussing the printing situa-   25
tion for next year, and we thought you would like to know if any-   38
thing important came from that meeting. It seems the schools of a   51
large city requested publishers to bid on a million copies of books,   65
and the question was raised whether the paper needed to print up an   79
order of this size would be available in time for opening of school   93
next year.   95

207. Alphabetic Speed Drill. Type 5 to 10 copies.

As often as we have made the trip between both those cities, we   13
cannot quite remember one occasion when we were able to get some   26
sleep. The first part of the night the train just seems to climb without   40
end, and we spend the time worrying that it is going to lose its grip   54
and roll back for half a day. The second part of the night the train   68
blazes down the other side of the mountain, and we spend the next   82
few hours worrying that the train will not be able to stop at our   95
station.   97

208. Perfect Speed Drill. Type at your best speed, striving for errorless typing.

It is the duty of all good men to have to work for jury pay. 12

209. Keyboard Recall Letter. Type 2 copies in block style, as shown in Lesson 51.

October 6, 1954
Mrs. T. R. Marsh
Jones Paper Company
340 East 87 Road
Seattle 26, Washington

Dear Mrs. Marsh:

Thank you for the confidence you have placed in our company 12
by purchasing our product. We are quite certain that over the 25
years it will give you value and extra service many times greater 38
than the amount of your original investment. ¶ Just as you are 50
proud of your products, we are proud of ours, and just as you prize 64
comments that tell how your products are faring when they get to 77
the customer, so do we. After a few months or so, if you care to 90
write us and give us your frank comments, or let us know what 102
service we may render, we shall deem it a pleasure to hear from you. 115

Cordially yours,
John A. Student

210. Alphabetic Speed Drill. Type 5 to 10 copies of the body of the letter, as instructed by the teacher.

General Products Company

100 GRAND CENTRAL AVENUE
NEW YORK 10, N. Y

January 30, 1954

Miss L. C. Adams
Croton Coal Company
874 West 26 Avenue
Pittsburgh 30, Pennsylvania

Dear Miss Adams:

   We certainly appreciate your inquiry about
our newest product, and we wish it were possible to
sell you one of our de luxe office models as we know
your office has an excellent application for that
machine

   As with all our products, we like to feel
certain that the improvement has no flaws; so
we are now in the process of placing a number of
machines on jobs in various offices. Although
machines marked for testing in your zone have now
been placed, we can arrange, in view of your
interest, to place one in your office if you so
desire

                    Very truly yours,

                    John A. Student

JAS:J

LESSON 61. SEMIBLOCK STYLE LETTER (ELITE TYPE)

211. **Keyboard Recall Letter.** Type 3 copies of the following letter in semi-block style, as shown on pages 45 and 46 (50-space elite line, 40-space pica).

(Date) Miss L. C. Adams   Croton Coal Company   874 West 26 Avenue
Pittsburgh 30, Pennsylvania   Dear Miss Adams: We certainly appreciate
your inquiry about our newest product, and we wish it were possible to sell
you one of our de luxe office models as we know your office has an excellent

45

January 30, 1954

Miss L. C. Adams
Croton Coal Company
874 West 26 Avenue
Pittsburgh 30, Pennsylvania

Dear Miss Adams:

We certainly appreciate your inquiry
about our newest product, and we wish it
were possible to sell you one of our de luxe
office models as we know your office has an
excellent application for that machine.

As with all our products, we like to
feel certain that the improvement has no
flaws; so we are now in the process of
placing a number of machines on jobs in
various offices. Although machines marked
for testing in your zone have now been
placed, we can arrange, in view of your
interest, to place one in your office if
you so desire

Very truly yours,

John A. Student

JAS:J

SEMIBLOCK STYLE LETTER (PICA TYPE)

application for that machine. ¶ As with all our products, we like to feel
certain that the improvement has no flaws; so we are now in the process of
placing a number of machines on jobs in various offices. Although machines
marked for testing in your zone have now been placed, we can arrange, in
view of your interest, to place one in your office if you so desire. Very truly
yours,   John A. Student

212. Typing Style Recall. Typing Style Point 6: Amounts of money, both dollars and cents, are written in figures. Type 1 copy.

The party will be given at the Lane & Lane Theatre (48 West 16 Court, Studio #6) on April 3, 1954, at 2:30 p.m. and again at 8 p.m. Eighty seats will sell at $3.30, 350 seats at $2, and about 10% of them at 75 cents. "Everyone," say the critics, "should see the first-rate hit, 'The Old West.' "

213. Alphabetic Speed Drill. Type 5 to 10 copies.

During the past two years the cover designs we have been sending   14
you have been based just on subjects related to the past ten years,   27
such cover designs being desirable because that period was a great   40
part of the life of everyone. We realize things have changed now and   54
our designs will now reflect the change, so that starting with the   67
series for the next month we are quickly releasing covers based on   81
themes such as the enclosed, dealing with the subject of business.   93

214. Alphabetic Speed Drill. Type 5 to 10 copies.

If a person has an original idea that he thinks is of value and that   14
he desires to submit to us, it is quite essential that he make an exact   27
report of the idea to us before we can decide whether or not we can   41
act on it. This company wants any person with such an idea to   54
protect himself just before he submits the idea to us, and he must   67
also understand that the company promises nothing other than to   79
analyze it and to decide whether it is interested in going ahead   91
with patents.   94

215. Perfect Speed Drill. Type at your best speed, striving for errorless typing.

It is the duty of all good men to have to work for jury pay.   12

216. Keyboard Recall Letter. Type 2 copies in semiblock style, as shown in Lesson 61.

November 28, 1954
Mr. C. D. Weston
Turner Shoe Company
438 North 60 Street
Birmingham 27, Alabama

Dear Mr. Weston:

The question of how comfortable your office chairs are may seem   12
like a very minor matter, but you must realize that your employees   26
may be working in a sitting position for as long as six to eight hours   40
a day. ¶ If the chair a worker uses causes the slightest discomfort   53
by reason of its being the wrong chair for the job, or the right chair   67
but improperly adjusted, you will lose efficiency from that one   80
employee. For that reason we should like to send a trained man to   93
make recommendations without cost for increasing the sitting   105
comfort of your employees.   110

Very truly yours,
John A. Student

217. Alphabetic Speed Drill. Type 5 to 10 copies of the body of the letter, as instructed by the teacher.

LESSON 64

218. Typing Style Recall. Typing Style Point 7: Even amounts of dollars are written without the decimal point and ciphers. Type 1 copy.

One hundred radios (Model #12), usually selling this year at $14.85, have been priced at $8 each, a reduction of about 45%. There are also 670 tubes at 60 cents each. "In this sale," the manager of Field & Cross states, "we must follow the age-old rule, 'first come, first served.' " The address is 33 South 14 Street, the date is January 2, 1954, and the time from 9 a.m. to 6:30 p.m.

219. Alphabetic Speed Drill. Type 5 to 10 copies.

To get action on important matters many men just turn to the	12
telephone, for they find that with it they can speed their voices	26
over many miles in any zone and get quick results. The telephone	38
is being used more and more today in selling and in every other	52
division of business, as its value is becoming more and more evident	66
to the person whose time is valuable. Managers in all fields of	79
business for a long time have seen in the telephone a quick means	92
for getting in extra selling.	98

220. Alphabetic Speed Drill. Type 5 to 10 copies.

Every so often I think back to the time when the most prized goal	13
to me was to be able to get on the squad of cheer leaders so that I	27
could kick my heels high in the air at the local high school meets.	41
After I had tried out with that team for a few weeks, the day came	55
when the top man of the team came before each of us just to see what	69
we could do. The grand moment came when I was to make that leap	81
high in the air, and in my excitement I am afraid my feet just froze	94
to the ground.	97

LESSON 65

221. Perfect Speed Drill. Type at your best speed, striving for errorless typing.

It is the duty of all good men to have to work for jury pay.   12

222. Keyboard Recall Letter. Type 2 copies in semiblock style, as shown in Lesson 61.

December 29, 1954
Mrs. S. W. Dunbar
703 East 46 Drive
St. Louis 28, Missouri

Dear Mrs. Dunbar:

Your letter explaining your interest in fine furniture is appreciated   14
and we feel complimented to know you chose to write to us about   27
your request. We have been in the business for more than ninety   41
years, and the type of skill we employ can be seen by the samples of   53
our work shown in the color booklet enclosed. ¶ Because of the size   66
of the job you are seeking to have done, we should like to suggest   79
that one of our designers call on you on whatever date you may   91
wish to set. Just note on this letter the time and date that would   105
best suit you.   108

Yours very truly,
John A. Student

223. Alphabetic Speed Drill. Type 5 to 10 copies of the body of the letter, as instructed by the teacher.

224. Perfect Speed Drill. Type at your best speed, striving for errorless typing.

It is the duty of all good men to have to work for jury pay.   12

225. Keyboard Recall Letter. Type 2 copies in semiblock style, as shown in Lesson 61.

February 2, 1954
Mr. John V. Hale
Hale Machine Company
834 East 76 Street
Dallas 20, Texas

Dear Mr. Hale:

We are happy to invite both you and your staff to attend a special   13
preview of a film dealing with a subject that is near to us today,   27
efficiency in the office. We must not tell you more than that, except   41
for the details of the showing which you will find on the enclosed   55
invitation cards. ¶ The special preview will be the very first showing   69
of this prize film and will be attended only by the press and by our   82
many customer friends of long standing, whom we consider part of   95
our official family. We look forward to seeing you next week at the   109
preview.   111

Sincerely yours,
John A. Student

226. Alphabetic Speed Drill. Type 5 to 10 copies of the body of the letter, as instructed by the teacher.

LESSON 67

227. Typing Style Recall. Typing Style Point 8: Amounts under $1 are written in figures with the word *cents* spelled out. Type 1 copy.

Fifty orders for Style #7 have been received and by January 1, 1954, we expect to have 350. Most remittances are from 25 cents to $2, but there was one for $14.50. "The one ever-popular item," says our order clerk, "is the book 'Wind at Sea,' for it accounts for 40% of our sales." Mail is now picked up at the Walsh & Company office (167 East 18 Street) at 10 a.m. and 4:30 p.m.

228. Alphabetic Speed Drill. Type 5 to 10 copies.

Perhaps you are the type that does not mind details and prefers to	13
do things his own way, with just a little help now and then from	27
those who have gone over the same road before. Should that be the	40
case, we have just the thing for you in our new office service plan,	53
through which you can quickly receive many suggestions that will	67
help you effect amazing savings in your office and at the same time	80
increase efficiency. We know you will find the enclosed text helpful	94
in your future planning.	99

229. Alphabetic Speed Drill. Type 5 to 10 copies.

We are not asking you to send any money at this time, but just to	14
tell us that we may send you the safe on trial and also what color	28
you would prefer. File your papers in it and use it for a few weeks,	42
and if you are then convinced that it is just the thing you have been	56
looking for, send us your remittance. But if you are not, just return	70
the safe to us at our expense. Please send in your card quickly, as we	84
have set aside only a small number of safes of this size for the special	98
offer.	99

230. Perfect Speed Drill. Type at your best speed, striving for errorless typing.

It is the duty of all good men to have to work for jury pay. 12

231. Keyboard Recall Letter. Type 2 copies in semiblock style, as shown in Lesson 61.

March 3, 1954
Mr. M. D. Greene
620 North 87 Drive
Los Angeles 34, California

Dear Mr. Greene:

We appreciate the many fine things you say about our line of 12
products and wish we were free to enter into an agreement whereby 26
you would handle our entire line; but as you know, we now have two 39
stores in your city representing us, and it would not be fair to those 53
stores if we were to grant another franchise just at this time. ¶ But 66
we have reason to believe that the present expansion of your 79
city will continue; if it does increase in size, we may be ready to 93
consider a third outlet in about two years, in which event we shall 107
be pleased to consider your request. 114

Yours truly,
John A. Student

232. Alphabetic Speed Drill. Type 5 to 10 copies of the body of the letter, as instructed by the teacher.

233. Typing Style Recall. Typing Style Point 9: In street addresses or dates, omit *rd, th, st*. Type 1 copy.

The store in the Stone & Company Building, at 63 North 14 Avenue, sells those time-tested pads (#803) at $2 and $3.75 and more than 25% of them as low as 75 cents. The store has been there since March 1, 1953, and is open daily from 8 a.m. to 10:30 p.m. "Our business at 'The Tablet Shop,' " says its manager, "is to serve your business." Five salesmen there serve about 600 customers a day.

234. Alphabetic Speed Drill. Type 5 to 10 copies.

If you are like quite a number of people who just put off planning	14
a vacation because you do not have time for an amazing number	27
of details, you will be happy to learn about the vacation tours we	41
plan for next spring. There will be many trips that will take from	55
seven days to a month, all depending upon the amount of time you	68
have available; and all you have to do is decide the trip you would	82
like to take and the amount to spend on the trip, and we will take	95
care of the rest.	98

235. Alphabetic Speed Drill. Type 5 to 10 copies.

During the boat outing someone got the dazzling idea that one of	13
the officers of the firm should take a turn at the steering wheel,	27
and it is said that to this day even those who proposed the idea still	41
flinch at the thought. First he would turn the wheel too far to the	55
right, and then, expecting to correct this, he would turn it too far	68
to the left, and this went on until our wake gave signs that ours was a	82
boat that did not quite know which way it was going, which was	95
correct, of course.	99

LESSON 70

236. Perfect Speed Drill. Type at your best speed, striving for errorless typing.

It is the duty of all good men to have to work for jury pay.   12

237. Keyboard Recall Letter. Type 2 copies in semiblock style, as shown in Lesson 61.

April 4, 1954
Mr. E. K. Hill
Lane Machine Company
807 East 24 Avenue
Detroit 36, Michigan

Dear Mr. Hill:

Replying to your recent letter, we do not think that the machines   14
coming out of your factory are causing us the service troubles, nor   28
the fact that some of the new models have undergone extensive   40
changes to make for faster office operation. ¶ We feel the difficulty   54
is with your service men and the condition has resulted from the   67
newer models. Acceptance of these models came so quickly that the   81
service men had not yet been properly schooled in their maintenance.   95
We realize, however, that this condition will resolve itself as your   109
men continue to gain experience on the job.   117

Cordially yours,
John A. Student

238. Alphabetic Speed Drill. Type 5 to 10 copies of the body of the letter, as instructed by the teacher.

May 15, 1954

Dear George:

As you know, the club members appointed me a committee of one to look into the possible purchase of new furniture when we redecorate the club next fall Although I have almost three months to get some good ideas, I am quite sure that is not going to be too long a time for the job

You know a lot more about furniture than I do, and I was wondering if you have time to go with me one day on a tour of furniture shops We could set the date at your best convenience. I realize how busy you are but hope you may have a free day to give me some of your good ideas

Sincerely

LESSON 71. PERSONAL LETTER

239. Alphabetic Recall Letter. Type 3 copies in the above style.

(Date) Dear George: As you know, the club members appointed me a committee of one to look into the possible purchase of new furniture when we redecorate the club next fall. Although I have almost three months to get some good ideas, I am quite sure that is not going to be too long a time for the job. ¶ You know a lot more about furniture than I do, and I was wondering if you have time to go with me one day on a tour of furniture shops. We could set the date at your best convenience. I realize how busy you are but hope you may have a free day to give me some of your good ideas. Sincerely,

56

240. Typing Style Recall. Typing Style Point 10: Hyphenate most compound adjectives preceding a noun. (Exception: adjectives formed with *ly* words—*a newly formed club*.) Type 1 copy.

Your order (#672) dated April 6, 1954, and addressed to Lee & Barnes, 784 North 13 Terrace, just reached us. Forty photographs, representing 10% of the shipment, were sent on the 10 a.m. direct-flight plane and the remaining 360 at 8:30 p.m. You will find most of them marked 75 cents, a few at $1.50 and $2. " 'The Three Bears' photograph," our art head states, "would be my first choice."

241. Alphabetic Speed Drill. Type 5 to 10 copies.

If you can just suggest the idea of working for us to someone you	14
know, you will not only help him earn good pay, but you will also	27
do a real service to the readers of our fine magazine. Your help will	40
make it possible to get copies of the magazines to them on time, and	54
that is why we are calling upon our friends in the city to put us in	67
touch with people who will give these readers the quick service they	81
expect. Without this help, we shall not be able to get issues out	94
at once.	96

242. Alphabetic Speed Drill. Type 5 to 10 copies.

The custom in the past has been to have a winter drive for members	13
in order to acquaint those who are now thinking of becoming full	27
members with the many things this club has to offer. We shall take	41
in winter members again this year; but we should like to say that	54
if any of your friends do wish to join, now is the time to do so, for	67
in this way they will save the entry fee. Since you have a sizeable	80
group of friends who wish to join next year, you can do these friends	94
a real service.	97

243. Perfect Speed Drill. Type at your best speed, striving for errorless typing.

It is the duty of all good men to have to work for jury pay.   12

244. Keyboard Recall Letter. Type 2 copies in block style, as shown in Lesson 51.

June 16, 1954
Mr. L. H. Lewis
Modern Fixture Company
608 West 47 Street
Buffalo 23, New York

Dear Mr. Lewis:

You may have already given thought on occasion to the possibility   13
of installing music in your offices, as is being done in many modern   27
offices around the country. But whether you have or not, we should   40
like to have the privilege of calling on you at this time. ¶ We just   53
want to put before you letters showing the reaction of those who   66
have used music, and exact figures that our customers submitted   79
showing the effect of music on office morale and production. If you   93
so request, we can also point out where music can make a sizeable   106
contribution in your offices.   112

Very truly yours,
John A. Student

245. Alphabetic Speed Drill. Type 5 to 10 copies of the body of the letter, as instructed by the teacher.

246. Typing Style Recall. Type 1 copy.

"While in town," visitors always say, "see 'Queen of the Sea.'" We will reopen Store #2 for fall business at the Sea & Fiske Building (54 North 13 Place) on September 1, 1954. Fifty ever-popular varieties of sea food are served to 500 customers a day between 11 a.m. and 9:30 p.m. Lunches are reasonably priced from 75 cents, dinners from $2 to $3.50, with a flat service charge of 10%.

247. Alphabetic Speed Drill. Type 5 to 10 copies.

Probably one of the most valuable features of our book is the simple	14
plan it gives for conserving time, a plan so easy that anyone can	28
quickly follow it. In addition, the book shows you how to organize	42
your day with a plan that is very flexible and can be followed by	55
almost any person regardless of the type of work in which engaged.	69
Once you start using this new plan, you will no longer have that	82
hurried feeling but will be able to take on all jobs with ease and	96
with much zeal.	99

248. Alphabetic Speed Drill. Type 5 to 10 copies.

The writing of a letter of just a few lines is certainly not a very	14
difficult task; yet so many of us, when it comes to sitting down and	28
writing a letter, even when it is to be a reply to a letter we have	42
received, can put the little job off for days and sometimes months.	55
It requires only a few minutes to do the actual writing, but it must	68
be that some human failing seizes us when it comes to sitting down	82
and organizing our thoughts so that they can be written down in a	96
few minutes.	99

249. Perfect Speed Drill. Type at your best speed, striving for errorless typing.

It is the duty of all good men to have to work for jury pay.   12

250. Keyboard Recall Letter. Type 2 copies in semiblock style, as shown in Lesson 61.

July 18, 1954
Mr. G. W. Stewart
Stewart Lumber Company
307 North 68 Street
Atlanta 24, Georgia

Dear Mr. Stewart:

The office furniture you ordered has been shipped and should arrive   14
a few days before you are ready to move to your new building.   27
¶ All the items shipped were those you requested in your order with   40
the exception of the club chair on which we took the liberty of   53
making a minor change. Although the model you will receive is not   67
the one you ordered, you will see that it is practically the same in   81
size and other respects, with certain good features added at no   94
increase in cost. We know you will enjoy this fine new furniture in   107
your new and larger offices.   113

Yours very truly,
John A. Student

251. Alphabetic Speed Drill. Type 5 to 10 copies of the body of the letter, as instructed by the teacher.

LESSON 76

252. Horizontal Centering. To center a line on standard-width paper:

1. Paper guide set at 0 on elite (small) type machines, at 7 on pica (large) type machines.

2. Paper inserted with left edge against the paper guide.

3. Center of the paper (50 on the scale) at the writing point.

4. One space back with backspacer for each two characters in the copy to be centered.

5. Copy typed from this point on the scale is correctly centered.

253. Centering Drill. Make a 3-line centered letterhead of each of the names below.

Chief Librarian   Library of Congress   Washington, D. C.
The New York Times   Times Building   New York, N. Y.
American Airlines   Airlines Terminal   Los Angeles
Harvard Bookstore   Harvard University   Cambridge, Massachusetts
Chicago Cubs   Wrigley Field   Chicago, Illinois

254. Vertical Centering. To center the copy in Vertical Centering Drill 255:

1. A full sheet of standard typing paper measures 8½″ x 11″ allowing 66 vertical line spaces.

2. A half sheet measures 8½″ x 5½″ and allows 33 vertical line spaces.

3. The copy in ¶255 contains 11 line spaces.

4. The 11 line spaces of copy subtracted from the 33 line spaces of the half sheet leaves 22 line spaces for blank space above and below the copy.

5. One-half the 22 spaces will be left blank above the copy as a top margin, one-half below as a bottom margin.

6. The first line, therefore, is centered on line 12 of the half sheet.

255. Vertical Centering Drill. Center on a half sheet. Use two hyphens, without space before or after, to indicate a dash.

TYPING AND SUCCESS

Typing is the modern way to write--by machine. Typing is not

only a valuable tool that will help you gain success in the

business office, but also a tool that will help you in your

many personal writing tasks at home. This same skill can

be an asset to you in both your business and personal life.

256. Typing Style Recall. Type 1 copy.

On February 3, 1954, Grant & Company will move to 46 West 78 Street (Room #72). Seven of us will be able to show you any of 600 items ranging from 10 cents to $89.50, and even some time-saving machines at $980, on which we allow a discount of 15%. As usual, our hours are from 9 a.m. to 9:30 p.m. "When you want fast delivery," as our slogan goes, "remember we are 'as near as your phone.'"

257. Alphabetic Speed Drill. Type 5 to 10 copies.

During the next few months we shall need a good deal of help, and 13
it occurred to us that you might be able to suggest someone who 26
would like to work for us at quite a good profit to himself. We 39
thought you would just like to know about our problem and as 53
one of our good friends in this zone you would help us. You will find 67
the type of person we are seeking in the ads, copies of which we are 81
giving you at this time, and, for your information, he need not have 95
business experience. 99

258. Alphabetic Speed Drill. Type 5 to 10 copies.

We receive a great many letters each year concerning ideas that 13
people hope may be of value to our company in conducting its 26
business; while quite a few of the writers submit their ideas to our 40
company without any thought of pay, often the writers realize they 53
have something of value for which they expect a fair payment. The 67
company wants such persons to protect their interests just as the 80
company likes to do with its interests, so that it may conduct its 94
business with no risk. 99

259. Perfect Speed Drill. Type at your best speed, striving for errorless typing.

It is the duty of all good men to have to work for jury pay.   12

260. Keyboard Recall Letter. Type 2 copies in block style, as shown in Lesson 51.

September 20, 1954
Mr. H. A. Wood
620 South 47 Avenue
Philadelphia 38, Pennsylvania

Dear Mr. Wood:

Your recent request addressed to our home office has been forwarded   14
to us with the notation that information has been mailed direct   28
to you. Your interest in our de luxe line is appreciated and we look   42
forward to helping you. ¶ One of our staff at this office has just been   56
assigned to analyze your travel plans and will get in touch with you   70
as soon as you have filled out and returned the enclosed card.   83
He will be able to furnish you with the total cost of any particular   97
tour or trip from and returning to your home station, and will   110
provide all necessary tickets.   116

Yours truly,
John A. Student

261. Alphabetic Speed Drill. Type 5 to 10 copies of the body of the letter, as instructed by the teacher.

262. Typing Style Recall. Type 1 copy.

On July 8, 1954, I talked to Clerk #7 at the 33 West 14 Avenue Branch of Penn & Penn sometime between 11:30 a.m. and 1 p.m. Twelve of the 102 questions on the two-colored form were not entirely clear. "To this form," you state, "you must attach 'stub' of ticket." I am attaching a stub for $1.75, another for $6, and a third for 45 cents (15% tax is included).

263. Alphabetic Speed Drill. Type 5 to 10 copies.

Now you can have on your desk every week a letter analyzing the   13
latest in the public relations field, a letter that will give you the   27
latest plans of other public relations men who have been effective   41
in winning the good will of the public. It will not just give you news   54
about men and events in your field but will keep you informed on   68
expected changes in the thinking of your readers. This letter is a per-   82
sonal report to you, and you will find it is a unique letter in your field   96

264. Alphabetic Speed Drill. Type 5 to 10 copies.

At some point in the quiet meeting the suggestion came to light that   14
the firm have a big outing, and the next thing we knew all had voted   28
in favor of the idea. This turned out to be a fine idea and all had a   42
good time, but somewhere along the line someone had thought it   55
would be nice to have races for prizes for all the children and that   69
was where we met our defeat. You can have as many starters and   82
judges as children racing, and still those managing the races will age   96
years in hours.   99

265. Perfect Speed Drill. Type at your best speed, striving for errorless typing.

It is the duty of all good men to have to work for jury pay.   12

266. Keyboard Recall Letter. Type 2 copies in semiblock style, as shown in Lesson 61.

October 12, 1954
Mr. J. L. Borden
J. L. Borden Company
237 East 80 Street
New York 46, New York

Dear Mr. Borden:

We appreciate receiving your recent letter asking for prices and   14
information on our de luxe products and are enclosing a booklet   27
which we believe will be helpful in answering any questions you   40
may have.   ¶ You will note the booklet does not include prices, as   53
there are several factors that affect the prices of any unit of this   66
type; and we feel that it is just fair to you to have these factors   79
analyzed so that an accurate estimate can be given, one that will   92
not obligate you in any way. We are therefore asking our local   105
manager to survey your needs promptly.   112

Cordially yours,
John A. Student

267. Alphabetic Speed Drill. Type 5 to 10 copies of the body of the letter, as instructed by the teacher.

WORD COUNT

The small figures given at the end of each line of practice material in Lessons 1—80 represent the total number of 5-stroke words in the copy. Beginning with Lesson 81, a second column of figures will be found in some of the exercises. The second column represents the *gross 5-stroke words a minute* written for a 5-minute writing. That is, the figure 49 at the end of the last line of copy completed in the 5-minute writing means that the typist has written 49 words a minute for 5 minutes. For every 5 words typed in an unfinished line, the typist adds 1 word a minute to his score.

268. Typing Style Recall. Type 1 copy.

"If you want that 'superservice,' " air-wise travelers will tell you,
"fly the Golden Route." Twenty-six big airliners are flown by our
185 seasoned pilots. Come to the air show and luncheon on June 16,
1954, between 11:30 a.m. and 1 p.m. at our offices in the Warner &
Sells Building, 43 North 17 Street (Room #1662). Single admission
will be 90 cents, couples $1.50, and families $2, plus 15% tax.

269. Alphabetic Speed Drill for 5-Minute Timed Writing. If you complete
typing this copy before the end of the timing, begin again.

		W·A·M	
		1m	5m
A	Thank you for writing us in such detail regarding the services	13	3
	charged on the machines we just installed in your office. I was out	26	5
	of town when you called, which is a matter of regret, because we feel	39	8
	that these matters can be settled much more quickly and satis-	52	11
	factorily when we can sit down and analyze them. We know that	65	13
	you are reasonable in your demands, and we are sure you also know	78	16
	that we expect to do the fair thing. You are entitled to a certain	91	19
	service, and we want to be sure that you get it.	99	20
B	We recall very distinctly our discussion on the servicing of the	13	22
	machines in your office. At that time we realized that we could make	27	25
	an arrangement whereby you would have a service man in your	39	28
	office at all times. Nothing was said, so far as we remember, about	52	30
	any charge for this extra service. For the first year there is no charge	66	33
	at all; and after the first year, the charge depends on the amount of	80	36
	work that is required in making the repairs you need in a year.	93	38
C	You will also recall that we discussed a change in the size of record	14	41
	card to be used with the clocks. Since that time we have given the	27	44
	matter a good deal of thought, and we sincerely believe that the	41	47
	stock you are now using will do the job in the most satisfactory	54	49
	manner. We wish that we could see our way clear to paying you a	67	52
	quick visit at your office, but it looks as though our staff will be	81	55
	tied down here for the next month or two.	89	57
D	You mention in your letter that the charges for delivery of the paper	14	60
	you ordered have been very high. You may remember that just a	26	62
	short time ago you asked us to send this paper quickly by special	40	65
	truck, and that is the way we sent it. As you say this method is	53	68
	rather expensive, I have looked into the cost of sending this paper	67	71
	to you by other means. After a little investigation I find that it	80	73
	probably would be best to send shipment to your zone by freight.	93	76

LESSON 82

270. Perfect Speed Drill. Your best speed, striving for errorless typing.

The just firm will give the men good pay for the right work.   12

271. Alphabetic Speed Drill. Lesson 81: 5 to 10 copies of ¶A, then ¶B.

LESSON 83

272. Centering Drill. Type 1 copy of the Notice below, centering it vertically and horizontally on a half sheet, 8½" x 5½". The underscore is the other character on the 6 key.

NOTICE

OPENING DAY DINNER

Free to Members

The Hobby Club is pleased to announce that its first meeting

of the new year will be held on September 10, 1953, at 6 p.m.

At that meeting, dinner will be served gratis to all members

attending. Mark this date on your calendar now. Then come!

START THE YEAR RIGHT

273. Alphabetic Speed Drill. Lesson 81: 5 to 10 copies of ¶C.

LESSON 84

274. Personal Letter Drill. Type 1 copy to each of these 7 persons: Bob, Jim, John, George, Helen, Peggy, Ed. (For style, see R-11, Reference Section.)

Dear——: You will remember that at Jim's house last month there 14
was some talk about a birthday party for Bill Boyd. We've made 27
some definite plans since then and have come up with the idea of 40
giving Bill a real surprise party at my house next Saturday, the 54
tenth, at 3 p.m. ¶ Alma will probably see you before then about 67
plans for a group gift. Sincerely, 73

275. Alphabetic Speed Drill. Lesson 81: 5 to 10 copies of ¶D.

LESSON 85

276. Perfect Speed Drill. Your best speed, striving for errorless typing.

The just firm will give the men good pay for the right work. 12

277. Alphabetic Production Letter. Type in block style, 1 copy to each of the 10 addresses given.

Dear Sir: As you have no doubt just heard from your home office, 13
Brill Brothers will carry our full line of goods within the next month 27
or two. As it has been planned to introduce the line with a full 41
window display in all stores, we are asking our representative in 54
your zone to call on you to make quick arrangements for your display 68
and to give you all the facts you will want concerning our products. 82
¶ We wish to co-operate with you in every way; so please feel free 95
to write us at any time, whether it is to offer a suggestion or to 108
request our service. Very truly yours, L. G. Mason, Treasurer 120

Manager, Brill Brothers, Boulder 3, Colorado
Manager, Brill Brothers, Whitefish 2, Montana
Manager, Brill Brothers, Austin 3, Texas
Manager, Brill Brothers, Atlanta 4, Georgia
Manager, Brill Brothers, Champaign 5, Illinois
Manager, Brill Brothers, Elmira 6, New York
Manager, Brill Brothers, Portland 7, Oregon
Manager, Brill Brothers, San Jose 8, California
Manager, Brill Brothers, Greenfield 9, Massachusetts
Manager, Brill Brothers, Euclid 2, Ohio

LESSON 86

278. Typing Style Recall. Type 1 copy.

On December 8, 1954, I remitted $3.75 to Jones & Franklin to cover the bills for 75 cents and $3. The check (#297) was addressed to your 4 South 16 Road office and mailed some time between 11 a.m. and 12:30 p.m. "Report these 'small' losses," your mail-claims agent has advised, "as they, too, must be investigated." Four such losses have now been reported out of about 120 payments.

279. Alphabetic Speed Drill for 5-Minute Timed Writing. If you complete typing this copy before the end of the timing, begin again.

	W·A·M	
	1m	5m
A		
Our studies analyzed reasons why people do not pay and what can	13	3
be done about it. One of the most important sections is the one that	27	5
takes up the matter of developing the correct credit policy for your	41	8
own business. But perhaps what you want to know quickly is what	54	11
the study will do for you, how it will help you speed up collections	68	14
and judge credits on a sounder basis. Examine the literature and	81	16
see how our information has helped credit managers.	92	18
B		
You will find any number of amazing little plans for bringing about	14	21
collections, plans that we know will get the money quickly without	28	24
losing the good will of the customer. We have for many years run	42	27
a variety of business enterprises and have suffered very few credit	55	29
losses, and we can show you how it is done, just how you can turn	68	32
your bad bills into cash. Our files contain many letters from credit	82	35
managers, extracts from which are printed in our booklets.	95	37
C		
We realize that the only way you can determine the value of those	13	40
suggestions quickly is by reading and testing the data. At this low	27	43
price for the service we cannot afford the expense of carrying	39	45
accounts; but we make the fair offer that if after receiving this	52	48
material you do not feel that it has been of any value to you, just	65	50
return it to us and we will immediately refund the entire price. These	79	53
booklets are new copies that have never been out of our files.	91	56
D		
If you are agreeable, we should just like to request about six names	14	58
for our mailing list. We would send them literature from time to	28	61
time, believing that in doing this we will be rendering them a real	42	64
service. Of course, you realize that we would not think of using your	56	67
name in this connection, unless you are willing; so you may rest	70	70
assured on that point. It should be a source of satisfaction to you to	83	73
include the names of some to whom our ideas would prove a service.	96	75

LESSON 87

280. Perfect Speed Drill. Your best speed, striving for errorless typing.

The just firm will give the men good pay for the right work. 12

281. Alphabetic Speed Drill. Lesson 86: 5 to 10 copies of ¶A, then ¶B.

LESSON 88

282. Centering Drill. Type 1 copy of the invitation below, centering it vertically and horizontally on a half sheet, 8½" x 5½".

The Hobby Club

requests the pleasure of your company

at its annual dinner

on Friday, the tenth of September

at six o'clock

at the Hobby Club House

12 Park Avenue

PLACEMENT PICTURE

283. Alphabetic Speed Drill. Lesson 86: 5 to 10 copies of ¶C.

LESSON 89

284. Interoffice Letter Drill. On an interoffice letterhead like the one shown, type 1 copy of the letter below to each of the 4 addresses listed. (See also Reference Section, R-9.)

TO —
FROM   General Sales Manager
SUBJECT   Hiring of Sales Personnel
DATE —

After much study it has been decided that the hiring of sales personnel should be decentralized by the first of next year. At

PLACEMENT PICTURE

70

that time, no further papers of applicants need be processed through 39
the home office. Each branch manager will have the complete author- 52
ity to hire according to the standards he sets for his office. ¶ While 66
our centralized plan seemed to offer certain advantages, such as 79
uniformity of standards, it was felt that the branch manager could 92
not fairly be held responsible for the operation of his unit unless he 106
completely controlled the selection of his personnel. Complete 118
detailed instructions regarding the new policy will reach you from 131
the personnel department. T. R. Callan 139

Branch Manager, Chicago
Branch Manager, San Francisco
Branch Manager, Dallas
Branch Manager, Boston

285. Alphabetic Speed Drill. Lesson 86: 5 to 10 copies of ¶D.

LESSON 90

286. Perfect Speed Drill. Your best speed, striving for errorless typing.

The just firm will give the men good pay for the right work.   12

287. Alphabetic Production Letter. Type in semiblock style, 1 copy to each
of the 10 addresses given.

Dear Madam: A number of our patterns this year have proved to be 13
extremely popular by actual test in several cities around the country. 27
We are arranging to have these patterns, as well as others in the 41
new season's line, shown to you shortly. ¶ We realize this is quite a 54
bit in advance of the season but since we anticipate a heavy demand 68
for some of the numbers, we are sure you will appreciate the oppor- 81
tunity to place your order in plenty of time to get in some early 94
sales. ¶ Our new catalog illustrating the complete line will reach 108
you in just a few days. Yours very truly, Alice G. Nelson 119

Fashions Buyer, Swanson Store, Toledo 6, Ohio
Fashions Buyer, Swanson Store, Muncie 3, Indiana
Fashions Buyer, Swanson Store, LaCrosse 4, Michigan
Fashions Buyer, Swanson Store, Birmingham 5, Alabama
Fashions Buyer, Swanson Store, Tacoma 6, Washington
Fashions Buyer, Swanson Store, San Diego 7, California
Fashions Buyer, Swanson Store, Denver 8, Colorado
Fashions Buyer, Swanson Store, Kansas City 9, Kansas
Fashions Buyer, Swanson Store, New Orleans 8, Louisiana
Fashions Buyer, Swanson Store, Richmond 7, Virginia

288. Typing Style Recall. Type 1 copy.

"I just read 'Above the Clouds,'" says Jane, "and I think you should all get copies soon." Her letter, dated August 4, 1954, mentioned a store at 36 North 87 Street (Clark & Weller, Department #62) where economy-bound editions can be had at 50 cents, $2, and $3.75, plus 1% sales tax. Thirty order blanks were delivered at 9:30 for those of our 175 members who may wish to order a copy.

289. Alphabetic Speed Drill for 5-Minute Timed Writing. If you complete typing this copy before the end of the timing, begin again.

	W·A·M	
	1m	5m
A		
Our journal will keep you equally informed on important develop-	14	3
ments that you might otherwise overlook. The important thing for	27	5
you and every other investor to do is just to keep an eye on not only	40	8
the market, but also the factors that determine market prices. This	54	11
amazing service should be of tremendous value in the weeks ahead	67	13
in helping you do this. At the same time, it will keep you informed	81	16
of opportunities with extra possibilities.	90	18
B		
Our editors are just now working on an interesting article that will	14	21
soon be available to every reader. Some time between now and the	27	23
middle of spring we shall publish the results of the careful researches	40	26
that are now being made, so that the three programs will represent	53	29
the composite views of our board as to the most attractive pur-	66	31
chases. The foregoing feature is typical of our policy to give our	79	34
readers research data that will be of maximum value to the investor.	93	37
C		
Believing that you will want to get your just share of the profits that	14	39
are now possible to buyers under present highly favorable conditions,	28	42
we wish to remind you that the next issues will have at least four or	42	45
five articles having quite a definite bearing on your investment	55	48
problems. Now that the business and market tide has definitely	68	50
turned, you will find the monthly issues of the magazine increas-	81	53
ingly valuable in keeping you in touch with securities.	93	55
D		
The most important advantage we offer is a result of increased mem-	13	58
bership, which has now reached such a figure that we can distribute	27	61
valuable data to our members. You need not spend a cent more for	40	63
sales data than you now do, so the advantage to you in joining is	53	66
thus quickly obvious. This insures you against missing the data in	67	69
which you are particularly interested. You must realize that this	80	71
service costs you nothing as there are no extra fees.	90	73

LESSON 92

290. Perfect Speed Drill. Your best speed, striving for errorless typing.

The just firm will give the men good pay for the right work.   12

291. Alphabetic Speed Drill. Lesson 91: 5 to 10 copies of ¶A, then ¶B.

LESSON 93

292. Centering Drill. Center 1 typed copy of the Menu below vertically and horizontally on a half sheet 8½" x 5½". Then center the Program below similarly, also on a half sheet.

MENU

Fruit Cup
Roast Maryland Turkey
Sweet Potatoes — String Beans.
Chocolate Ice Cream
Beverage

PLACEMENT PICTURE

PROGRAM

Songs by the Hobby Glee Club
Welcome by the President
"The Oddest Hobbies", described by R. Frazer
Closing Remarks by W. L. Beals

PLACEMENT PICTURE

293. Alphabetic Speed Drill. Lesson 91: 5 to 10 copies of ¶C.

LESSON 94

294. Manuscript Typing Drill. Type 1 copy of the following page of manuscript, corrected as indicated. In typing footnotes, use the automatic line finder which makes possible automatic return to the original line of writing (illustrated in Reference Section, R-66 to R-70.)

295. Alphabetic Speed Drill. Lesson 91: 5 to 10 copies of ¶D.

REAL

A study of 1,000 companies of every type ~~and kind~~ that keep accurate records of salesmen's calls developed some realistic facts to show that the salesman who quits does not succeed.[1] There is an old saying that goes, "Victory goes to the one who hangs on a second longer than his opponent."

Selling Not a Contest

Selling is not a contest that one participant wins and the other loses, for a proper sale makes a profit for the buyer and the salesman. Nevertheless, there are facts to show ~~show~~ that the salesman who does not follow through and call back with sound arguments and with abundant sales helps is wasting time, money, and effort. Persistence does pays off! One of the country's biggest sales school executives has this to say to his men:

> Perseverance, persistence and perception are the
> qualities that will make your sales success increase.
> You must perceive that there is a real user benefit
> to your product. Then you must persist in calling
> back until your customer is educated to see what
> your proposal offers him.

Must Win Acceptance

How can ~~he~~ You expect to impart ~~his~~ Your superior product knowledge, develop the proper applications of ~~his~~ Your products, and win the acceptance ~~he~~ you wants and get the order in one call, two calls, or three calls? If ~~he does~~ You do, it is more or less accidental!

---

[1]J. P. Stevens, "Salesmen Who Win," Sales Research Quarterly 18: 122-123. December, 1950.

296. Perfect Speed Drill. Your best speed, striving for errorless typing.

The just firm will give the men good pay for the right work.　　12

297. Alphabetic Production Letter. Type in block style, 1 copy to each of the 10 addresses given.

Dear Sir: You have no doubt seen the excellent national advertising　14
that has appeared recently on our handy utility kit for car owners.　28
To give you the opportunity of introducing this new product in your　42
territory without any obligation on your part, we are happy to offer　56
you the supply you will need on consignment. In other words, you　70
will be billed only for those you sell; any unsold units may be re-　83
turned. ¶ Hundreds of service stations are realizing new profits　96
under this plan. Write us today and just specify how many units　109
you will require. Yours truly, Edward A. Race　　118

Manager, Liberty Service Station, Warren 6, Pennsylvania
Manager, Liberty Service Station, Macon 3, Georgia
Manager, Liberty Service Station, Redwood City 4, California
Manager, Liberty Service Station, Elizabeth 5, New Jersey
Manager, Liberty Service Station, Key West 6, Florida
Manager, Liberty Service Station, Shreveport 7, Louisiana
Manager, Liberty Service Station, Memphis 6, Tennessee
Manager, Liberty Service Station, Butte 5, Montana
Manager, Liberty Service Station, Tucson 7, Arizona
Manager, Liberty Service Station, Evanston 9, Illinois

LESSON 96

298. Typing Style Recall. Type 1 copy.

This check for $180.75 represents $180 for the machine parts and 75 cents for delivery. Please make delivery after May 4, 1954, any time between 10 a.m. and 3:30 p.m. at our new Barnes & Crane Building address, 660 West 10 Street (Room #1302). Six people have recommended your product, including one who uses 128 of them. "If you want the best buy of all," he says, "a 100% time-proven 'Champion' is the answer."

299. Alphabetic Speed Drill for 5-Minute Timed Writing.

	W·A·M	
	1m	5m

A

	1m	5m
We cannot give you a full account of our new and amazing product	14	3
in a letter. The enclosed circular describes it with illustrations and	28	6
gives a partial idea of its working. Many of the pictures will be	42	8
familiar to you, and every one of them will give you extra ideas on	55	11
how to use the product. It is easy to see why this development is so	68	14
popular. You will quickly get ideas on how to apply the product in	82	16
your plans to speed up selling and save money.	92	18

B

Now, just to introduce our product to several thousand dealers, we	14	21
are setting a special price on quantity orders. At a nominal resale	28	24
price, you should realize a good profit on your investment. Each	41	27
carton contains different styles and different patterns to give you a	55	29
complete stock for your needs. Our terms are net thirty days and	69	32
the postage is paid at your end. If your check is sent with the order,	83	35
we pay the parcel post to your store, as we save on extra bookkeeping.	97	38

C

We are enclosing reprints of the first two ads on the new product	14	41
and the publication dates and the magazines in which the ads are	27	43
to appear. The third ad in the current series will appear in several	41	46
issues during the spring. The fourth ad is scheduled to appear just	55	49
in the fall. To make it possible for companies to run a local ad, we	69	52
can quickly provide a copy of the main illustration and text and	82	54
suggest that the local company build the ad around the reprints.	96	57

D

We have been working for quite a long time on some method of	13	60
providing mats to local companies, but the cost of doing this is	27	62
considerable. During the first part of the year we did provide such	41	65
mats, but the response was so poor that we had to drop it, the chief	54	68
difficulty being that we could not reproduce accurately any of the	68	71
national ads in a space smaller than four columns. Companies	81	73
quickly objected to an ad of that extra size.	90	75

300. Perfect Speed Drill. Your best speed, striving for errorless typing.

The just firm will give the men good pay for the right work.   12

301. Alphabetic Speed Drill. Lesson 96: 5 to 10 copies of ¶A, then ¶B.

LESSON 98

302. Centering Drill. Center 1 copy of the Title Page below vertically and horizontally on a full sheet, 8½″ x 11″, as shown in the miniature model.

POINTS FOR STAMP COLLECTORS

by

William J. Wells

Secretary, The Hobby Club

Helpful information for the new hobbyist, compiled from files of famous stamp collectors

Published by

THE HOBBY CLUB OF NEW YORK

PLACEMENT PICTURE

303. Alphabetic Speed Drill. Lesson 96: 5 to 10 copies of ¶C.

LESSON 99

304. Addressing Drill. Type 3 envelopes or index cards for each of the following names and addresses. To save time and motion, insert the next card

General Products Company
100 GRAND CENTRAL AVENUE
NEW YORK 10, N. Y.

The Manager
Brill Brothers
Boulder, Colorado

PLACEMENT PICTURES
Large envelope (left)
Index card (below)

Manager
Lee Hardware Company
Tucson 2, Arizona

or envelope as you turn the cylinder knob to remove the last one typed. (See "Chain Feeding" and model addresses, Reference Section, R-74, R-14, R-17.)

Manager, Brill Brothers, Boulder 2, Colorado
Manager, Brill Brothers, Whitefish 3, Montana
Manager, Brill Brothers, Austin 4, Texas
Manager, Brill Brothers, Atlanta 5, Georgia
Fashions Buyer, Swanson Store, Denver 3, Colorado
Fashions Buyer, Swanson Store, Kansas City 4, Kansas
Fashions Buyer, Swanson Store, New Orleans 2, Louisiana
Fashions Buyer, Swanson Store, Richmond 1, Virginia
Manager, Liberty Service Station, Warren 2, Pennsylvania
Manager, Liberty Service Station, Macon 3, Georgia
Manager, Liberty Service Station, Redwood City 4, California
Manager, Liberty Service Station, Elizabeth 3, New Jersey

305. Alphabetic Speed Drill. Lesson 96: 5 to 10 copies of ¶D.

LESSON 100

306. Perfect Speed Drill. Your best speed, striving for errorless typing.

The just firm will give the men good pay for the right work.   12

307. Alphabetic Production Letter. Type in semiblock style, 1 copy to each of the 7 addresses given.

Dear——: We are happy to enclose two invitations to our annual   14
exhibit of book bindings and sincerely hope that you and some   27
member of your production staff can be with us during the show.   41
¶ Last year, you will remember, the display was a complete success, 55
and we received many comments from our customers as to how   68
much they had realized just from reviewing everything that is new   82
in book binding. We can say without reservation that this year the   96
show will be an even bigger success for there are quite a few surprises 110
in store for you. ¶ We look forward to seeing you the day of the   124
show. Sincerely yours, S. P. James.   131

Mr. J. L. Hudson, Carver Book Company, Philadelphia 13, Pennsylvania
Mr. E. Sloane, Servel Publishing Company, Yonkers 9, New York
Mr. E. L. Koppers, Jr., Koppers Book Company, Peekskill 17, New York
Mr. Fred L. Meyer, Kraft Publishing Company, Jersey City 5, New Jersey
Mr. O. E. Helm, Rodman Book Company, Newark 7, New Jersey
Miss W. G. Blaine, Harris Press, Trenton 6, New Jersey
Mr. W. E. Ponter, Little Book Company, Boston 18, Massachusetts

LESSON 101

308. Typing Style Recall. Type 1 copy.

On June 6, 1954, between the hours of 2 p.m. and 3:30 p.m. we held the monthly price conference with Stone & Stone at 84 East 17 Street (Room #126). Thirty-five more (about 20% more) than the expected 160 came from the industry and paid from $2 to $7.50 to attend, in addition to a tip of 75 cents. "It was the 'meeting of the year,' " writes year-end chairman Lewis, "and I am proud."

309. Alphabetic Speed Drill for 5-Minute Timed Writing.

	W·A·M	
	1m	5m

A

	1m	5m
Enclosed are samples of some of the shoes we manufacture, and	13	3
since we want several thousand additional dealers to try our shoes,	26	6
we have just decided to make a special offer on all those styles and	40	8
sizes now in demand. Our shoes are of excellent quality, as you will	54	11
see from these samples. They are made from finest leather and are	68	14
manufactured complete in our own factory. The styles and colors go	82	16
with the fashions of the season, and the quality is high.	93	19

B

	1m	5m
You will probably be quite interested in any suggestions that will	14	21
help to make your advertising on these shoes a success. At the	27	24
request of our eastern manager, we will just try to include a few	40	27
such suggestions in this letter, and also to tell you something about	54	29
the large advertising drive that the company is putting on during	68	32
the current year. Our dealers who have had extra success recognize	81	35
the effectiveness of this plan.	87	36

C

	1m	5m
We know of one dealer who sent a letter to all the members of	13	39
several clubs in his zone, advising them of the special sale and of his	27	41
extra fine service. In special mailings or even in distribution of	41	44
circulars, it is always a good idea to plan to put your message before	55	47
a group of people with whom you do not ordinarily do business. By	69	51
sending invitations to your regular mailing list, you are giving this	83	53
information to people who are already quite well informed.	95	55

D

	1m	5m
We are just going to send any supply of shoes you order with no	14	58
obligation on your part. Please inspect the samples carefully and	28	61
notice the difference between them and the stock you now have.	42	63
Before our present stock runs out, please tell us quickly which of	55	66
the colors and styles you wish, and the brief size information we	68	69
need to guarantee stocking a balanced line. When we send the	81	71
order, there is no extra hurry on your part to pay for the goods.	94	74

310. Perfect Speed Drill. Your best speed, striving for errorless typing.

The just firm will give the men good pay for the right work.   12

311. Alphabetic Speed Drill. Lesson 101: 5 to 10 copies of ¶A, then ¶B.

LESSON 103

312. Personal Letter Drill. Type 1 copy to each of these 9 persons: Bob, Jim, John, George, Helen, Peggy, Ed, Alma, Harry.

Dear——: I certainly want to thank you again for the wonderful sur-   14
prise party and for your share in the very practical gift. ¶ As you   27
know, my brother has just returned from a trip and brought back   41
for me a number of beautifully colored calendars. I want you to have   54
one, so come to my house and take your choice. Sincerely,   65

313. Alphabetic Speed Drill. Lesson 101: 5 to 10 copies of ¶C.

LESSON 104

314. Tabulation. Before beginning a tabulation, clear any present tab stops on the machine by holding down the "Clear" key while moving the carriage from side to side with the carriage release. Then follow these steps:

1. For each column in the tabulation, make a penciled bracket, thus: (Tabulation Drill 315, opposite page, used as example.)

⌐‾⌐   ⌐‾⌐   ⌐‾⌐

2. In each bracket, place the number of characters in the longest item in the column.

⌐ 8 ⌐   ⌐ 10 ⌐   ⌐ 6 ⌐

3. Between brackets, place the number of spaces to be allowed between the columns, 10 spaces in this tabulation.

⌐ 8 ⌐ 10 ⌐ 10 ⌐ 10 ⌐ 6 ⌐

4. Add the total number of spaces.

$$8 + 10 + 10 + 10 + 6 = 44$$

5. Insert paper in machine with center of the paper (50 on the scale) at the writing point.

6. Backspace one-half the total number of spaces—one-half of 44, or 22 in this case, setting left marginal stop at this point, 28.

7. Tap out on the space bar the number of characters in the first bracket (8) plus the 10 spaces allowed between columns, a total of 18 spaces. Set a tab stop at this point, 46 on scale.

8. Tap out on the space bar the number of characters in the second bracket (10) plus the 10 spaces allowed between columns, a total of 20 spaces. Set a tab stop at this point, 66 on scale.

315. Tabulation Drill. Type 1 copy of the following tabulation as explained above. Center it vertically and horizontally on a half sheet, 8½" x 5½".

BALANCED HAND WORDS

duty	form	than
with	firm	then
city	usual	panels
aught	quantity	when
turns	title	wish
amend	proficient	rush
problems	auditor	spent

LESSON 105

316. Perfect Speed Drill. Your best speed, striving for errorless typing.

The just firm will give the men good pay for the right work.   12

317. Alphabetic Production Letter. Type in block style, 1 copy to each of the 7 addresses given. (For style of signature, see R-2, Reference Section.)

Dear——: Thank you for your recent inquiry regarding our dinette   14
sets. We are pleased to enclose a folder that presents the full line   28
and gives you the outstanding qualities for which our line is justly   42
recognized. ¶ These sets have a quality in construction which is un-   56
surpassed in the entire field. While styling is a matter of taste,   69
millions of customers, through their purchases, have already testified   82
that our styling is in the best taste. Our dinette sets are also priced   96
to fit every budget. ¶ Visit your nearest dealer and see a demon-   109
stration. Very truly yours, G. S. Greene, Sales Promotion

Mr. C. D. Hiller, 979 South Broadway, Denver 6, Colorado
Mr. A. Oliver, 501 Lark Lane, Worcester 2, Massachusetts
Mrs. H. P. Hood, 452 Center Street, Akron 7, Ohio
Mrs. O. E. Fairbanks, 567 Fairlawn Place, Baton Rouge 2, Louisiana
Mr. Harry Gibson, 65 Norris Heights, Minneapolis 3, Minnesota
Mrs. E. Goodyear, 430 Ninth Street, Fresno 4, California
Mrs. R. S. Fuller, 63 South Main Street, Newark 7, New Jersey

318. Typing Style Recall. Type 1 copy.

Two books were mailed to you on December 3, 1954, at Ronald & Bailor, 24 West 16 Street. They were billed (Invoice #2616) at $6.50 and $10, and 90 cents was added for mailing, as well as 2% for taxes. About 700 such books are mailed from here daily between 8:30 a.m. and 5 p.m., and only a very few are lost. "However," says our mailing department, "these time-consuming little 'incidents' will occur occasionally."

319. Alphabetic Speed Drill for 5-Minute Timed Writing.

	W·A·M 1m	5m
A		
If you want to retire some day and are willing to lay aside a portion	14	3
of your income every month, you can have freedom from many	27	5
worries. You can have all the joys of recreation or travel at the time	41	8
when every man wants them most. The plan is not limited to men,	54	11
for similar plans are available to women. When we know your exact	67	13
age, what size income you will need, and how soon it should begin,	81	16
we will tell you the cost.	86	17
B		
It makes no difference if your exacting plans for saving have been	14	20
upset during the past few years, and it makes no difference if you	27	23
are worth half as much today as you were ten years ago. At the pres-	41	25
ent time, by following a simple retirement plan, you can arrange to	55	28
quit work fifteen years from today, with a sizeable monthly income	69	31
guaranteed you for life. Not only that, but if you should die before	83	34
that time, we just pay your wife a good monthly income.	94	36
C		
This company was organized to reduce insurance costs by pre-	13	39
venting losses and by controlling expenses. It has always lived	26	41
within its income, it has recorded a steady increase in assets and	40	44
surplus, and it has followed a quiet policy in the handling and	54	47
investing of its funds. Last year its income and the number of	67	49
accounts protected were at the highest level in the history of the	80	52
company. It has aided many to enjoy large savings.	90	54
D		
Just a few points have been raised rather frequently so far with	13	57
regard to our plan, and in order to avoid answering these same	27	59
questions over and over again for numerous individuals, and in the	40	62
interest of uniformity, they are covered in this letter. You realize	54	65
that there are no exceptions to the requirement that the insured	68	68
must have lived in this state for a continuous period of not less than	82	70
two years prior to the effective date of the policy.	93	73

320. Perfect Speed Drill. Your best speed, striving for errorless typing.

The just firm will give the men good pay for the right work.   12

321. Alphabetic Speed Drill. Lesson 106: 5 to 10 copies of ¶A, then ¶B.

LESSON 108

322. Telegram Drill. On the telegram blank forms that will be supplied to you, type 1 copy of the full rate telegram below to each of the 5 addresses.

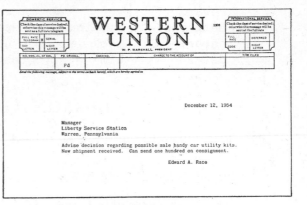

Advise decision regarding possible sale handy car utility kits. New shipment received. Can send one hundred on consignment.

Edward A. Race

Manager, Liberty Service Station, Warren, Pennsylvania
Manager, Liberty Service Station, Macon, Georgia
Manager, Liberty Service Station, Elizabeth, New Jersey
Manager, Liberty Service Station, Shreveport, Louisiana
Manager, Liberty Service Station, Butte, Montana

323. Alphabetic Speed Drill. Lesson 106: 5 to 10 copies of ¶C.

LESSON 109

324. Centering Column Headings in Tabulation. Column headings are centered over the longest item in the column. Follow these steps: (Tabulation Drill 325, below, used as example.)

1. Plan the tabulation as described in ¶314, Lesson 104.
2. Type the centered main heading.
3. The first bracket of your plan shows the figure "8" for the word *bettered* in the first column.
4. The word *Left*, the first column heading, contains 4 letters.

5. The difference between 4 (the number of letters in *Left*), and 8 (the number of letters in *bettered*), is 4.

6. One-half of 4 is 2. Therefore 2 spaces should be allowed on either side of the heading *Left*.

325. Tabulation Drill. Type 1 copy of the following tabulation as explained in ¶314 and ¶324. The tabulation is to be centered vertically and horizontally on a half-sheet, 8½″ x 5½″.

WORDS TYPED WITH ONE HAND

Left	Right	Left	Right
erred	join	date	only
reward	you	case	nylon
bettered	million	recesses	pupil
career	look	steer	upon
deter	him	tests	minimum

LESSON 110

326. Perfect Speed Drill. Your best speed, striving for errorless typing.

The just firm will give the men good pay for the right work. .12

327. Alphabetic Production Letter. Type in semiblock style, 1 copy to each of the 7 addresses given.

Dear——: In response to your request concerning office flooring, we 14
are forwarding, under another cover, our booklet describing the com- 28
plete line of excellent flooring we carry for business offices. ¶ Our 42
products are sold by your dealer who specializes in floor coverings. 56
He will be glad to discuss your plans with you, show you the ma- 69
terials he has in stock, and give you a quick estimate. The office 82
whose address is on the enclosed card is responsible for the distribu- 96
tion of our products in your area and will be glad to give you a list 110
of flooring contractors near you and help you in every way. Yours 123
very truly, C. G. Donald, Advertising Department 133

Mr. O. Carlson, H. C. Clements Company, Portland 6, Oregon
Mr. J. G. Bruce, Holmes Supply Company, Jacksonville 4, Florida
Mr. C. Uhler, French & James Company, Indianapolis 2, Indiana
Mr. L. C. Cott, Cott Manufacturing Company, Pittsburgh 5, Pennsylvania
Mr. F. T. Gray, James & Dunn Company, Inglewood 3, California
Mr. William C. Hay, Denton & Price Company, Arkansas City 5, Arkansas
Mr. T. E. Thomas, LaSalle Supply Company, Utica 2, New York

328. Typing Style Recall. Type 1 copy.

"The new game known as 'Black Magic,' " say the newspapers, "is really taking hold." Eighty leather-bound sets a day, approximately, have been sold by us, a total of 800 since the game was announced on August 13, 1954. Sets sell for 60 cents, $2, and the deluxe at $8.50, 10% for tax. We are open from 8:30 a.m. to 9 p.m. Come and see us at the Flint & Steel Building, 46 South 17 Avenue (Counter #26).

329. Alphabetic Speed Drill for 5-Minute Timed Writing.

	W·A·M	
	1m	5m

A

	1m	5m
Many persons who at one time handled their own investments now	13	3
use our services because the lack of time and the lack of facilities	27	5
have resulted in losses to them. The fees for this service are just	41	8
moderate. We cannot quote the fees in this letter because we do	54	11
not know in advance just what you would require us to do, but we	67	13
shall be glad to quote our fees if you will tell us what you want the	81	16
service to cover and what details you expect to entrust to our care.	95	19

B

	1m	5m
To the man who has wide interests and who must seize every	12	21
minute of his time for the promotion of those interests, this service	26	24
is a lifesaver. It takes care of his banking and helps him maintain	40	27
proper records, and it also quickly handles for him all details that	54	30
come up in connection with the supervision of his investments. To	67	32
the person who has just had little or no experience in business	80	35
matters, the services of this bank should be invaluable.	91	37

C

	1m	5m
As you have ordered investment data from us from time to time,	13	40
perhaps you will be interested to hear that we are now selling our	27	43
financial handbook at a special price. We are selling it at this low	41	45
price as we intend to discontinue its sale after next month. The	54	48
books have been selling quickly since our special announcement,	68	51
and we have just a limited supply left. If you care to have any of	82	54
these at this amazingly low price, please write me as soon as possible.	96	56

D

	1m	5m
Members of our bank receive our monthly investment forecasts	13	59
without charge. This is a service that just cannot be offered to very	27	62
many people, for the membership has been limited; but the directors	41	65
have decided to increase membership at this time. Costs of printing	54	67
are already extremely high and we wish to offset these increases by	68	70
larger printings for our members. We hope you will quickly take	81	73
advantage of this opportunity and accept this membership.	93	75

LESSON 112

330. Perfect Speed Drill. Your best speed, striving for errorless typing.

The just firm will give the men good pay for the right work.   12

331. Alphabetic Speed Drill. Lesson 111: 5 to 10 copies of ¶A, then ¶B.

LESSON 113

332. Tabulation Drill. Type 1 copy of the following tabulation. Center it vertically and horizontally on a half sheet, 8½″ x 5½″.

RUG SUPPLY IN WAREHOUSE

Make	Color	No.
Wilton	Rose	37
Alexander	Beige	129
Smithson	Taupe	661
Olson	Dark Green	342
Royale	Maroon	260
Royale	Light Green	32

333. Alphabetic Speed Drill. Type 5 to 10 copies of ¶C, Lesson 111.

LESSON 114

334. Manuscript Typing Drill. Type 1 copy of the following page of manuscript, corrected as indicated.

335. Alphabetic Speed Drill. Lesson 111: 5 to 10 copies of ¶D.

~~GOOD~~ *PROPER* SEATING FOR OFFICE WORKERS

Office techniques have advanced considerably since people
used to *do their* work standing up. Chairs, ~~at one time~~ *it would seem,* were reserved
for use by kings and royalty. Fifty years ago clerks labored
at "stand-up" desks. Then some bright lad discovered that he
could do more work sitting down--so office chairs began to come
into general use.

Scientific Seating Is *practically* New

Until recently, however, office chairs did not keep pace
with scientific progress. Individual comfort was ignored and
no effort was made to adjust the chair to the worker, to the
desk, or to the job.

Seating Affects Production

We know now that, Workers do not produce as much when they are tired. For
most efficient performance, an office worker--whether he *is* the
top executive or the lowest clerk--requires a chair which offers
support where the body needs it. Note what Dr. Coleman *L.* Maze,
noted management authority, has to say about the importance of
proper seating *in the business office:*

> Chairs have come in for increasing study. The
> so-called posture chair has demonstrated its worth
> in giving body support and comfort to the office
> worker. Posture chairs have been designed for
> certain operations as posting and typing. They
> have made their contribution in increasing job
> output and reducing fatigue.[1]

---

[1]Coleman L. Maze, Office Management, New York, The Ronald
Press Company, 1947.

336. Perfect Speed Drill. Your best speed, striving for errorless typing.

The just firm will give the men good pay for the right work.   12

337. Alphabetic Production Letter. Type in block style, 1 copy to each of the 7 addresses given.

Dear——: These are not usual times in the history of our industry.   14
Never before has our company or any other released two entirely   28
new quality products in a single month. Such an unusual occasion   41
calls for an extra effort on our part. ¶ It is important to dealers   55
that every possible minute be spent in the presence of new pros-   68
pects. We realize that reports are necessary, but these may be   82
relegated to the early and late hours when it is not possible to call   96
on your customers and prospects. ¶ Whether you are about to   109
make your quota or have just secured it, for the sake of tomorrow   122
be sure to make those important new calls today. Yours truly,   135
O. R. Harrington, Dealer Sales   141

Mr. G. Gregor, Gregor Equipment Company, Detroit 17, Michigan
Mr. J. B. Walter, Walter Equipment Company, San Francisco 16, California
Mr. D. P. Prescott, Prescott Sales Company, New Haven 4, Connecticut
Mr. F. T. Grayson, Quality Appliance Company, Chicago 12, Illinois
Mr. J. B. Blythe, Blythe Sales, Inc., Odessa 2, Texas
Mr. W. D. Dayton, Price & Company, Davenport 3, Iowa
Mr. H. D. Allen, Allen Equipment Company, Denver 4, Colorado

LESSON 116

338. Typing Style Recall. Type 1 copy.

The new Cross & Sprain Building, 460 North 87 Street, will open March 2, 1954. The renting office (Room #234), open from 8 a.m. to 5:30 p.m., states they expect to be almost 100% rented. "We are proud," says the renting manager, "of our 'safety-type' elevators." Twenty-six floors will be serviced by a staff of 112 trained persons. Office space rents from $3.50 to $5, with storage space at 90 cents.

339. Alphabetic Speed Drill for 5-Minute Timed Writing.

	W·A·M	
	1m	5m

A

	1m	5m
Every man knows that you can buy goods on a charge account and	13	3
just pay for them later; but many men, especially the younger ones	27	5
who do not have a sizeable bank account, are nervous about the	41	8
questioning one is expected to submit to in order to open a charge	55	11
account. If you are one of these men, you will be glad to know about	69	14
our company. Here you can open a charge account quickly. You can	82	16
open a charge account with a minimum of red tape.	92	18

B

	1m	5m
All you have to do is just to come into any one of our branches and	14	21
ask to open a charge account. The salesman will quickly give you	28	24
a very simple form to fill out; and when this form has been examined	42	27
by our credit office, you will receive a notice that your account has	56	30
been opened and you may start charging your purchases. When you	70	32
start buying here, you will discover that we do everything we can	84	35
to serve you best at an amazingly low cost.	93	37

C

	1m	5m
Our prices are always fixed at a point that makes it profitable for a	14	40
customer to buy our goods. It has always been our firm contention	28	43
that just and lasting business must always produce a quick and	41	45
lasting profit to the buyer as well as to the seller, and of the two, the	55	48
profit for the buyer must be the larger one. Drop in at our nearest	69	51
branch and let them show you some of our newest prize models.	82	53
There are many from which to choose.	89	55

D

	1m	5m
Our customers include quite a few friends of ours who had just put	14	58
off opening an account from day to day, who had no reserve fund to	27	60
call on for the extra purchases that are sometimes necessary. Thanks	41	63
to their friends and to our own vigorous efforts, many of these people	55	66
have just recognized the value of opening an account. Many of	68	69
these people have been able to pay only a very moderate sum every	82	71
month but in the meantime have enjoyed the goods they bought.	95	74

LESSON 117

340. Perfect Speed Drill. Your best speed, striving for errorless typing.

The just firm will give the men good pay for the right work.   12

341. Alphabetic Speed Drill. Lesson 116: 5 to 10 copies of ¶A, then ¶B.

LESSON 118

342. Tabulation Drill. Type 1 copy of the following tabulation. Center it vertically and horizontally on a half sheet, 8½″ x 5½″.

OLDEST UNIVERSITIES IN AMERICA

Name	City	State	Date
Harvard	Cambridge	Massachusetts	1636
William & Mary	Williamsburg	Virginia	1693
Yale	New Haven	Connecticut	1701
Pennsylvania	Philadelphia	Pennsylvania	1740
Princeton	Princeton	New Jersey	1746

343. Alphabetic Speed Drill. Lesson 116: 5 to 10 copies of ¶C.

LESSON 119

344. Addressing Drill. Type 3 envelopes or index cards for each of the following names and addresses.

Manager, Liberty Service Station, Key West 3, Florida
Manager, Liberty Service Station, Shreveport 2, Louisiana
Manager, Liberty Service Station, Memphis 4, Tennessee
Manager, Liberty Service Station, Butte 5, Montana
Manager, Liberty Service Station, Tucson 7, Arizona
Mr. C. D. Hillen, 979 South Broadway, Denver 6, Colorado
Mr. A. Oliver, 501 Park Lane, Worcester 2, Massachusetts
Mrs. H. P. Hood, 452 Center Street, Akron 7, Ohio
Mrs. O. E. Fairbanks, 567 Fairlawn Place, Baton Rouge 2, Louisiana
Mr. Harry Gibson, 65 Norris Heights, Minneapolis 3, Minnesota
Mrs. E. Goodyear, 430 Ninth Street, Fresno 4, California
Mrs. R. S. Fuller, 63 South Main Street, Newark 7, New Jersey

345. Alphabetic Speed Drill. Lesson 116: 5 to 10 copies of ¶D.

346. Perfect Speed Drill. Your best speed, striving for errorless typing.

The just firm will give the men good pay for the right work.   12

347. Alphabetic Production Letter. Type in semiblock style, 1 copy to each of the 7 addresses given.

Dear——: The fifth edition of our manual on banking and finance 14
is just off the press and ready for distribution to colleges and other 28
institutions offering courses in those subjects. A copy of this fifth 42
edition is being mailed to each member bank today. ¶ You will 55
notice that we offer a free copy of this new textbook to any in- 68
structor requesting it. All such requests should be referred by 82
member banks to the Banking Research Institute at this office and 96
they will be filled immediately. ¶ The Institute will send you a 109
notice of all requests received just as soon as they have been filled. 123
Be sure to follow up all such requests and offer whatever services 137
you can as it will pay dividends in the form of good will for the 150
banking profession. Sincerely yours, O. W. Worth, Educational 163
Services 165

Mr. J. V. Peterson, Bank of Los Angeles, Los Angeles 19, California
Mr. Edward A. Richards, Bank of Denver, Denver 7, Colorado
Mr. B. R. Bruce, Bank of New Orleans, New Orleans 3, Louisiana
Mr. C. W. Bates, Bank of Cincinnati, Cincinnati 6, Ohio
Mr. C. V. Belknap, Bank of Pittsburgh, Pittsburgh 7, Pennsylvania
Mr. G. K. Bell, Bank of Washington, Washington 8, D. C.
Mr. O. R. Sturtevant, Bank of Boston, Boston 16, Massachusetts

348. Typing Style Recall. Type 1 copy.

Grosset & Riggs will hold their sales show at 234 West 56 Street (Room #8) on April 7, 1954, between 9:30 a.m. and 5 p.m., and they expect almost 50% of those invited to attend. "Everyone will want to see," says Mr. Grosset, "our latest 'cost-cutting' office equipment." Three floors of displays will be manned by a staff of 106, and while admission ordinarily costs $2.50 to $5, we will have to pay only the tax of 75 cents.

349. Alphabetic Speed Drill for 5-Minute Timed Writing.

	W·A·M	
	1m	5m

A

	1m	5m
The enclosed plan is just a suggestion, and if any extra changes are	13	3
necessary, they can easily be made. As long as you maintain the	27	5
general plan, the price will not be greatly affected if you make any	41	8
small changes. The installation will involve the supervision of our	54	11
men who are familiar with the cost of installing machines of this	68	14
size. We would say that your total cost should not exceed the price	82	16
quoted, but you understand that this is just an estimate on our part.	95	19

B

We hope we have not gone into too much detail in explaining the	13	22
situation, but it is important that offices understand the situation	27	24
clearly, so that no doubt will exist as to the prices, sizes, and styles	41	27
of the various types of machines ordered. If the enclosed proposal	55	30
fails to cover the details in which you are interested, we shall be	68	33
more than pleased to answer any questions you may have regarding	81	35
these machines if you will just write us.	90	37

C

If you decide definitely to go ahead with the work, we can readily	13	40
give a final estimate; and if you feel that the men in your own plant	27	42
could handle the actual installation, you will be able to make an	40	45
extra saving. The men, of course, will have our blueprints to work	54	48
with. We hope this is just the information that you want and that	68	51
you will feel quite free to make any changes you wish on the blue-	82	53
print. We shall appreciate your analyzing and returning it.	94	56

D

Also, as far as plant building, we have constructed and installed	14	59
most of the plants in your area, and we are ready to build for you	27	61
at any time. We also have parts for immediate replacement should	41	64
this ever become necessary. The experience we have had in equip-	54	67
ping these plants with our systems has been utilized in the design of	68	70
our plans. We will construct and install to your complete acceptance	82	72
and satisfaction the plant outlined in your specifications.	93	75

LESSON 122

350. Perfect Speed Drill. Your best speed, striving for errorless typing.

The just firm will give the men good pay for the right work.   12

351. Alphabetic Speed Drill. Lesson 121: 5 to 10 copies of ¶A, then ¶B.

LESSON 123

352. Tabulation Drill. Type 1 copy of the following tabulation. Center it vertically and horizontally on a half sheet, 8½″ x 5½″.

MAILING ADDRESSES FOR H. D. BROWN

Date	City	State	Hotel
March 11-16	Rochester	New York	Weaver
March 17-31	Detroit	Michigan	Cadillac
April 1-15	Chicago	Illinois	Palmer House
April 16-30	Los Angeles	California	Ambassador
May 1-5	Seattle	Washington	Olympic

353. Alphabetic Speed Drill. Lesson 121: 5 to 10 copies of ¶C.

LESSON 124

354. Personal Business Letter Drill. Type 1 copy for each of the 5 addresses listed. (See also Reference Section, R-10.)

PLACEMENT PICTURE

Gentlemen: We are planning to remodel our 9 home in the spring and are therefore inter- 17 ested in receiving your literature containing 26 ideas on the subject. ¶ Would you be good 35 enough to send me a copy of your booklet, 43 and if there is any charge bill me or send the 52 booklet C.O.D. If you can include literature 60 giving prices, it will help us in our planning. 69 Cordially yours, John A. Student   75

93

Ayers Lumber Company, Ayers Building, Muncie 4, Indiana
Baylor Fixtures, Inc., Baylor Building, Des Moines 6, Iowa
Standard Paints Company, 654 Gennessee Building, Cleveland 3, Ohio
Hanover Furniture Company, 16 Geddes Square, Greensboro 1, North Carolina
Johnson Door Company, 135 Spring Street, Seattle 4, Washington

355. Alphabetic Speed Drill. Lesson 121: 5 to 10 copies of ¶D.

LESSON 125

356. Perfect Speed Drill. Your best speed, striving for errorless typing.

The just firm will give the men good pay for the right work.   12

357. Alphabetic Production Letter. Type in block style, 1 copy to each of the 7 addresses given. Note placement of addressee's title.

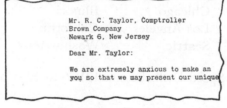

PLACEMENT PICTURE

Dear——: We are extremely anxious to make an appointment with   14
you so that we may present our unique plan for cutting your costs on   28
office supplies. ¶ This is not just another request to make a sales   41
demonstration, but a sincere offer to send one of our trained supplies   55
experts who will thoroughly analyze your office supplies needs. He   69
will give you a confidential report explaining just which supplies are   83
best suited for each of your office tasks and pointing out where costs   97
may be cut. ¶ Please write when we may have the privilege of calling   111
on you. Very truly yours, T. S. Rhodes, Research Director   122

Mr. R. C. Taylor, Comptroller, Brown Company, Newark 6, New Jersey
Mr. S. E. Knowles, Treasurer, Bell Power Company, Portland 6, Oregon
Mr. T. D. Sanford, Comptroller, Arned Company, Durham 4, North Carolina
Mr. G. L. Berger, Treasurer, Riggs Corporation, Detroit 17, Michigan
Mr. O. W. Kinley, General Manager, Otis, Inc., Pierre 4, South Dakota
Mr. P. T. Payne, Treasurer, Wilcox Company, Washington 7, D. C.
Mr. Ernest White, Comptroller, Ames Company, Boston 13, Massachusetts

LESSON 126

358. Typing Style Recall. Type 1 copy.

"A real contribution," states the commissioner, "for the 'travel-minded' public." Turner & Crane will formally announce the road opening in their offices at 356 South 42 Avenue (Suite #1720) on May 8, 1954, between 4:30 and 6 p.m. Ninety-three newspapers out of 120 have accepted invitations, almost 75%. Approximately $300 will be spent for dinners costing $3.25 each, and souvenir booklets will be distributed costing 90 cents each.

359. Alphabetic Speed Drill for 5-Minute Timed Writing.

W·A·M
1m 5m

A

You will recall that just a few days ago you phoned this office and 14 3
informed us that the proofs for our book would be ready for inspec- 28 6
tion next week. Our editor called to look at the plates at that time, 42 8
with the understanding that all of them were quite ready and that 55 11
he would inspect all of them at one time. It appears that only three 69 14
of the four were completed, and that it will be necessary to make 82 16
another trip. You realize this will mean a delay in going to press. 96 19

B

As it is six months since we have printed any books, and as the sale 14 22
of the books is showing an amazing increase, we should appreciate 28 25
it very much if you would move this job along quickly in order that 42 27
we may have the revised edition on hand in the next month or two. 55 30
If necessary, we will pay overtime in order to get the job done in 68 33
time. When the job is complete, ship half the order to this office, 82 36
the remainder to our warehouse. 89 37

C

Your man promised us that he would take up with you the highly 13 40
unsatisfactory service we have received on our book shipments 26 43
from your bindery to this zone. Your plant has not corrected the 40 45
condition in spite of the fact that quite a few months ago we informed 54 48
you that an order was coming through, and that when it did come 67 50
through, we expected no unnecessary delays. When we gave him 81 53
the order we let him set his own date for the deliveries. 92 55

D

We realize it would be to the interest of all of us if you would call 14 58
on the bindery at the very next opportunity. It is surely most im- 28 61
portant for us to keep on good terms with that company, for, as 41 64
you know, they handle thousands of dollars worth of our book 54 66
business. We are one of their best customers and always meet 67 69
their bills promptly, so you can readily see how much we value 80 71
prompt and dependable service. Just have a talk with them. 92 74

360. Perfect Speed Drill. Your best speed, striving for errorless typing.

The just firm will give the men good pay for the right work. 12

361. Alphabetic Speed Drill. Lesson 126: 5 to 10 copies of ¶A, then ¶B.

LESSON 128

362. Tabulation Drill. Type your Monday Class Program in tabular form with all the necessary information. Center the tabulation vertically and horizontally on a half sheet.

363. Alphabetic Speed Drill. Lesson 126: 5 to 10 copies of ¶C.

LESSON 129

364. Interoffice Letter Drill. On the interoffice letterhead shown, type 1 copy of the letter below to each of the 4 addresses listed.

TO   — — —
FROM   Sales Promotion Department
SUBJECT   Obsolete advertising literature
DATE   — — —

A few of our branches have called attention to the fact that their 14
stock of advertising literature is growing constantly and is creating 28
a storage problem. We have therefore adopted the following policy: 42

    1. Advertising literature will be distributed in limited 53
quantities hereafter, on a quota basis. 61

    2. A list of literature to be destroyed will be distributed 73
monthly to each branch. 78

To bring you up to date, please dispose of all literature not listed as 92
current on the attached sheet. T. D. Martin 101

Branch Manager, Chicago
Branch Manager, Los Angeles
Branch Manager, New Orleans
Branch Manager, New York

365. Alphabetic Speed Drill. Lesson 126: 5 to 10 copies of ¶D.

LESSON 130

366. Perfect Speed Drill. Your best speed, striving for errorless typing.

The just firm will give the men good pay for the right work.   12

367. Alphabetic Production Letter. Type in semiblock style, 1 copy to each of the 5 addresses given. (See Reference Section, R-1, for help in arranging letters.)

PLACEMENT PICTURE

Dear——: Thank you for your request for information concerning   14
office lighting. Due to an unforeseen demand, our present supply of   28
our professional bulletin on this subject has been exhausted. Our   41
printers, however, have promised us a delivery of additional copies   55
within the next few days, and as soon as the booklet is received, we   69
shall send you one in the mails. ¶ In the meantime, you may find the   83
attached catalog folder of interest. It analyzes and pictures each   96
type of office lighting fixture we manufacture and explains where it   110
fits in the office situation. ¶ Our lighting fixtures are found in the   124
offices and plants of leading manufacturers throughout the country.   138
If you are looking for scientific lighting which will make for greater   152
efficiency of office workers, our products are an excellent choice. ¶ If   165
we may be of further service to you, please write us and we shall be   179
glad to furnish you with whatever additional information you may   193
wish. Yours very truly, L. E. Zook, Chief Engineer   203

Mr. T. V. Alexander, President, Leland Foundry, Gary 7, Indiana
Mr. Hugh V. Kevy, Treasurer, The Bates Company, Black River 2, New York
Mr. C. V. Foster, President, Foster Company, Boston 18, Massachusetts
Mr. T. W. Chase, President, Green & Green, Louisville 7, Kentucky
Mr. Warren Cain, Treasurer, Todd Company, Sacramento 9, California

368. Typing Style Recall. Type 1 copy.

On June 4, 1954, from 11:30 a.m. to 5 p.m., the Bross & Sprague Museum will have a showing of modern art. The address is 657 East 80 Road (Studio #14). Seventy paintings will be exhibited to about 800 visitors, who will pay 90 cents, $1.50, and $2 for various types of admissions, and 50% of the proceeds will go to the Annual Art Fund. "Such a collection of 'history-making' art," says Mr. Johnson, "should be seen by all."

369. Alphabetic Speed Drill for 5-Minute Timed Writing.

	W·A·M	
	1m	5m

A

There are many smart economy moves to be made in connection 12 | 2
with the use of telephones for advertising and promotion. Because of 26 | 5
our varied and long experience in this phase of advertising and in 39 | 8
sales promotion, we are well prepared to be useful to you in making 52 | 10
these moves. Our range of experience enables us to provide the plan 66 | 13
for telephone selling best suited to your requirements. One company 80 | 16
has just realized a quick profit. 87 | 17

B

If you are planning to move your offices this fall, let us know about 14 | 20
it quickly so that we can avoid any delay in arranging for your 27 | 23
special services for long distance in your new offices. Just tell us 41 | 26
when you are moving and where you are moving to, and we will 54 | 28
do the rest. Many people are amazed at the low cost of making 67 | 31
such telephone calls over long distances. It is really surprising how 81 | 34
little extra it costs to keep in touch with branches and customers. 94 | 36

C

And speaking of cost, if you check to see how little extension tele- 14 | 39
phones cost, you will find that for a few cents a day you can have 28 | 42
telephones anywhere in your offices where they may be needed 41 | 44
quickly. Just call our business office for more information. And if 55 | 47
you are building your new offices, be sure to tell your builder that you 69 | 50
want telephone pipes installed which permit your telephone wiring to 83 | 53
be concealed. We can tell you more about some amazing services. 96 | 55

D

We do not have to look very hard these days to realize that spring 14 | 58
is with us again. For one thing, you are probably much busier than 28 | 61
you have been in a good many months with that new office planning 41 | 64
and all the various extra details that come at this time of the year. 55 | 66
But there is no reason for being too busy to keep in mind that you 69 | 69
can save yourself lots of time and money when you do business 82 | 72
quickly and easily by telephone. 89 | 74

LESSON 132

370. Perfect Speed Drill. Your best speed, striving for errorless typing.

The just firm will give the men good pay for the right work.   12

371. Alphabetic Speed Drill. Lesson 131: 5 to 10 copies of ¶A, then ¶B.

LESSON 133

372. Tabulation Drill. Type 1 copy of the following tabulation. Center it vertically and horizontally on a half sheet, 8½″ x 5½″.

SALES FOR JANUARY, 1954

Salesman	Territory	Quota	Sales
Ellery	Northeast	$10,000	$12,800
Whitman	Southeast	8,000	7,600
Rockefeller	Central	7,500	8,200
Wynn	Northwest	12,500	11,400
Havemeyer	Southwest	11,000	12,500

373. Alphabetic Speed Drill. Lesson 131: 5 to 10 copies of ¶C.

LESSON 134

374. Manuscript Typing Drill. Type 1 copy of the following page of manuscript, corrected as indicated.

375. Alphabetic Speed Drill. Lesson 131: 5 to 10 copies of ¶D.

The executive who goes ahead is not the executive who is satisfied with his job as it is, but the executive who is ambitious. The enterprising executive is determined to reach the top. He is ambitious *not only* for his company ~~as well as~~ *but also* for himself He thinks of the business as a whole and explores all angles rather than just those affecting his own department. He is receptive to new ideas *because they mean new business.*

To his boss or his company he is a key man. He means the difference between profit and loss. Although he commands a high salary, he knows how to make money for his employers--he earns every dollar he is paid--and more.

Today there is a real shortage of enterprising executives *!*

What It Takes

Leading executives will say, "It takes the kind of ability that will give any man an edge on competition." In this light, I. J. Kirwin *, an authority on these matters,* says:

> The man who would get ahead must be able to see the
> management picture as a whole and understand the broad
> principal of business operation: organization, human
> relations, manufacturing control, and distribution.[1]

Modern Methods
Uses

The enterprising executive will not hesitate to use profit-making methods actually used by other successful firms, modern purchasing and inventory controls. ~~and plans for setting up a~~

---

[1]I. J. Kirwin, <u>Management Today</u>, Chicago, Crane Publishing Company, 1950.

376. Perfect Speed Drill. Your best speed, striving for errorless typing.

The just firm will give the men good pay for the right work.   12

377. Alphabetic Production Letter. Type in block style, 1 copy to each of the 4 addresses given. (See Reference Section, R-1, for help in arranging letters.)

Dear——: We should like to know more about your films for office use. Our main interest at the present time is to secure films showing the function of different office machines, the standards of quality set by different offices around the country, the degree of skill necessary for performing various routine duties of the office. We have been told that this is the type of film that your organization makes available through sale or rental. ¶ We have for some time considered the idea of using motion pictures to train new employees. We realize how effective a film can be in showing the proper clothes to wear, the proper way to greet callers,   136 the proper way to answer the telephone. We can also imagine the   150 interest of new employees in learning office behavior through real   164 office situations pictured on the screen. ¶ If there is a representative   178 of your company in our territory, perhaps the best plan would be   192 just to have him call here so that we may discuss the whole matter   206 in person. We are sure he will probably have some excellent recom-   220 mendations once he learns what we are trying to do. ¶ We know we   233 can obtain office films from manufacturers of the various business   247 machines, but we find these are written mostly from the point of   261 view of operation and not from the point of view of efficiency of use.   275 One of the first things we are trying to do, of course, is to show new   289 employees how inefficiency costs money. ¶ We shall appreciate infor-   303 mation about your films as soon as possible. Yours truly, C. G. Wells,   317 Training Director   319

PLACEMENT PICTURE

Mr. W. W. Barker, Editor, Office Films, Inc., 330 Delmar, Columbus 7, Ohio

Mr. K. S. Ward, Editor, Business Films, 660 North Avenue, Chicago 22, Illinois

Mr. C. M. White, Director, Efficiency Films, 438 South Street, Dallas 3, Texas

Mr. E. E. White, Editor, Acme Film Company, 111 West Street, Utica 3, New York

378. Typing Style Recall. Type 1 copy.

We called on Hamilton & Smith at 856 North 70 Avenue (Rooms #42 and #43) between 11:45 a.m. and 1 p.m. on July 7, 1954, and explained that a return of 3% was considered good in advertising. Three thousand circulars will therefore be mailed instead of the previously planned 1,500, and they will list items from $6.50 to $200 and even some at 50 cents. "This hand-picked mailing list," they say, "should give us 'first-hand' information."

379. Alphabetic Speed Drill for 5-Minute Timed Writing.

	W·A·M	
	1m	5m

A

For the past several months we have had three members of your	13	3
staff in our office, and we have found them very tactful in dealing	27	5
with difficult situations. They have made every effort to solve quickly	41	8
the problems that have confronted us for many years and that	55	11
have been costing our company a lot of extra money every year.	68	14
Your men have just made some changes in the personnel of our	80	16
office and our factory, and they have done it in an amazing way.	93	19

B

They gave considerable attention to the problem of reducing our	14	21
costs in the shop, and installed a cost system that has given us a	28	24
better position to meet competition. As you may know, competition	42	27
in our line of business is very keen, and during the past few years we	55	30
have lost considerable business. Although your men worked on our	69	32
problem at a time when conditions were uncertain and profits were	82	35
quite small, they succeeded in doing an amazing job.	93	37

C

While making these changes in our office and factory, we have main-	14	40
tained our extra high standard of quality. In fact, in some cases we	28	43
have improved methods without increasing production cost. This is	42	46
another factor that will be helpful in meeting the keen competition	56	48
we mentioned above. We realize it is too early for us to say what our	70	51
yearly savings will be as a result of the plan, but we have gone far	84	54
enough with it at present to feel thoroughly satisfied with the job.	98	57

D

We have stocked the new box they recommended for quite a while	13	59
now, and we have found it most satisfactory. As a matter of fact, we	27	62
do not think we will have much occasion to mail our goods any other	41	65
way. The use of the same type carton for all our orders will mean	55	68
considerable saving, as it will just eliminate the manufacture of the	69	71
special cartons. We are holding certain orders here until we receive	83	73
your approval of the mailing cartons, as expressed in your letter.	96	76

LESSON 137

380. Perfect Speed Drill. Your best speed, striving for errorless typing.

The just firm will give the men good pay for the right work.　　　12

381. Alphabetic Speed Drill. Lesson 136: 5 to 10 copies of ¶A, then ¶B.

LESSON 138

382. Tabulation Drill. Tabulate the holidays you can remember (at least 6), using the main heading ANNUAL HOLIDAYS and the column headings Month, Day, Holiday. Center the tabulation vertically and horizontally on a half sheet.

383. Alphabetic Speed Drill. Lesson 136: 5 to 10 copies of ¶C.

LESSON 139

384. Addressing Drill. Type 3 envelopes or index cards for each of the following names and addresses.

Mr. F. T. Gray, James & Dunn Company, Hudson Street, Inglewood 3, California

Mr. T. E. Thomas, LaSalle Supply Company, Utica 2, New York

Mr. G. Gregor, Gregor Equipment Company, Pontiac 17, Michigan

Mr. J. B. Walter, Walter Equipment Company, San Francisco 8, California

Mr. D. P. Prescott, Prescott Sales Company, New Haven 4, Connecticut

Mr. F. T. Grayson, Quality Appliance Company, Chicago 12, Illinois

Mr. J. B. Blythe, Blythe Sales, Inc., 456 Main Street, Odessa 2, Texas

Mr. W. D. Dayton, Price & Company, 45 High Street, Davenport 4, Iowa

Mr. H. D. Allen, Allen Equipment Company, Denver 6, Colorado

Mr. J. V. Peterson, Bank of Los Angeles, Los Angeles 19, California

385. Alphabetic Speed Drill. Lesson 136: 5 to 10 copies of ¶D.

386. Perfect Speed Drill. Your best speed, striving for errorless typing.

The just firm will give the men good pay for the right work.   12

387. Alphabetic Production Letter. Type in semiblock style, 1 copy to each of the 2 addresses given. The heading for the second page reads: "National Supply Corporation, September 15, 1954, page 2."

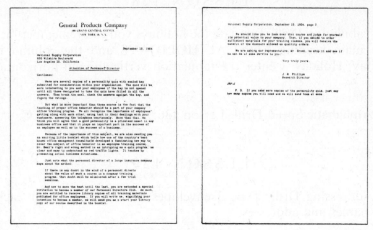

PLACEMENT PICTURES

Attention of Personnel Director, Gentlemen: Here are several   12
copies of a personality quiz with sealed key submitted for consider-   26
ation within your organization. The quiz will be more interesting   40
to you and your employees if the key is not opened until all those   53
designated to take the quiz have filled in all the answers. Then   67
break the seal, check the answers against the key, and figure the   80
ratings. ¶ But what is more important than those scores is the fact   94
that the teaching of proper office behavior should be a part of your   108
company training program. We all recognize the importance of   120
employees' getting along with each other, using tact in their deal-   133
ings with customers, answering the telephone courteously. More   147
than that, we think you will agree that a good personality is a   150
priceless asset in any business office and that it plays an important   164
part in the success of an employee as well as in the success of a   177
business. ¶ Because of the importance of this subject, we are also   191
sending you an exciting little booklet which tells how one of the   205
country's best known office management consultants developed a   219
fascinating new way to cover the subject of office behavior in an   232
employee training course. Dr. Beal's right and wrong method is as   246
intriguing as a quiz program, as clear and easy to understand as red   259

traffic lights. It teaches by presenting actual business situations. 273
¶ Just note what the personnel director of a large insurance com- 286
pany says about the method: 292

> If there is any doubt in the mind of a personnel director 303
> about the value of such a course in a company training 314
> program, that doubt will be eliminated after a few trial 325
> sessions. 327

¶ And now to save the best until the last, you are extended a special 340
invitation to become a member of our Personnel Directors Club. As 353
such you are entitled to receive library copies of all training ma- 367
terials published for office employees. If you will write us, signifying 381
your intention to become a member, we will send you as a start 394
your library copy of our course described in the booklet. ¶ We 407
should like you to look over that course and judge for yourself its 420
potential value to your company. Then, if you decide to order 433
sufficient materials for your training classes, you will receive the 446
benefit of the discount allowed on quantity orders. ¶ We are asking 460
our representative, Mr. Brown, to stop in to see if he can be of 473
some service to you. Very truly yours, J. R. Phillips, Research 486
Director, P. S. If you need more copies of the personality quiz, just 500
say how many copies you will need and we will send them at once. 513

National Supply Corporation, 620 Wilshire Boulevard, Los Angeles 25,
California
Carver Equipment Company, 220 West 43 Street, New York 9, New York

LESSON 141

388. Typing Style Recall. Type 1 copy.

The executives of Kane & Homer like the location at 708 West 65 Street (Room #369). They plan to visit that location again on August 9, 1954, between 10:30 a.m. and 1:30 p.m., and there is a 50% chance they will take the space. Rates quoted were $2.50 and $3 a foot, 80 cents for storage. Eighty to 125 persons will have to be accommodated. "There is every reason to believe," says Kane, "these 'sound-conditioned' offices are ideal."

389. Alphabetic Speed Drill for 5-Minute Timed Writing.

	W·A·M	
	1m	5m

A

	1m	5m
It is our policy to give the customer a bill for work done just the first	14	3
year, but no actual charge is made, and for that reason he thought	28	6
that your man was to handle the service without cost. We told him	42	8
however, that this was not our understanding at all; for if I remem-	56	11
ber correctly, we decided that the man who was taking care of the	69	14
rest of this copy editing would also take care of the promotion in	83	17
this zone. This would reduce the future cost of extra ad work.	97	19

B

	1m	5m
It is quite possible that we were not careful enough in making our	14	22
terms clear, or you may have additional information that would	28	25
make the services invoiced to you not allowable. We have just asked	42	28
our representative in your city to call on you early next week. We	56	31
should like to have you analyze the situation with him freely, and we	70	33
hope you can work out an early solution of this matter that will be	83	36
mutually satisfactory. If you are not satisfied, please write me.	97	39

C

	1m	5m
As none of your invoices will be due for some weeks, we suggest	13	41
that you just send us a note quickly for the total of the invoices,	27	44
which will permit us to fill the present requests for service. You may	41	47
feel that we are being extra strict over this matter, but if you will	55	50
analyze it we believe you will see that what is a safe credit for us to	69	53
give is a safe credit for you to take, and anything over that is a bad	83	55
risk for you to assume in the present state of the market.	94	58

D

	1m	5m
The cost of the service is really nominal when you consider it is	13	60
through your advertising that buyers will ask for just your goods	27	63
when they go to select gifts for their friends. Plan definitely to in-	41	66
clude this issue in your advertising campaign, to realize a profitable	55	69
season. The enclosed report will quickly show you how easy it is to	69	71
reach our more than one million readers. We can still take care of	83	74
your ad in good shape if all the material is in our hands by next week.	96	77

390. Perfect Speed Drill. Your best speed, striving for errorless typing.

The just firm will give the men good pay for the right work.   12

391. Alphabetic Speed Drill. Lesson 141: 5 to 10 copies of ¶A, then ¶B.

LESSON 143

392. Personal Business Letter Drill. Type 1 copy to each of the 3 addresses listed. (See also Reference Section, R-10.)

Attention of Personnel Director, Gentlemen: May I have the   12
privilege of an interview to discuss my qualifications for a secretarial   25
position in your company? The attached personal data sheet will   39
give you the details of my training, background, and experience.   53
¶ Although my actual experience has been limited to summer work,   66
you will note I have had the benefit of very extensive training in   80
secretarial work, which has helped me gain an above-average skill   94
in both shorthand and typing. ¶ Please use the enclosed envelope   107
to let me know when I may call. Very truly yours, John A. Student   120

The Price Radio Company, 51 First Avenue, St. Louis 4, Missouri
The Diamond Sales Company, 345 Harrison Street, St. Louis 15, Missouri
The Jewel Electric Company, 342 South Main Street, St. Louis 14, Missouri

393. Alphabetic Speed Drill. Lesson 141: 5 to 10 copies of ¶C.

LESSON 144

394. Billing Drill. On duplicated billheads like the one shown below, type the 5 copies of the following bill needed for the 5 addresses given. Set tabular stops according to the columns on the billhead.

Rollo Duplicator at $125
Rollo Service Kit at $25

Life and Casualty Insurance
1540 Brewster Avenue
Cincinnati 6, Ohio
Invoice No. 3257,
Quantity: 1 each

General Products Company
100 GRAND CENTRAL AVENUE
NEW YORK 10, N. Y.

Life and Casualty Insurance
1540 Brewster Avenue
Cincinnati 6, Ohio

DATE   May 22, 1954
INVOICE NO.   3247

Quantity	Description	Unit Price	Amount	Total
1	Rollo Duplicator	125 00	125 00	
1	Rollo Service Kit	25 00	25 00	150 00

King Records Company, Koppers Building, Pittsburgh 17, Pennsylvania
    Invoice No. 3258, Quantity: 2 each
Johnson Foods Company, 501 Peshtigo Court, Chicago 34, Illinois
    Invoice 3259, Quantity: 2 each
Servel Motor Company, 561 Main Street, Detroit 6, Michigan
    Invoice No. 3260, Quantity: 1 each
Lee, Jordan & Jordan, 58 Maiden Lane, New York 34, New York
    Invoice No. 3261, Quantity: 2 each

395. Alphabetic Speed Drill. Lesson 141: 5 to 10 copies of ¶D.

LESSON 145

396. Perfect Speed Drill. Your best speed, striving for errorless typing.

The just firm will give the men good pay for the right work.   12

397. Alphabetic Production Letter. Type in block style, 1 copy to each of the 7 addresses given. Note style of company signature.

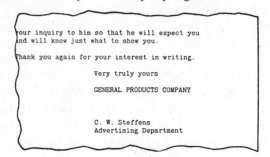

```
your inquiry to him so that he will expect you
and will know just what to show you.

Thank you again for your interest in writing.

              Very truly yours

              GENERAL PRODUCTS COMPANY



              C. W. Steffens
              Advertising Department
```

Dear——: Thank you for writing us about our new model home-   13
type organ. We want you to know all about it and hope it will be   26
possible for you to see one soon. ¶ We are sending you a booklet   39
that contains several illustrations of our new home organ, and   53
attached to this letter is a card with the name of our dealer in your   67
zone. We are forwarding your inquiry to him so that he will expect   81
you and will know just what to show you. ¶ Thank you again for   94
your interest in writing. Very truly yours, General Products Com-   108
pany, C. W. Steffens, Advertising Department   118

Mrs. C. W. Babcock, 48 High Street, South Bend 4, Indiana
Mr. E. G. Smythe, 78 Trunk Road, St. Joseph 7, Missouri
Mrs. B. T. Quinn, 17 Hudson Street, New Haven 16, Connecticut
Mrs. Fred Leasley, 571 Park Lane, Salt Lake City 17, Utah
Mr. R. C. Hayes, 42 Fulton Street, Atlanta 14, Georgia
Mr. W. N. Brigham, 46 North Main Street, Houston 32, Texas
Mrs. H. Belgraves, 49 Northern Boulevard, Des Moines 12, Iowa

398. Typing Style Recall. Type 1 copy.

Our shipping department in Room #416 has outgrown its space and is being moved to the Cross & Snell Building (250 South 87 Street), a space about 50% larger. Twenty people will handle 125 bags of mail daily from 8 a.m. to 5:30 p.m. and will be paid from 75 cents an hour to $1.60, with the head receiving $2. "We could no longer work under those conditions," says Mr. Lee, "and still be expected to do a 'top-notch' job."

399. Alphabetic Speed Drill for 5-Minute Timed Writing.

	W·A·M	
	1m	5m

A

If you will analyze the enclosed carbon of my letter to your general	14	3
manager, you will note we have a large amount of our work in your	27	5
plant right now. I should like some sort of schedule, so that we may	41	8
know the time we may expect these different jobs. I have told your	55	11
salesman and general manager quite a few times that only the fact	69	14
that you have no serious delays on our type of work keeps that work	82	16
in your plant. The shop has always done excellent work.	93	19

B

We are surely pleased to hear that the letter printed in your columns	14	21
in the last issue aroused so much favorable comment. It is evident	28	24
that the subject of using this system on testing the motor is a timely	42	27
one. Let us just emphasize that no fuel can remedy a defect, and that	56	30
the motor itself should be quickly checked before putting it to work.	70	33
If after you have examined our findings you care to go into the sub-	84	35
ject further, please do not hesitate to correspond with us.	96	38

C

The idea has already been an amazing success, and as our present staff	14	41
is anxious to enlarge the field of its influence and to increase quickly	28	43
its use in the field, we are now applying to the board to make it	41	46
possible for one member and one or more guests from our company	54	49
to attend the motors convention. We have just reviewed the many	68	51
advantages that accrue from attendance at conventions of the nature	82	54
of this one, but we are particularly attracted to clinics.	94	57

D

The committee of men who selected the device we requested had	13	59
some difficulty in deciding just which would be most helpful to us	27	62
in our work. They recognized that although we are working with	41	65
skilled help, it would be desirable for you to send a number of extra	55	68
devices for use by those who have had little or no training. They	69	70
felt that that would take over as much of the training of those men	83	73
as possible. We hope that most of these devices will be quite suitable.	97	76

LESSON 147

400. Perfect Speed Drill. Your best speed, striving for errorless typing.

The just firm will give the men good pay for the right work.   12

401. Alphabetic Speed Drill. Lesson 146: 5 to 10 copies of ¶A, then ¶B.

LESSON 148

402. Telegram Drill. On the telegram blank forms that will be supplied to you, type 1 copy of the night letter below to each of the 5 addresses listed.

New supply of bulletins on office lighting just received and copies you requested have been mailed. Our lighting engineer, Mr. W. Taylor, now in your territory and will contact you within ten days to offer his services.

> L. E. Zook
> Chief Engineer
> Crowell Electric Company

Mr. T. V. Alexander, President, Leland Foundry, Gary, Indiana
Mr. Hugh V. Kevy, Treasurer, The Bates Company, Black River, New York
Mr. C. V. Foster, President, Foster Company, Brookline, Massachusetts
Mr. T. W. Chase, President, Green & Green, Louisville, Kentucky
Mr. C. W. Barton, Comptroller, Alden Company, Port Chester, New York

403. Alphabetic Speed Drill. Lesson 146: 5 to 10 copies of ¶C.

LESSON 149

404. Billing Drill. On the duplicated billheads that will be supplied, type the 6 copies of the following bill needed for the 6 addresses given. Set tabular stops according to the columns on the billhead.

> Reynolds Range #100 at $120
> Reynolds Timer at $5

Gotham Builders, 51 Lark Lane, Worcester 3, Massachusetts
    Invoice No. 7535, Order No. 5968, Quantity: 2 each.
Grove City Sales, 536 Trinity Place, St. Paul 4, Minnesota
    Invoice No. 7536, Order No. 9481, Quantity: 4 each.
Goodyear Sales Company, 3 Harrison Street, San Francisco 27, California
    Invoice No. 7537, Order No. 9375, Quantity: 2 each.

Flinkote Corporation, Main Street, Montclair 4, New Jersey
   Invoice No. 7538, Order No. 4841, Quantity: 3 each.
Hood & Sons, Inc., Remway Park, Ashtabula 6, North Carolina
   Invoice No. 7539, Order No. 2847, Quantity: 3 each.
General Building Co., 243 South Broadway, Denver 12, Colorado
   Invoice No. 7540, Order No. 2643, Quantity: 2 each.

405. Alphabetic Speed Drill. Lesson 146: 5 to 10 copies of ¶D.

LESSON 150

406. Perfect Speed Drill. Your best speed, striving for errorless typing.

The just firm will give the men good pay for the right work.   12

407. Alphabetic Production Letter. Type in semiblock style, 1 copy to each of the 5 addresses given.

Dear——: Continued market research and careful analysis of office   14
requirements seem to indicate an increasing need for adding ma-   27
chines of larger capacity. To care for the special applications and   41
markets involved and to meet this apparent need, we are considering   54
the addition of a new machine line to include the features needed   67
with that type of machine. ¶ You will surely appreciate that such   80
a move is a larger undertaking and would involve expenditures of   94
considerable sums of money for development and production. Before   108
making a definite decision, therefore, we should like to obtain an   122
expression of opinion from you, since your organization is and has   136
always been a heavy user of just this type of equipment. We feel   150
that, because your organization has so many applications for adding   163
machines, you would know from a really practical standpoint   176
whether the proposed product would serve a good purpose. ¶ We   189
know we can count on your co-operation, as we have in the past, and   202
on your treating this matter in confidence. Yours very truly,   215
Grayson Office Machine Company, T. G. Howard, Director of   227
Product Development   231

Mr. P. S. Robertson, Treasurer, Porter & Company, Cleveland 32, Ohio
Mr. Albert S. Pohl, Comptroller, Fiske & Company, Tacoma 16, Washington
Mr. J. N. Robbins, President, Robbins & Company, Portland 7, Oregon
Mr. T. R. Van Dyke, Treasurer, Ferris Tool, Inc., Larchmont 5, New York
Mr. S. A. Wheatly, Comptroller, Tucker Oil Company, Tulsa 2, Oklahoma

LESSON 151

408. Typing Style Recall. Type 1 copy.

We were in the neighborhood of the Ashland & Brown store at 542 North 67 Drive on September 8, 1954, and saw the machines you wanted (Model #8) at $15.50 and $20, with refills at 50 cents a package. Eighty sheets are in the small pad and 160 in the large, the latter priced to save 25%. "Come between 8:30 and 10 a.m.," says the manager, "and we will give you a 'sure-fire' demonstration."

409. Alphabetic Speed Drill for 5-Minute Timed Writing.

W·A·M
1m 5m

A

	1m	5m
We realize just how happy you must be, planning to build your new	14	3
home, and how proud you will be of all the modern equipment that	27	5
makes owning a home a pleasure. We just want you to continue to	41	8
feel proud of all your new modern appliances and assure you that	54	11
we will co-operate with your builder to assure you the very best serv-	68	14
ice from those units. One of our expert heating engineers will call	82	16
at your home to go over the whole situation with your builder.	95	19

B

	1m	5m
Every appliance that comes into our store is marked with our lowest	14	22
possible price, and that price just stays on for good. The price tag	28	25
on each machine is so low that we do not have to reduce prices in	41	27
order to move it. We do not have many sales—our machines are	54	30
priced just as low now as they will be next year. When you want	68	33
home appliances, you will get an amazing bargain in our store. Even	82	35
after your home is complete, stop in occasionally and see the fine	94	38
values we have to offer for quick clearance.	99	39

C

	1m	5m
I think this is quite a good opportunity to tell you about the sale our	14	42
store is planning to celebrate our tenth anniversary. Just before this	28	44
sale is open to the public, we extend a cordial invitation to our	42	47
friends to visit us one day previous to the official opening of the sale,	56	50
in order to give them an opportunity to be the first to take advantage	70	53
of the amazing offers we are making. I am enclosing a card that will	84	56
admit you to this special sale. We will therefore expect to see you.	98	58

D

	1m	5m
You could just go to the office of this building, and they would	14	61
quickly tell you that we have been in this same store for years. We	27	64
could next take you to an advertising department and show you that	41	67
we advertise in many papers and magazines anywhere from large	55	70
ads down to very small ads. We could show you letters that could	69	72
not fail to convince you that our goods certainly help a lot of people.	83	75
Thus you can readily see how easily we sell customers our service.	96	78

LESSON 152

410. Perfect Speed Drill. Your best speed, striving for errorless typing.

The just firm will give the men good pay for the right work.   12

411. Alphabetic Speed Drill. Lesson 151: 5 to 10 copies of ¶A, then ¶B.

LESSON 153

412. Billing Drill. On the duplicated billheads that will be supplied, type the 6 copies of the following bill needed for the 6 addresses given. Set tabular stops according to the columns on the billhead.

Moderne Sectional Bookcase at $20
Set of Bookcase Legs at $1

Warner Paper Company, 509 West Main Street, Waterbury 12, Connecticut
    Invoice No. 5637, Order No. 7648, Quantity: 5 each.
Dayton Library, 234 Main Street, Dayton 3, Ohio
    Invoice No. 5638, Order No. 9403, Quantity: 3 each.
Clements Bookstore, 55 High Terrace, Wappingers Falls 2, New York
    Invoice No. 5639, Order No. 7954, Quantity: 2 each.
DeVry Hospital, 141 Holmes Avenue, Los Angeles 32, California
    Invoice No. 5640, Order No. 3754, Quantity: 5 each.
Rio Grande Western Company, 46 Center Street, Indianapolis 4, Indiana
    Invoice No. 5641, Order No. 3246, Quantity: 3 each.
The Dunn Library, Hudson Street, Inglewood 3, California
    Invoice No. 5642, Order No. 3769, Quantity: 4 each.

413. Alphabetic Speed Drill. Lesson 151: 5 to 10 copies of ¶C.

LESSON 154

414. Theme Typing Drill. Type 1 copy of the following theme.

415. Alphabetic Speed Drill. Lesson 151: 5 to 10 copies of ¶D.

FAST SHIPPING BY AIRFREIGHT

Airfreight is a new low-cost basic method of shipping designed to move merchandise at air speed in a regular flow on a volume basis. It is a new and revolutionary business tool opening up new merchandising channels, offering possibilities for wider markets, for developing new products and distributing existing products in new ways.

It benefits shippers and receivers, buyers and sellers, *as well as others.*

Miles-a-Minute ~~Speed~~ *Delivery*

~~Airfreight~~ Shipments *by airfreight* travel on fast cargo planes along the most direct routes to and from most cities. Beyond these points, shipments can be made via connecting airlines or surface transportation. This new mode of shipping has made it possible for many large companies to change their distribution policies and ~~thereby~~ *at the same time* realize new sales possibilities.

No Limits to Markets

With such fast shipping, markets are limited only by the imagination of the producer and *by* the demand for his product. No matter where he is located in the country, if there is a use for his product anywhere in this country or overseas, this fast *modern* method of shipping can get it there. Neither time nor distance need stand in the way.[1]

---

[1] Abstracted from "A Factual Study of the Advantages of Airfreight," American Airlines, New York, N. Y.

416. Perfect Speed Drill. Your best speed, striving for errorless typing.

The just firm will give the men good pay for the right work.   12

417. Alphabetic Production Letter. Type in block style, 1 copy to each of the 4 addresses given.

Dear——: We have just prepared and are now distributing to a   14
selected list of newspaper executives a special case history report. A   28
copy is being reserved for you should you, after reading this letter,   41
decide it is of interest to your organization. ¶ As a financial execu-   55
tive, you should be particularly interested in this report. It is   68
actually an intimate analysis of management and accounting prob-   81
lems common to most large newspapers. And it tells you specifically   94
what the Washington Chronicle is doing to solve them. ¶ For   106
example, that newspaper's executives had been looking for a method   119
that would give them more direct control over newsprint and wage   132
costs, a method that would simplify procedures and save money in   146
advertising and circulation accounts receivable operation. Also,   160
they wanted a method that could quickly produce a variety of   173
statistical reports required for closer executive control. ¶ This report   187
explains how the flexibility of a new accounting method is meeting   191
the requirements with many economies and profitable advantages.   204
Condensed for quick reading, the report is well documented with   218
exhibits of forms now used by that newspaper. ¶ We believe you   231
will want to have this report for its timely value in connection with   245
cutting accounting costs and establishing more effective manage-   258
ment control. More than likely it will bring you welcome information   272
and suggestions of similar advantages applicable to your own ac-   285
counting procedures, both now and in the future. ¶ We shall be glad   299
to send you the copy reserved for you. To get that copy promptly,   312
just fill in and start the enclosed postpaid reply card back to us   325
today. Yours truly, Accounting Sales, Inc., K. E. Reamer, Director   339
of Methods.   341

Mr. H. S. Peters, Treasurer, The Baltimore Record, Baltimore 18,
    Maryland
Mr. E. V. Bachmann, Comptroller, Dallas Chronicle, Dallas 8, Texas
Mr. J. M. Tarkington, Treasurer, St. Louis News, St. Louis 7, Missouri
Mr. T. G. Sloane, Treasurer, Seattle News, Seattle 21, Washington

LESSON 156

418. Typing Style Recall. Type 1 copy.

We visited the Mark & Jewel store at 845 South 26 Terrace on October 7, 1954, from 11:30 a.m. to 2 p.m. and saw the machine (Model #8) but found it marked at $17.50 and $25, with refills at 60 cents. Ninety sheets are in the pad, however, with 180 in the large size, the latter saving 35% in price. "Though the price is slightly higher," was the explanation, "this will give you 'top-quality' work."

419. Alphabetic Speed Drill for 5-Minute Timed Writing.

	W·A·M	
	1m	5m

A

In this course, each of you is an individual whose progress is limited — 14 — 3
solely by your ability. Your reading program is fitted just to your — 28 — 6
needs and, contrary to the usual method of adapting the student to a — 41 — 8
set program, we make the program fit the student. Next, the occa- — 54 — 11
sional class meetings are quite small, averaging about twelve stu- — 67 — 13
dents to the instructor, giving you close personal contact with your — 80 — 16
teacher. At the same time you have the advantage that discussion — 93 — 18
in classes that size provides. — 99 — 20

B

You will receive your first study book just as soon as your applica- — 14 — 23
tion reaches my desk. For five months thereafter, you will receive — 27 — 25
a very beautiful and desirable book at a price you would ordinarily — 41 — 28
pay for a novel. You will be delighted when you recognize the fine — 55 — 31
literature you have always intended to read but for some queer — 68 — 33
reason or other, have kept putting off. Never has a greater bargain — 82 — 36
been offered to the person truly interested in reading. — 93 — 38

C

Now, at the time people are searching for ways to increase their — 14 — 41
knowledge and skill, to increase earnings for a new car or a new — 27 — 44
home, this organization is bringing out books full of suggestions for — 41 — 47
everybody. They are just on sale at book dealers everywhere. A — 54 — 49
fine article this month is enclosed, which points out that the little — 68 — 52
things are often the most vital. Strangely enough, the biggest re- — 82 — 55
wards are paid for everyday things that most people can learn. — 95 — 58

D

All students taking our insurance course are quite eligible for merit — 14 — 60
rating if they wish to be written at the private rates, but are not — 28 — 63
recognized for merit rating if they must be written at the commercial — 42 — 66
rates. If a student owning a car that is being covered at the merit — 56 — 69
rate sells the car to another student, it is necessary to determine — 69 — 71
whether the new owner is entitled to the merit rate. If the new owner — 82 — 74
is not, the policy should provide for the extra rates. — 93 — 76

116

LESSON 157

420. Perfect Speed Drill. Your best speed, striving for errorless typing.

The just firm will give the men good pay for the right work.   12

421. Alphabetic Speed Drill. Lesson 156: 5 to 10 copies of ¶A, then ¶B.

LESSON 158

422. Billing Drill. Using half sheets of stationery, center a billhead as shown, substituting your name and address, then type the 6 copies of the following bill needed for the 6 addresses given.

Care of lawn and grounds for May $10

```
                    RALPH W. WILLIAMS
                    120 Locust Avenue
                    Auburn 13, Illinois



                                                    June 1, 1964

    Mr. T. R. Leight
    27 Brook Drive
    Auburn 2, Illinois
    _____

    Care of lawn and grounds for May...............................$10
```

Mr. T. R. Leight, 27 Brook Drive, Auburn 2, Illinois
Mrs. R. W. Tierney, 325 Plann Avenue, Auburn 3, Illinois
Mrs. W. L. French, 31 Stout Street, Auburn 2, Illinois
Mr. C. C. Durec, 345 Main Street, Auburn 1, Illinois
Mr. R. G. James, 143 Locust Avenue, Auburn 13, Illinois
Mr. W. C. Dayton, Harrison Park, Auburn 4, Illinois

423. Alphabetic Speed Drill. Lesson 156: 5 to 10 copies of ¶C.

LESSON 159

424. Addressing Drill. Type 3 envelopes or index cards for each of the following names and addresses.

Mr. T. V. Alexander, President, Leland Foundry, Leland Square, Gary 7, Indiana

117

Mr. Hugh V. Kevy, Treasurer, The Bates Company, 680 Broadway, Black River 2, New York

Mr. C. V. Foster, President, Foster Company, 8686 Griffin Park Place, Boston 18, Massachusetts

Mr. Warren Cain, Treasurer, Todd Company, 65 Easton Avenue, Sacramento 9, California

Mr. W. W. Barker, Editor, Office Films, Inc., 320 Delmar, Columbus 7, Ohio

Mr. K. S. Ward, Editor, Business Films, 660 North Avenue, Chicago 22, Illinois

Mr. E. E. White, Editor, Acme Film Company, 111 West Street, Utica 3, New York

Carver Equipment Company, 220 West 43 Street, New York 9, New York

National Supply Corporation, 620 Wilshire Boulevard, Los Angeles 25, California

425. Alphabetic Speed Drill. Lesson 156: 5 to 10 copies of ¶D.

LESSON 160

426. Perfect Speed Drill. Your best speed, striving for errorless typing.

The just firm will give the men good pay for the right work.   12

427. Alphabetic Production Letter. Type in semiblock style, 1 copy to each of the 2 addresses given.

PLACEMENT PICTURE

Dear——: Subject: Writing Aptitude. Your inquiry is very much   14
appreciated, since we are anxious to place in the hands of everyone   28
who is seriously interested in writing full information about our   42
training program and service. ¶ We hope you will pardon this form   56
letter. We wish it were possible to avoid generalities and get right   69
down immediately to a discussion of your particular situation, but of   82

course we cannot do that at this stage. ¶ You may never have at- ₉₅
tempted to write a line for publication, yet feel that with proper ₁₀₉
guidance you could succeed in some branch of writing. Or perhaps ₁₂₂
you have been writing for a long time and are seeking a way to ₁₃₆
improve so that your work will sell more regularly and bring higher ₁₅₀
prices. ¶ In either case, if you have the necessary natural talent and ₁₆₄
are willing to do your part, our service will help you surely and ₁₇₇
quickly to reach the goal you have set for yourself. Our students have ₁₉₁
successfully sold the following: ₁₉₈

Magazine Articles	437	202
Short Stories	298	206
Newspaper Columns	137	210
Radio Scripts	212	214

¶ Regardless of your particular aims, our training provides a logical ₂₂₈
short cut to an interesting and profitable writing career. Here for ₂₄₂
the first time actual situations are used to teach practical writing. ₂₅₆
¶ So that we may learn more definitely where you stand and more ₂₇₀
intelligently reach a decision as to what we may be able to do to be ₂₈₃
of help to you, our faculty has devised the writing aptitude test ₂₉₇
inclosed. ¶ If you will just answer the test questions to the best of ₃₁₁
your ability, as directed in the printed instructions, and return it to ₃₂₄
us in the addressed envelope, your answers will be analyzed carefully ₃₃₈
and we shall report to you frankly just what the future may hold for ₃₅₂
you as a writer. ¶ With our report on your test we shall send our ₈₆₆
recommendations as to the steps you can best take now toward a ₃₇₉
writing career. If in our opinion our training will be of immediate ₃₉₃
help to you, we shall send at the same time a book that will provide ₄₀₆
you with some valuable instruction on writing. This book presents ₄₂₀
writing to you in an entirely new aspect and inspires you with the ₄₃₄
many profitable opportunities that are open to men and women in ₄₄₈
this field. ¶ Our report will be of value to you as a guide in the ₄₆₂
future even though you do not act on it now. Sincerely yours, ₄₇₅
General Products Company, E. J. Kendall, Dean, P. S. All papers ₄₈₈
will be returned to you after we have made our report. ₄₉₈

Mrs. G. C. Glacer, 75 North Street, Camden 13, New Jersey
Mr. D. S. Shelley, 326 West 121 Street, Lexington 5, Kentucky

428. Typing Style Recall. Type 1 copy.

They were in the vicinity of the Laden & Smith store at 452 West 76 Drive on September 18, 1954, and saw the model you wanted (Model #5) at $35.50 and $40, with spare parts at 90 cents a kit. Fifty parts are in the small kit and 125 in the large, the latter priced to save 35%. "If you can come between 9:30 and 11 a.m.," says Mr. Laden, "we will give you a 'tailor-made' demonstration."

429. Alphabetic Speed Drill for 5-Minute Timed Writing.

W·A·M
1m 5m

A

	1m	5m
Unless your store can afford to spend extra sums at frequent inter-	13	3
vals to keep an old demonstration player adjusted and working, and	27	5
this is a daily problem created by changing temperature and humid-	41	8
ity, it is well to consider how to eliminate the problems of tuning	54	11
and maintenance. If your store has no music, now is the time to look	68	14
into the possibility of securing one of our players. There are a number	82	16
of amazing little models, one for every store.	91	18

B

There is a player in a size that is quite within the reach of even the	14	21
smallest business. Because of the extra large number of our players	27	24
being constantly bought by stores, more than all other comparable	40	26
instruments combined, ours is the lowest priced complete one known	53	29
on the market. And ours is the only one in the world that just cannot	66	31
go out of tune, and that therefore is always ready to provide hun-	80	34
dreds of beautiful true tones in any weather, anywhere.	91	36

C

Your dealer will be glad to demonstrate the unique player to you,	14	39
without obligation, of course. It is believed that the recognized	28	42
capacity of our player to provide suitable music under just any cir-	41	45
cumstances had much to do with the recent success in the last inter-	54	47
national show. We have been doing the finest type of designing for	68	50
many years. The men we employ are experienced and careful and	81	53
they are very highly skilled.	87	54

D

The extra efficiency and skill with which our men make your player	14	57
will not only reduce your promotion worries to a minimum but will	28	59
surprise and delight you. With your order in our care, you may rest	42	62
assured that everything will be delivered quickly and in top condi-	55	65
tion. In any event, we assume full responsibility and will insure you	69	68
against any possible loss or damage. Each van in your zone is insured	83	70
against loss by fire and theft while it is on the job.	94	73

LESSON 162

430. Perfect Speed Drill. Your best speed, striving for errorless typing.

Those men will do work just for us if we give them good pay.   12

431. Alphabetic Speed Drill. Lesson 161: 5 to 10 copies of ¶A, then ¶B.

LESSON 163

432. Addressing Drill. Type 3 envelopes or index cards for each of the following names and addresses.

Mrs. James A. Beals, Deerfield 2, Massachusetts
Mrs. M. J. Starr, Rushville 3, Ohio
Mr. H. J. Brunner, Willimantic 4, Connecticut
Mr. J. Harold Brown, Milford 4, New Jersey
Mrs. O. T. Cooper, Elmsford 3, New York
Mr. V. D. Stacey, Woodstock 3, New York
Mrs. G. L. Gallup, Wilton 2, Maryland
Miss Alice M. Ely, Spring Lake 3, Pennsylvania
Mrs. J. J. Colt, Cottsville 4, Delaware
Mr. A. V. Luke, East Stroudsburg 3, Pennsylvania

433. Alphabetic Speed Drill. Lesson 161: 5 to 10 copies of ¶C.

LESSON 164

434. Tabulation Drill. Set up the following tabulation attractively on a full sheet, 8½" x 11".

AMERICAN JUNIOR EXECUTIVES' ASSOCIATION
Executive Board

Ralph A. Bryson	Herbert M. Grumman	Mildred J. Sheats
L. A. Beals	R. M. Hunsaker	Paul H. Reid
William G. Colt	H. Y. McCallister	Mildred J. Starr

Executive Council

Frank I. Bigelow	R. A. Beard	Edward J. Carman
Roy G. Ambler	Charles A. Hunter	Harry J. Brunner
W. S. Bradford	F. W. Brigham	B. M. Chivers
L. P. Bittner	H. F. Bennion	W. R. Cherrington

435. Alphabetic Speed Drill. Lesson 161: 5 to 10 copies of ¶D.

436. Perfect Speed Drill. Your best speed, striving for errorless typing.

Those men will do work just for us if we give them good pay.   12

437. Alphabetic Production Letter. Type in block style, 1 copy to each of the 10 addresses given.

Dear Sir: As you probably know by this time, next month is the   12
period that your home office has designated for featuring our line   26
of paints. ¶ This year we have planned a display that is even more   39
attractive than those of previous years, and the sales for your store   53
should be proportionately greater. We again have a specially trained   67
crew for the job of setting up attractive window displays for the   80
campaign, and one of those specialists will be calling at your store   94
within the next three weeks. ¶ As usual, we will welcome any in-   108
quiries or suggestions from our dealer outlets for increasing the   121
effectiveness of our displays. Very truly yours, R. H. Merrick,   134
Sales Promotion.   137

Manager, Lee Hardware Company, Tucson 2, Arizona
Manager, Lee Hardware Company, Odessa 4, Texas
Manager, Lee Hardware Company, Utica 9, New York
Manager, Lee Hardware Company, Evanston 7, Illinois
Manager, Lee Hardware Company, Louisville 8, Kentucky
Manager, Lee Hardware Company, San Jose 4, California
Manager, Lee Hardware Company, Pierre 5, South Dakota
Manager, Lee Hardware Company, Lewiston 2, Maine
Manager, Lee Hardware Company, Helena 3, Montana
Manager, Lee Hardware Company, Spokane 6, Washington

LESSON 166

438. Typing Style Recall. Type 1 copy.

Our order department in Room #614 has expanded and is being moved to the Bowman & Lane Building (520 North 87 Street) in 40% larger quarters. Thirty clerks will handle 950 orders daily from 8:30 a.m. to 5 p.m. and will receive from 85 cents to $1.85 an hour, with the supervisor receiving $2. "We had definitely outgrown that space," says the supervisor, "and could no longer do a 'top-quality' job."

439. Alphabetic Speed Drill for 5-Minute Timed Writing.

	W·A·M 1m	5m
A		
There are three important factors to be recognized when planning	14	3
the most important part of a room. The first is that it last. You are	27	5
interested not only in the length of service your flooring material	41	8
will give you, but equally important, the kind of service and just how	55	11
this service meets your needs. The next factor is saving. This, too, is	69	14
important, because you should not pay more than you have to in	82	16
order to obtain the flooring that will do the best job for you.	94	19
B		
Then you must analyze style and the appearance of your floor	12	21
because it is so important in home styling. Planning your home	24	24
begins with basic parts of the house that will be with you always,	37	26
those parts that you will live with as long as you live in your home.	51	29
These interior parts must be chosen with extra skill for they must	64	32
be adaptable to just any decor and gracefully complement your	77	34
furnishings. Your floor is quite the most important part of your room.	91	37
C		
You must realize that you and your guests look at floors more than	13	40
the walls, ceilings, and even furniture. Everyone looks where he	26	43
steps, for it is a fixed habit as well as a safety measure. Our plant	40	45
has prepared more than a hundred smart patterns from which you	53	48
can select just the right ones to enhance each room of your house. To	67	50
add quite another touch of individuality, your flooring will have	81	53
your initial printed on it as part of the design.	91	55
D		
You may be amazed that it is possible for us to do this in these	13	58
times of rising costs. First, we make this special offer to you by mail,	27	61
with no extra money for salesmen and dealers. Second, we had the	41	63
beautiful goods that we use on these coverings made for us last	54	66
February just before the big jump in price. We also ordered the	67	69
binding to match the flooring early last spring. We should have to	81	71
pay much more for the work if we ordered it now.	91	73

LESSON 167

440. Perfect Speed Drill. Your best speed, striving for errorless typing.

Those men will do work just for us if we give them good pay.   12

441. Alphabetic Speed Drill. Lesson 166: 5 to 10 copies of ¶A, then ¶B.

LESSON 168

442. Centering Drill. Set up the following title page attractively on a full sheet, 8½″ x 11″. To "letterspace," as in the title, space once between letters, three times between words.

THE MARKET FOR WRITERS

J. Hartley Linton
Professor of Literature
Wembley Institute
Boston

An evaluation of today's market for fiction and nonfiction writing intended as a possible guide for those interested in the writing profession.

**THE HANLEY SMITH
PUBLISHING COMPANY**
Boston, Massachusetts

PLACEMENT PICTURE

443. Alphabetic Speed Drill. Lesson 166: 5 to 10 copies of ¶C.

LESSON 169

444. Manuscript Typing Drill. Type 1 copy of the following page of manuscript, corrected as indicated.

445. Alphabetic Speed Drill. Lesson 166: 5 to 10 copies of ¶D.

THE ~~MARKET~~ REAL MARKET FOR WRITERS

New writers often decide that fiction writing is the only field where rewards are high and outlets plentiful. It is true, of course, that at the very top of the market fiction stories bring ~~unusually high~~ very good prices. But the market for nonfiction ~~non-fiction~~ also is a broad one that ~~grows~~ is growing broader all the time.

The Market for ~~Non-Fiction~~ Nonfiction

The modern reader is more interested in facts than was the reader of a decade ago. In recent times, many famous fiction writers have turned to writing ~~non-fiction~~ nonfiction, not because the fiction market was failing but because it is so much easier to gather facts and put them directly on paper.

The newspaper syndicates, the Sunday newspapers, the weekly magazines—all ~~these~~ of them want facts. Just note what D. D. Brown, noted fiction writer, ~~has to say~~ said recently:

> There is rich writing material in every corner of the
> country. Often all that is required is the gathering
> of facts and their simple direct presentation. No
> intense study of technique is demanded, no literary
> frills. A keen eye, an alert ear, and an understanding
> of markets may be combined to produce a good income.[1]

The Market for Fiction

"The pulp market itself has ~~broadened a great deal,~~ come a long way," states O. R. Norton, famous short story writer.[2] The demand is for more and more short stories and new names.

---

[1] D. D. Brown, Writing for Success, New York, O. F. Little Company, 1948.
[2] O. R. Norton, Selling Short Stories, Boston, D. D. Wright Publishing Company, 1949.

446. Perfect Speed Drill. Your best speed, striving for errorless typing.

Those men will do work just for us if we give them good pay.   12

447. Alphabetic Production Letter. Type in semiblock style, 1 copy to each of the 10 addresses given.

Dear Sir: One of our representatives will call on you within the next   14
month to show you our new and improved selection of school sup-   27
plies. We have endeavored to put these school items before you   40
early in the season just to give you an opportunity to stock up and   54
plan displays well in advance of school opening. ¶ When our man   67
calls, you will note that quite a few of the items are selling well   80
below last year's prices. You will also note that the line includes a   94
few novelty items with which you are bound to create special   107
interest among students and realize a greater sales volume. Yours   120
very truly, Edward G. Wise, School Manager.   129

Manager, The White Company, Des Moines 11, Iowa
Manager, The White Company, New Rochelle 6, New York
Manager, The White Company, South Bend 8, Indiana
Manager, The White Company, Asbury Park 7, New Jersey
Manager, The White Company, Vernon 6, Texas
Manager, The White Company, Reno 3, Nevada
Manager, The White Company, Clearwater 7, Florida
Manager, The White Company, Racine 3, Wisconsin
Manager, The White Company, Tacoma 9, Washington
Manager, The White Company, Inglewood 4, California

LESSON 171

448. Typing Style Recall. Type 1 copy.

The officers of Ramey & Horn are pleased with the space at 807 South 56 Street (Room #936). They plan to move on July 9, 1954, between 8 a.m. and 8:30 p.m. and there is a 50% chance they will later need more space. The rent will be between $1.50 and $2 a foot, and 90 cents for storage space. Ninety to 115 persons will occupy the offices. "These 'color-conditioned' offices," says Mr. Horn, "always make for high morale."

449. Alphabetic Speed Drill for 5-Minute Timed Writing.

	W·A·M	
	1m	5m

A

	1m	5m
We realize that when a shop owner builds a wall around his property	14	3
he wants good protection and a trim wall for many years to come. So	27	5
when we build for you, we build every part of it as sturdy as we can	41	8
and we try to give you the kind of quality that means extra beauty.	55	11
At the same time we try to keep prices down to where every owner	68	14
can afford our work. Our walls are built by our own trained crews.	82	16
These men are not only skilled at their work, but they know how to	95	19
do the job right.	98	20

B

	1m	5m
First you will find that our men are the type of men whom you will	13	22
be glad to have working around your place of business. Next in im-	26	25
portance is the quality of work, and then the type and size of gate to	40	28
go with your new wall. The purpose of a gate is to swing open and	53	30
shut, and that is its whole job. When a gate drags or sticks it is a	67	33
first-class nuisance. That is why we build your gates as rugged as	81	36
possible and why we equip them with strong hinges and catches.	94	38

C

	1m	5m
If you want to keep children safely outside your factory yard, the	14	41
gate to use is one that closes by itself with perfect safety. When you	28	44
pass through the gate it closes behind you, smoothly and quickly. A	42	47
strong spring is encased in the hinge itself and closes the gate. You	56	49
can always recognize one of our gates by its sturdiness, and by the	69	52
fact that we mount them on extra heavy posts, which hold up even	82	55
under the most unusual traffic conditions.	91	57

D

	1m	5m
When an insurance man looks at plant property, he looks for theft	13	59
hazards. Your shop is well kept and quite free from just such hazards.	27	62
It is what we insurance men call a preferred risk. By insuring in our	41	65
company, a company that accepts preferred risks only, you can get	54	67
an extra dividend on your insurance. Our company is a mutual	68	70
company operating according to life insurance methods.	79	72

127

LESSON 172

450. Perfect Speed Drill. Your best speed, striving for errorless typing.

Those men will do work just for us if we give them good pay.   12

451. Alphabetic Speed Drill. Lesson 171: 5 to 10 copies of ¶A, then ¶B.

LESSON 173

452. Addressing Drill. Type 3 envelopes or index cards for each of the following names and addresses.

Manager, Lee Hardware Company, Evanston 7, Illinois
Manager, Lee Hardware Company, Louisville 8, Kentucky
Manager, Lee Hardware Company, San Jose 4, California
Manager, Lee Hardware Company, Pierre 5, South Dakota
Manager, Lee Hardware Company, Lewiston 2, Maine
Manager, Lee Hardware Company, Helena 3, Montana
Manager, Lee Hardware Company, Spokane 6, Washington
Manager, The White Company, Des Moines 11, Iowa
Manager, The White Company, New Rochelle 6, New York
Manager, The White Company, South Bend 8, Indiana

453. Alphabetic Speed Drill. Lesson 171: 5 to 10 copies of ¶C.

LESSON 174

454. Tabulation Drill. Set up the following tabulation attractively on a full sheet, 8½″ x 11″.

HIGHEST AND LOWEST RECORDED TEMPERATURES

State	Station	Highest	Lowest
Arizona	Phoenix	118	16
California	Los Angeles	109	28
Florida	Miami	96	27
Illinois	Chicago	105	—23
Massachusetts	Boston	104	—18
Montana	Helena	103	—42
North Dakota	Bismark	114	—45
New York	New York	102	—14

455. Alphabetic Speed Drill. Lesson 171: 5 to 10 copies of ¶D.

456. Perfect Speed Drill. Your best speed, striving for errorless typing.

Those men will do work just for us if we give them good pay.   12

457. Alphabetic Production Letter. Type in block style, 1 copy to each of the 6 addresses given.

Dear Mr.——: There is a good job waiting for you, which should be   14
of interest to you. We want to talk to you about it immediately.   28
For your convenience, our employment office will be open until   41
8 p.m. every day next week. ¶ You should be fully qualified for one   55
of the many positions available here because we are doing the same   69
type of sheet steel fabrication as is done in the organization where   83
you were recently employed. ¶ Working conditions and scale of pay   96
are equal to or better than for similar work anywhere in this area.   110
Besides helping us maintain important production you will have   123
every opportunity for advancement. ¶ The job you can have is one   136
with a definite future. We have a steady, dependable business   149
which has been built up through many years of experience in our   162
line. ¶ Please get in touch with us as quickly as possible so that   176
we may talk to you personally about this opportunity for steady   190
work now, with a future for you which is limited only by your own   203
ability. Sincerely yours, Elvin Merrill, Personnel Manager.   215

Mr. C. Rodman, Vine Street, Orange 2, New Jersey
Mr. S. T. Hudson, Maple Avenue, Teaneck 4, New Jersey
Mr. V. E. Carlson, Spring Road, Butler 3, New Jersey
Mr. R. Blaine, Cedar Street, Ridgefield 1, New Jersey
Mr. W. Roberts, Vale Avenue, Menlo Park 6, New Jersey
Mr. C. C. Race, Lincoln Road, Fairlawn 4, New Jersey

LESSON 176

458. Typing Style Recall. Type 1 copy.

The men called on Leed & Taylor at 685 North 40 Avenue (Room #72) between 10:30 a.m. and 1 p.m. on August 2, 1954, to talk about the possibility of a 3% return on the mailing. Twenty thousand folders will be mailed instead of 17,500, and they will show items from $8.50 to $25 and a few at 85 cents. "This 'blue-book' mailing list," says Mr. Arnold, "should give us a very high return."

459. Alphabetic Speed Drill for 5-Minute Timed Writing.

	W·A·M	
	1m	5m

A

The real comfort of hot water service comes from always having — 13, 3
enough. This depends both on the kind of heater you buy and the — 26, 5
size in its relation to your needs. From a very efficient heater such — 40, 8
as the one shown here, you can draw a greater quantity of the hot — 54, 11
water before it is diluted with cold. But the best of heaters cannot do — 68, 14
the job if it is not exact in size. Actually, that would save you nothing — 82, 16
in the operating cost, and might require earlier replacement. — 94, 19

B

A water heater with margin to spare is always a good investment. — 13, 21
Just what size of heater for your home will depend upon the type, — 26, 24
upon the number of people in your family, the appliances you would — 40, 27
like to own, and your customary way of living. The average adult — 54, 30
uses hundreds of gallons of hot water a month. This includes water — 68, 32
for personal use and the extra quantity necessary to meet the needs — 82, 35
of food preparation and other household uses in the average family. — 96, 38

C

Most families fall into one of two groups in their use of hot water. — 13, 41
Those who live in extra large homes are the liberal users. Hot water — 27, 43
is more frequently used in several places in the house at once without — 41, 46
thought as to amount. In addition to the size of your family and the — 55, 49
quantity of water needed, it is just as necessary to know when im- — 68, 52
portant uses of hot water overlap. It is best, therefore, to have a sur- — 82, 54
vey of your needs done by an engineer in the field. — 92, 56

D

Because of the changing conditions in the world today, you must — 13, 59
realize that the cost of equipment like this will rise during the years — 27, 62
just ahead. In fact, during the last two or three years, the cost of — 41, 65
living has already increased to some extent. This rising cost of living — 55, 67
makes the planning of spending of vital importance. In fact, it is es- — 69, 70
sential if you are to get those things that you really need for the — 82, 73
comfort and convenience of your family, and get them now. — 94, 75

LESSON 177

460. Perfect Speed Drill. Your best speed, striving for errorless typing.

Those men will do work just for us if we give them good pay. 12

461. Alphabetic Speed Drill. Lesson 176: 5 to 10 copies of ¶A, then ¶B.

LESSON 178

462. Centering Drill. Set up the following contents page attractively on a full sheet 8½" x 11".

THE MARKET FOR WRITERS

CONTENTS

Chapter		Page
I	The Nonfiction Market	2
II	The Fiction Market	6
III	Newspaper Writing	7
IV	Magazine Writing	9
V	Special Feature Writing	12
VI	Short Story Writing	13
VII	Editorial Writing	17
VIII	Schools	18
IX	Case Histories	20

PLACEMENT PICTURE

463. Alphabetic Speed Drill. Lesson 176: 5 to 10 copies of ¶C.

LESSON 179

464. Telegram Drill. On the telegram blank forms that will be supplied to you, type 1 copy of the full rate telegram below to each of the 10 addresses listed.

Annual display featuring our paints and arrival date our representative delayed two weeks.

R. H. Merrick

Manager, Lee Hardware Company, Tucson, Arizona
Manager, Lee Hardware Company, Odessa, Texas
Manager, Lee Hardware Company, Utica, New York
Manager, Lee Hardware Company, Evanston, Illinois
Manager, Lee Hardware Company, Louisville, Kentucky
Manager, Lee Hardware Company, San Jose, California

Manager, Lee Hardware Company, Pierre, South Dakota
Manager, Lee Hardware Company, Lewiston, Maine
Manager, Lee Hardware Company, Helena, Montana
Manager, Lee Hardware Company, Spokane, Washington

465. Alphabetic Speed Drill. Lesson 176: 5 to 10 copies of ¶D.

LESSON 180

466. Perfect Speed Drill. Your best speed, striving for errorless typing.

Those men will do work just for us if we give them good pay.   12

467. Alphabetic Production Letter. On the interoffice letterhead form that will be supplied to you, type 1 copy of the letter below to each of the 6 addresses given.

TO   —
FROM   Director, Mechanical Service Training
SUBJECT   Proposed Training Classes
DATE   —

We have analyzed the repair calls made nationally in connection   13
with the Model 7 Package Mailer, and they reveal the need for   26
further mechanical training of our field staff on this new product.   40
It was found that there is nothing basically wrong with the con-   54
struction of the equipment and that the more than normal number   67
of service calls is due to the fact that our men are using expedients   81
of their own when they are not too sure of the source of trouble.   95
These difficulties can be solved through proper instruction. ¶ Three   108
different training classes will be held in the very near future, each   122
of one week's duration. Will you please submit the names of those   136
of your men who will attend these classes, specifying in each case   149
whether the man will attend the first, second, or third class. Classes   163
will be held at the home office as usual. Further details will be sent   177
just as soon as definite dates have been set. S. D. Allen.   189

Mechanical Service Manager, Cleveland
Mechanical Service Manager, Boston
Mechanical Service Manager, Chicago
Mechanical Service Manager, Dallas
Mechanical Service Manager, Los Angeles
Mechanical Service Manager, Atlanta

468. Typing Style Recall. Type 1 copy.

On July 14, 1954, from 11:30 a.m. to 5 p.m., the Sprague & Sprague showroom will feature modern furniture. The address is 756 East 14 Road (Showroom #8). Ninety pieces will be exhibited to about 1,800 visitors who will pay 85 cents, $1.25, and $2 for admission, 50% of which will go to a special fund. "Everyone should make it a point," says Mr. Laidlow, "to 'explore' each of these history-making designs."

469. Alphabetic Speed Drill for 5-Minute Timed Writing.

	W·A·M·	
	1m	5m

A

	1m	5m
If one were to ask you exactly how many days in the year the sun	13	3
shows his face in your back yard, you would probably say something	27	5
to the effect that at times you see him often, but at other times he	40	8
seldom appears. The point is that you cannot count on him to dry	54	11
your wash, and often, after putting it out, you then quickly rush out	68	14
and recover it through the rain. And in winter the sun does little to	81	16
warm the wintry blasts or melt the clothes that freeze as fast	92	18
as they are hung.	96	19

B

	1m	5m
In summer, colors quickly fade pale and drab when exposed at	12	22
length to the torrid stare of the sun. In freezing winter or hot summer	26	24
weather, your new clothes dryer is ready to serve you. Never again	40	27
will you be concerned about weather changes. Never again will you	54	30
dig paths through the snow to your drying line, exposing yourself to	68	33
the wintry winds. With your new dryer, you just dry your clothes	81	35
indoors anytime, as fast as you can wash, while you relax.	93	38

C

	1m	5m
Rain or shine, your dryer gives your laundry that sunshine and	13	40
breeze freshness, and in the equally controlled sunlight of your dryer	27	43
even the most delicately tinted fabrics cannot fade. A large part of	41	46
each wash can just be folded and put away without ironing. This	54	49
saves you from extra work, and your clothes from outdoor damage	68	51
and abuse. Just think how much time you can save with this new	81	54
machine for your many other household duties.	90	56

D

	1m	5m
If you are wondering about payments, familiarize yourself quickly	14	59
with our credit plan. During the past four years, this plan has helped	28	61
thousands of our customers to enjoy the better things of life without	41	64
extending and without straining the family budget. We believe that	55	67
this plan is founded on a sound principle of good business. We also	68	69
believe firmly that to encourage anyone to overspend or to live	81	72
beyond his means is against public interest.	90	74

LESSON 182

470. Perfect Speed Drill. Your best speed, striving for errorless typing.

Those men will do work just for us if we give them good pay.   12

471. Alphabetic Speed Drill. Lesson 181: 5 to 10 copies of ¶A, then ¶B.

LESSON 183

472. Addressing Drill. Type 3 envelopes or index cards for each of the following names and addresses.

Manager, The White Company, Reno 3, Nevada
Manager, The White Company, Clearwater 7, Florida
Manager, The White Company, Racine 3, Wisconsin
Manager, The White Company, Tacoma 9, Washington
Manager, The White Company, Inglewood 4, California
Mr. C. L. Rodman, Vine Street, Orange 2, New Jersey
Mr. S. T. Hudson, Maple Avenue, Teaneck 4, New Jersey
Mr. V. E. Carlson, Spring Road, Butler 3, New Jersey
Mr. R. Blaine, Cedar Street, Ridgefield 1, New Jersey
Mr. W. J. Roberts, Vale Avenue, Menlo Park 6, New Jersey
Mr. C. C. Race, Lincoln Road, Fairlawn 4, New Jersey
Mr. R. W. Williams, Crest Avenue, Asbury Park 2, New Jersey

473. Alphabetic Speed Drill. Lesson 181: 5 to 10 copies of ¶C.

LESSON 184

474. Billing Drill. On the duplicated billheads that will be supplied, type the 8 copies of the following bill needed for the 8 addresses given. Set tabular stops according to the printed columns on the billhead.

Leatherette Schoolbags #42 at $5 Doz.

The White Company, Des Moines 11, Iowa
    Invoice No. 2931, Order No. 3758, Quantity: 5 Doz.
The White Company, New Rochelle 6, New York
    Invoice No. 2932, Order No. 5896, Quantity: 7 Doz.
The White Company, South Bend 8, Indiana
    Invoice No. 2933, Order No. 3290, Quantity: 6 Doz.
The White Company, Asbury Park 7, New Jersey
    Invoice No. 2934, Order No. 8456, Quantity: 10 Doz.

The White Company, Vernon 6, Texas
Invoice No. 2935, Order No. 4958, Quantity: 5 Doz.
The White Company, Reno 3, Nevada
Invoice No. 2936, Order No. 9584, Quantity: 8 Doz.
The White Company, Clearwater 7, Florida
Invoice No. 2937, Order No. 4365, Quantity: 7 Doz.
The White Company, Racine 3, Wisconsin
Invoice No. 2938, Order No. 0985, Quantity: 8 Doz.

475. Alphabetic Speed Drill. Lesson 181: 5 to 10 copies of ¶D.

LESSON 185

476. Perfect Speed Drill. Your best speed, striving for errorless typing.

Those men will do work just for us if we give them good pay.   12

477. Alphabetic Production Letter. Type in semiblock style, 1 copy to each of the 10 addresses given.

Dear Sir: We are glad to note from your repeat orders that you have   14
done so well with the sale of our handy utility kit, which you intro-   28
duced just recently. We are about to announce an amazing new   41
product, a chemical car window cleaner, and we feel quite sure this   54
will be another good seller in your line of auto supplies. ¶ Within   68
the next few days you will receive a small supply of samples, which   81
you may wish to distribute among your favorite customers as a   94
means of introducing the product. We are attaching our price list   107
and will be happy to send your first shipment on consignment.   120
Very truly yours, George F. Haley, Sales Manager.   129

Manager, Liberty Service Station, Macon 2, Georgia
Manager, Liberty Service Station, Warren 7, Pennsylvania
Manager, Liberty Service Station, Redwood City 4, California
Manager, Liberty Service Station, Elizabeth 3, New Jersey
Manager, Liberty Service Station, Key West 1, Florida
Manager, Liberty Service Station, Shreveport 7, Louisiana
Manager, Liberty Service Station, Memphis 8, Tennessee
Manager, Liberty Service Station, Butte 6, Montana
Manager, Liberty Service Station, Tucson 2, Arizona
Manager, Liberty Service Station, Evanston 3, Illinois

478. Typing Style Recall. Type 1 copy.

"For the 'art-minded' public," says the director, "this is a dream come true." Opening of the new Monroe & Freel Museum will be announced at the old building at 635 South 24 Avenue (Suite #27) on May 18, 1954, between 2:30 and 3 p.m. Sixty editors out of 125 will attend, almost 50%. More than $500 will be spent at the opening, which will include dinners costing $5.50 each and souvenirs at 50 cents each.

479. Alphabetic Speed Drill for 5-Minute Timed Writing.

W·A·M
1m 5m

A

	1m	5m
With a power tool you can enhance your fine furniture jobs with all	13	3
the detailed smartness that marks the work of a person who is skilled	27	5
in the trade. The versatility of the smaller power tool, the quickness	41	8
and ease with which it handles work on chairs and other furniture	54	11
and does all your storm and screen sash work, make it one of the	67	13
most practical tools you can have in your shop. You can turn out	80	16
excellent work amazingly quickly with one of these tools.	91	18

B

	1m	5m
The table for the power tool raises and lowers amazingly fast without	14	21
disturbing the solid base and speed wheel. Controls are conveniently	28	24
located, and every feature is provided for quick, accurate setting	42	27
and smooth finishes. It is built to handle extra heavy work and has	56	29
big ball bearings to insure long and good service. Every feature is	69	32
provided for simple operation. Just make it a point to see this new	83	35
tool at your local store.	88	36

C

	1m	5m
You will agree our power tool is the quality tool you will be proud to	14	39
have in your shop for many years to come. Once you have experi-	27	41
enced the fun of making some of the wood furniture for your own	40	44
home, you will be sure to consider working with these tools a hobby.	54	47
Besides being practical, and easy to use, the tools are just the right	68	49
size and economical. To appreciate the ease with which you can work	82	52
with these tools, and also their efficiency, you must actually use	95	55
them.	96	55

D

	1m	5m
We want to make it possible for you to compare our products with	13	58
those you are now using, and we shall be glad to send you some tools	27	60
for examination. You will be put to no expense in making this com-	41	63
parison. Give us, as accurately as you can, the information called for	55	66
on the enclosed card. If you are not quite sure of the exact size of	69	69
the tools needed, just check the attached list. You cannot make a	82	71
mistake in accepting this offer.	88	73

480. Perfect Speed Drill. Your best speed, striving for errorless typing.

Those men will do work just for us if we give them good pay.   12

481. Alphabetic Speed Drill. Lesson 186: 5 to 10 copies of ¶A, then ¶B.

LESSON 188

482. Centering Drill. Set up the following announcement attractively on a full sheet, 8½″ x 11″.

ANNUAL FALL CONCERT
The Community High School Orchestra
proudly presents
"MUSICAL TREASURES"
on Saturday, November 13, 1954
at 8 o'clock
High School Auditorium

PLACEMENT PICTURE

Remember what a huge success last year's concert was? Remember all the fine comments and reviews? This year the high school orchestra has planned a musical program that is going to make this concert the biggest and best of them all. Besides orchestral selections from the very best in music, there will be two surprise vocal and instrumental solos. Get your tickets now, before they are all sold out!

Tickets 50 cents   School Library

483. Alphabetic Speed Drill. Lesson 186: 5 to 10 copies of ¶C.

LESSON 189

484. Manuscript Typing Drill. Type 1 copy of the following page of manuscript, corrected as indicated.

485. Alphabetic Speed Drill. Lesson 186: 5 to 10 copies of ¶D.

an interesting

"The history of printing is ~~a~~ story of the advancement

of universal education."[1] The more one learns about the

conditions before the invention of printing, and of the

subsequent beneficial influence it has exerted, the more clearly

one understands that the social structure of today is largely

dependent upon printing. These truths are proved as we compare

the historical record of the last few centuries with the ages

before printing.

Printing and Modern Civilization

double space

Seldom do we realize when we read a newspaper, a magazine,
or a book that we owe our present intellectual, social, economic
and spiritual development to the thoughts which we have thus
received--through the printed word.

The printed records of pioneer work in science and research
have given us the foundation for modern invention. Invention
has formed the foundation for present-day manufacture. Here
again, printing steps in to co-ordinate manufacturing with
marketing, so that through advertising desire may be created
for those wonderful new products which make life more ~~worthwhile~~.

worth while.

Printing and Education

stop to evaluate

Let us ~~truly evaluate~~ the importance of printing. Printing

interprets all arts and human knowledge. Upon the efforts of

almost

printers rests the education of everyone. One noted educator

gone so far as to say

has ~~pointed out~~ that printing extends the intellectual horizon

of the youth of our land and is the very basis of our whole

system of universal education.

———

[1]Bruce G. Meadows, Printing Education, Albany, Stevenson
Publishing Company, 1951.

486. Perfect Speed Drill. Your best speed, striving for errorless typing.

Those men will do work just for us if we give them good pay.   12

487. Alphabetic Production Letter. Type in block style, 1 copy to each of the 10 addresses given.

Dear Mr.——: You will receive shortly samples of the two new   12
wallboards announced to our dealers last month. National adver-   25
tising on these products will begin appearing during the next few   39
weeks and the demand for these time-saving building materials   52
should be quite brisk. Copies of some of the major ads are enclosed.   65
¶ It would be well for you to place your order for the materials im-   79
mediately, so as to be prepared to fill orders once the advertising is   93
released, also to insure your getting stock before any possibility of   107
our main supply running low. Your order will as always be filled   121
promptly. Yours very truly, Richard T. Reynolds, Sales Manager   134

Mr. S. T. Pine, Pine Supply Company, Elkhart 7, Indiana
Mr. S. V. Conklin, Lane Lumber Company, Nashville 2, Tennessee
Mr. V. K. Lindley, Builders Supply Corporation, Houston 8, Texas
Mr. A. N. Neal, Fiber Board Company, Berkeley 4, California
Mr. O. V. Scott, Scott Lumber Company, Seattle 4, Washington
Mr. C. V. Snedder, Ferris Supply Company, Wichita 6, Kansas
Mr. N. D. Poole, Poole Lumber Company, Erie 11, Pennsylvania
Mr. John H. Richards, Rand Building Supply, Utica 6, New York
Mr. J. W. Barker, White Supply Company, Lowell 4, Massachusetts
Mr. C. C. Finch, Finch Supply Company, Memphis 2, Tennessee

488. Typing Style Recall. Type 1 copy.

Cramer & Freel will hold a sales show at 423 West 65 Avenue (Section #7) on April 8, 1954, between 9 a.m. and 5:30 p.m. and they have planned on 30% of those invited to attend. "Every cost-minded executive will want to examine," says Mr. Freel, "the full line of 'Superior' products." Thirty exhibits will be manned by 140 persons, and while the show is worth $3.50 to $5 to see, the charge is only 50 cents.

489. Alphabetic Speed Drill for 5-Minute Timed Writing.

	W·A·M	
	1m	5m

A

	1m	5m
There is something which, more than anything else, sets apart a	13	3
very successful person. That fact has been proved by surveys con-	27	5
ducted by leading colleges around the country, studies analyzing	40	8
careers of quite a number of successful persons. They have brought	53	11
out this truth, that the one single thing that persons with successful	67	13
jobs have in common above all others is the ability to speak and	81	16
write well. This ability is worth thousands of dollars in extra	94	19
earning power.	97	19

B

	1m	5m
This is one ability you should try to develop quickly, regardless of	14	22
what field of work you choose for your career. You can easily recog-	27	25
nize why this should be so, for in any line of business or profession,	41	27
your progress depends largely upon how well you get along with	54	30
other persons. And that means how well you express yourself to	67	33
create a favorable impression and to influence others in your behalf,	81	36
on the job and in your social life.	88	38

C

	1m	5m
The doctor must exact the confidence of his patients, while the	13	41
lawyer must plead his case in court. The engineer must sell his ideas	27	43
to his clients. And in business, from the time you apply for a job until	41	46
you reach your top salary level, the success you realize will depend	55	49
upon your skill in selling yourself in words. This becomes more true	69	52
the higher you advance in business. It so happens that the higher you	83	55
go, the more you will require these skills.	92	57

D

	1m	5m
We urge you to enroll now, before we receive our full quota of mem-	14	59
bers. Just as soon as we receive your enrollment, you are put on our	28	62
list to receive free each month a copy of the news letter that we issue.	42	65
This organization offers you an unusual opportunity. You may think	56	68
it is too good to be true. But investigate for yourself at no expense to	70	70
you. Accept our service free for five weeks. We are sure you will be	84	73
well satisfied.	87	74

LESSON 192

490. Perfect Speed Drill. Your best speed, striving for errorless typing.

Those men will do work just for us if we give them good pay.   12

491. Alphabetic Speed Drill. Lesson 191: 5 to 10 copies of ¶A, then ¶B.

LESSON 193

492. Addressing Drill. Type 3 envelopes or index cards for each of the following names and addresses.

Manager, Liberty Service Station, Elizabeth 3, New Jersey
Manager, Liberty Service Station, Key West 1, Florida
Manager, Liberty Service Station, Shreveport 7, Louisiana
Manager, Liberty Service Station, Butte 6, Montana
Manager, Liberty Service Station, Tucson 2, Arizona
Manager, Liberty Service Station, Evanston 3, Illinois
Manager, Liberty Service Station, Memphis 8, Tennessee
Mr. S. T. Pine, Pine Supply Company, Elkhart 7, Indiana
Mr. S. V. Conklin, Lane Lumber Company, Nashville 2, Tennessee
Mr. V. K. Lindley, Builders Supply Corporation, Houston 8, Texas

493. Alphabetic Speed Drill. Lesson 191: 5 to 10 copies of ¶C.

LESSON 194

494. Tabulation Drill. Set up the following tabulation attractively on a full sheet, 8½" x 11".

WELLER HOME DEVELOPMENT COMPANY

Homes Still Available for Sale

No.	Construction	Rooms	Heating	Price
1	Brick	5	Oil	$10,500
2	Shingle	5	Oil	10,900
5	Clapboard	6	Gas	12,500
8	Clapboard	5	Gas	11,400
9	Stucco	7	Gas	14,600
11	Brick	7	Oil	16,500
14	Brick	5	Oil	12,300

495. Alphabetic Speed Drill. Lesson 191: 5 to 10 copies of ¶D.

496. Perfect Speed Drill. Your best speed, striving for errorless typing.

Those men will do work just for us if we give them good pay.　　12

497. Alphabetic Production Letter. Type in semiblock style, 1 copy to each of the 5 addresses given.

Dear Mr.——: Our directories, as you know, are revised periodically, 13
and the job of getting them promptly into the hands of users is a big 26
one. As the contractors in charge of distribution, we are confronted 39
with the very difficult problem of securing sufficient people to 53
deliver the books, which will be ready for distribution in your zone 67
in approximately two weeks. ¶ It is essential that these newly 80
revised directories be delivered promptly in order to provide good 94
service to plants and offices and to the many people engaged directly 107
or indirectly in business. It has occurred to us that you may know 120
someone with an automobile whom you would recommend for this 133
work. ¶ This job is temporary, pays well, and consists of an average 146
delivery of 300 directories involving approximately ten to twelve 160
hours of working time. The arrangements permit those now en- 173
gaged in other jobs and having free time during the day to accept 187
a supplementary job of this nature. Also, gasoline for such work is 200
now authorized by us and can be obtained from local service 212
stations upon presentation of a letter from this company. We are 225
enclosing a return post card on which we should appreciate your 238
noting the name, address, and telephone number of any acquaintance 251
who you think would be interested. ¶ Your co-operation in this 264
respect will be greatly appreciated and will assist us in solving a 277
problem. Sincerely yours, V. E. Brennan, Personnel Department 290

Mr. O. G. Wiley, Oak Road, Greenwich 3, Connecticut
Mr. H. G. Smith, Williams Drive, Teaneck 2, New Jersey
Mr. R. T. Pauley, Brook Lane, Lake Placid 3, New York
Mr. O. W. Gilbert, Lake Drive, Milford 2, Connecticut
Mr. E. L. Perrine, Forest Park, Spring Lake 4, New York

LESSON 196

498. Typing Style Recall. Type 1 copy.

The new Brown & Brown office building, 604 North 78 Street, will be ready March 22, 1954. The renting office (Room #423), which remains open from 9 a.m. to 4:30 p.m., states it is already 60% rented. "Our biggest feature," say the renting agents, "is our 'day-light-type' windows." Thirty floors will be made into 450 offices. Space is from $3 to $5.50 a foot, with storage space at 95 cents.

499. Alphabetic Speed Drill for 5-Minute Timed Writing.

		W·A·M	
		1m	5m
A	When you enclose your property with a quality fence you must	13	3
	realize you are making a permanent improvement that not only	26	5
	provides a great protection and peace of mind for you but also makes	39	8
	your property just that more valuable. A sturdy fence is an attrac-	52	10
	tive addition to any yard as it makes an excellent background for	65	13
	tall shrubs and a good trellis for climbing flowers and vines. Hun-	79	16
	dreds of home owners around the country own our fences.	90	18
B	Our fence is a lighter weight fence than the usual and has been	14	21
	designed to satisfy the need of so many property owners for a fence	27	23
	that gives full protection at the lowest possible cost. In choosing	41	26
	between our two sizes of fence, the chief difference to be remembered	55	29
	is lasting quality, not just for resistance to weather or corrosion, but	69	32
	for the ability to withstand rough treatment. If the fence is to be	82	34
	used where there are many children, the heavy de luxe fence should	95	37
	be chosen.	97	37
C	The choice between the two sizes depends entirely on the conditions	14	40
	under which it will be used. Line posts can be set in concrete, if it	27	43
	is desired, at small extra cost, but all corners and gate posts must be	41	46
	set in concrete bases. Many who chose our fences have written us in	55	48
	the past to the effect that they should have had the work done a long	69	51
	time ago. Quite a few others have written saying they had the job	82	54
	done years ago and their fence is still like new.	92	56
D	For years our company has specialized in making loans to families of	14	59
	just average means when a loan could be used to advantage toward	28	61
	the purchase of one of our fences. We are well known for friendly	41	64
	service and low rates and terms. As it is our policy to try to serve	54	67
	everyone who comes to us, we have developed a service that can	67	69
	quickly take care of your exact home improvement needs. There is	81	72
	no extra charge for this friendly service.	90	74

143

LESSON 197

500. Perfect Speed Drill. Your best speed, striving for errorless typing.

Those men will do work just for us if we give them good pay.   12

501. Alphabetic Speed Drill. Lesson 196: 5 to 10 copies of ¶A, then ¶B.

LESSON 198

502. Centering Drill. Set up the following invitation attractively on a full
sheet, 8½" x 11".

The Community High School Orchestra
cordially invites you to attend
its Annual Fall Concert
featuring
"MUSICAL TREASURES"
Saturday, November 13, 1954
at eight o'clock
High School Auditorium
Dancing   Dress informal

503. Alphabetic Speed Drill. Lesson 196: 5 to
10 copies of ¶C.

PLACEMENT PICTURE

LESSON 199

504. Billing Drill. On the duplicated billheads that will be supplied, type
the 8 copies of the following bill needed for the 8 addresses given. Set tabular
stops according to the printed columns on the billhead.

Wallboard #65 at $2 each
Wallboard #66 at $1 each

Mr. S. T. Pine, Pine Supply Company, Elkhart 7, Indiana
    Invoice No. 6132, Order No. 8745, Quantity: 25 #65, 25 #66
Mr. S. V. Conklin, Lane Lumber Company, Nashville 2, Tennessee
    Invoice No. 6133, Order No. 8574, Quantity: 30 #65, 30 #66
Mr. V. K. Lindley, Builders Supply Corporation, Houston 8, Texas
    Invoice No. 6134, Order No. 3526, Quantity: 30 #65, 30 #66
Mr. A. N. Neal, Fiber Board Company, Berkeley 4, California
    Invoice No. 6135, Order No. 3947, Quantity: 20 #65, 20 #66

Mr. O. V. Scott, Scott Lumber Company, Seattle 4, Washington
    Invoice No. 6136, Order No. 3246, Quantity: 50 #65, 50 #66
Mr. C. V. Snedder, Ferris Supply Company, Wichita 6, Kansas
    Invoice No. 6137, Order No. 2643, Quantity: 25 #65, 25 #66
Mr. N. D. Poole, Poole Lumber Company, Erie 11, Pennsylvania
    Invoice No. 6138, Order No. 1237, Quantity: 40 #65, 40 #66
Mr. John H. Richards, Rand Building Supply, Utica 6, New York
    Invoice No. 6139, Order No. 2138, Quantity: 25 #65, 25 #66

505. Alphabetic Speed Drill. Lesson 196: 5 to 10 copies of ¶D.

LESSON 200

506. Perfect Speed Drill. Your best speed, striving for errorless typing.

Those men will do work just for us if we give them good pay.　12

507. Alphabetic Production Letter. Type in block style, 1 copy to each of the 3 addresses given.

Dear Mr.——: Subject: Packard Electric Company. Since writing 12
you last month, we have had some additional dealings with this 25
organization, and as a result we now attach a specimen copy of a 38
special net price quotation, which is to apply uniformly to all branch 52
and district offices of this company. ¶ The specimen quotation will 65
assist you in presenting to this customer the services that we offer 78
as the most effective, the most rapid, and the most economical means 92
of obtaining for them efficient inventory control. ¶ Here is a fine 106
opportunity for all branch and district offices of this organization to 120
secure professional results at a price substantially below our normal 134
selling price. The decision to establish this special price is the result 148
of our desire to make these conversions as quickly as possible and 161
in a manner that will produce the best results for the customer. 174
¶ These special prices are probably less than they would have to pay 187
for overtime work by their own employees. It is a recognized fact, 200
too, that more errors are made in overtime hours, and the next day's 213
work usually suffers through lowered efficiency. You might also 225
suggest that with the tax situation as it is, the net cost will run 238
nearly 40% under what they pay for our services. ¶ Our Los Angeles 251
office has worked very closely with the home office of Packard 263
Electric Company in developing the improvements with which you 276
are now familiar. The entire program will be sponsored and recom- 290
mended by their Home Office; but the decision in regard to adoption 304
of the new system and the acceptance of our service proposal will 318
rest with the local branch offices of that company. ¶ We feel, how- 331

ever, in view of the fact that the entire program, including service, 344
will have the endorsement of the Los Angeles home office, some 356
recognition should be accorded to our dealer in Los Angeles, and it 368
has therefore been decided that the total commission of 5% on the 381
net service is to be split 80% to the salesman securing the order and 394
20% to that dealer. Please note that where travel expense is required 407
this expense will be billed at cost on the basis of one supervisor at 421
each work location. ¶ The many inquiries that have already reached 434
us indicate a very lively interest in our equipment and service. We 447
suggest you see your Packard Electric people immediately so that 460
orders may be scheduled to meet the individual requirements of 472
each location. Yours truly, P. S. Langley, General Sales Manager 484

Mr. C. V. Jenkins, Manager; Park Equipment Company, Austin 6, Texas
Mr. G. Arthur White, Manager, White Business Services, Portland 8, Oregon
Mr. H. W. Hageney, Manager, Crane Office Equipment Company, Trenton
4, New Jersey

508. Typing Style Recall. Type 1 copy.

"A new book entitled 'River Edge' is really setting sales records," say the booksellers, "and this is just the beginning." Ninety paper-bound copies were sold in one store in a day, 860 since the book came off the press on August 27, 1954. They sell for 90 cents, $2, and $2.50 for the leather edition, plus 2% tax. Our store is open from 8:30 a.m. to 9 p.m. and is located at the Bell & Field Building, 64 South 71 Avenue (Entrance #3).

509. Alphabetic Speed Drill for 5-Minute Timed Writing.

	W·A·M 1m	5m

A

	1m	5m
In this training, you may work on any of several forms of writing.	14	3
If fiction is your prime interest, then you may request to do just	28	6
fiction from start to finish. If you are seeking news training, your	42	8
editor will send carefully chosen newspaper lessons, which will	55	11
give you newspaper desk experience. If you wish to specialize in	68	14
some other field, your lessons will be chosen in that field; or you	82	16
may sample a number of fields if that is what you prefer.	93	19

B

Every student is invited to submit, from time to time, a number of	13	21
original manuscripts outside the regular lessons, which will be ana-	27	24
lyzed and commented on fully by the instructor. When students	40	27
need more time to enable them to complete all the work of the	53	29
course, we will gladly arrange for it. Except in specific cases, which	67	32
are clearly indicated when you enroll, there is no time limit on any	81	35
job. Our editors stand ready at all times to answer all your	93	37
questions.	95	38

C

This service is open to you without additional fees all during your	14	40
training. We do not just grade your work and answer questions. We	28	43
suggest how to improve your work, and we give suggestions for out-	42	46
side reading or practice. We also send you each month free of	55	49
charge our writing guide. This saves time because of the condensa-	69	51
tions by an expert staff. It makes spare moments valuable to you	82	54
because the convenient size enables you to carry it anywhere.	94	56

D

This monthly letter will come in handy in spare moments on busses	13	59
or trains, while waiting for people, or between jobs. It helps in your	27	62
work because many of the ideas in its articles may be used quite	40	64
profitably in your profession. It continues your education by giving	54	67
you a broad knowledge of the expert writing from the leading books	68	70
and magazines. It brings you a book a month, because each issue	81	73
contains the condensation of at least one book.	90	75

LESSON 202

510. Perfect Speed Drill. Your best speed, striving for errorless typing.

Those men will do work just for us if we give them good pay.   12

511. Alphabetic Speed Drill. Lesson 201: 5 to 10 copies of ¶A, then ¶B.

LESSON 203

512. Addressing Drill. Type 3 envelopes or index cards for each of the following names and addresses.

Mr. C. V. Snedder, Ferris Supply Company, Wichita 6, Kansas
Mr. N. D. Poole, Poole Lumber Company, Erie 11, Pennsylvania
Mr. John H. Richards, Rand Building Supply, Utica 6, New York
Mr. J. W. Barker, White Supply Company, Lowell 4, Massachusetts
Mr. C. C. Finch, Finch Supply Company, Memphis 2, Tennessee
Mr. O. G. Wiley, Oak Road, Greenwich 3, Connecticut
Mr. H. G. Smith, Williams Drive, Teaneck 2, New Jersey
Mr. R. T. Pauley, Brook Lane, Lake Placid 3, New York
Mr. O. W. Gilbert, Lake Drive, Milford 2, Connecticut
Mr. E. L. Perrine, Forest Park, Spring Lake 4, New York

513. Alphabetic Speed Drill. Lesson 201: 5 to 10 copies of ¶C.

LESSON 204

514. Tabulation Drill. Set up the following tabulation attractively on a full sheet, 8½" x 11".

NOTABLE BRIDGES

Bridge	Location	Span in Feet
San Francisco-Oakland	San Francisco Bay	9,500
Golden Gate	San Francisco Bay	4,200
Huey P. Long	Mississippi River, New Orleans	3,524
George Washington	Hudson River, New York City	3,500
Bronx-Whitestone	East River, New York City	2,300
Ambassador	Detroit-Canada	1,850
Quebec	St. Lawrence River	1,800
Delaware River	Philadelphia-Camden	1,750
Queensferry	Firth of Forth, Scotland	1,710

515. Alphabetic Speed Drill. Lesson 201: 5 to 10 copies of ¶D.

516. Perfect Speed Drill. Your best speed, striving for errorless typing.

Those men will do work just for us if we give them good pay.   12

517. Alphabetic Production Letter. Type in semiblock style, 1 copy to each
of the 10 addresses given.

Dear Mr.——: This office has planned an unusual display of com-   13
mercial photography equipment that we feel will be of interest to   27
you and your associates. Please accept the two enclosed invitations   41
with our compliments. ¶ The purpose of the exhibit is to introduce   55
cost-cutting methods and equipment to organizations such as yours,   69
which we know are continually striving to give greater service to   83
their customers with the greatest economy. ¶ We look forward to   96
seeing you at the exhibit. If you desire additional invitation cards,   110
we will be happy to send them. Very truly yours, W. A. Crane,   122
President   124

Mr. John V. McCabe, Apex Studio, New Haven 2, Connecticut
Mr. N. V. Bullard, Bullard Photo Shop, Stamford 6, Connecticut
Mr. C. C. Romer, Romer Art Studio, Orange 3, New Jersey
Mr. O. N. Backer, Regal Art Studio, Montclair 9, New Jersey
Mr. B. B. Grail, Grail Studios, Hartsdale 2, New York
Mr. J. V. Whyte, Lee Commercial Photographers, White Plains 3, New York
Mr. A. E. Newman, Newman Art Studio, Providence 2, Rhode Island
Mr. R. F. Weyer, The Crane Studio, Lynbrook 8, New York
Mr. T. G. Dunn, Dunn & Dunn, Yonkers 11, New York
Mr. S. N. Amberg, Seal Photograph Company, Pearl River 4, New York

518. Typing Style Recall. Type 1 copy.

Two copies were mailed on December 15, 1954, to Miller & Jones, 42 West 61 Street. They were billed (Invoice #9621) at $8.50 and $15, with 45 cents added for mailing and 2% for tax. We mail about 850 copies a day between 9:30 a.m. and 4 p.m. and very few are damaged. "But," says our shipping department head, "even our well-bound shipments can run 'afoul.' "

519. Alphabetic Speed Drill for 5-Minute Timed Writing.

	W·A·M	
	1m	5m

A

Fishing ranks as one of the favorite sports. Most of the mountain	14	3
streams offer amazingly fine trout fishing, and lakes are dotted	27	5
through the high areas for those who enjoy fishing from a boat or	41	8
casting from shore, especially in the southern part of the state	54	11
around the several lakes. In addition, one seeking a light form of	67	13
sport may ride the high mountain trails on a dude ranch pack trip,	81	16
hike over well-marked paths, or just loaf and relax in a wooded	94	19
area by a mountain stream.	99	20

B

Tennis is available, golf courses may be found just within walking	14	23
distance, and the golfer may experience the thrill of knowing his	28	25
worst tee shot is a dazzling thousand feet high at the start. Hunting	41	28
in season calls the lovers of guns to the hills where the deer make	55	31
their home and to the sweeping plains where quail are plentiful.	68	33
For the hardy sportsman who likes to follow the bay of hounds,	81	36
bear may be hunted with dogs during a few weeks of the season.	94	39

C

If you care for more daring sports, mountain lions offer a challenge	14	42
the year round, since the season never closes on them. Also there are	28	44
some twelve areas in the state that offer amazingly good skiing, and	42	47
extra slopes are being developed as the popularity of this sport	55	50
quickly spreads. We can go on page after page with types of sport	68	52
and other recreation that many have enjoyed and that you can	81	55
enjoy here. But come and see for yourself.	90	57

D

Make your plane reservation now, but please be sure to let us know	14	60
quickly if you change your plans. We realize that now and then a	28	62
change of plans cannot exactly be avoided and that there may be	41	65
very good reasons for not being able to use the space you have re-	55	68
served. But, as a rule, it is seldom impossible for passengers to	69	70
notify us in advance when they will not be able to use the seats	82	73
they have reserved. Their failure to do so costs us thousands of	95	76
dollars.	97	76

520. Perfect Speed Drill. Your best speed, striving for errorless typing.

Those men will do work just for us if we give them good pay.   12

521. Alphabetic Speed Drill. Lesson 206: 5 to 10 copies of ¶A, then ¶B.

LESSON 208

522. Centering Drill. Set up the following program attractively on a full sheet, 8½″ x 11″.

PLACEMENT PICTURE

ANNUAL FALL CONCERT
The Community High School Orchestra
presenting
"MUSICAL TREASURES"

PROGRAM

Selections from Pinafore (Gilbert and Sullivan)........Orchestra
Scottish Fantasy (Bruch)............Albert S. Truex, Violinist
Selections from The Bartered Bride (Smetana)........Orchestra
Beyond the Sun (Browne)..................G. V. Leed, Tenor

Intermission

Selections from Madam Butterfly (Puccini)...........Orchestra
Warsaw Concerto (Addinsell)...............G. V. Davi, Pianist
One Fine Day (Puccini)................Miriam Green, Soprano
Bolero (Ravel)...................................Orchestra

John V. Butler, Conducting

523. Alphabetic Speed Drill. Lesson 206: 5 to 10 copies of ¶C.

524. Telegram Drill. On the telegram blank forms that will be supplied to you, type 1 copy of the night letter below to each of the 10 addresses listed.

Order for Chemical Car Window Cleaner received but only part shipment made due to stock shortage. Remainder of shipment following in ten days.

George F. Haley

Manager, Liberty Service Station, Macon, Georgia
Manager, Liberty Service Station, Warren, Pennsylvania
Manager, Liberty Service Station, Redwood City, California
Manager, Liberty Service Station, Elizabeth, New Jersey
Manager, Liberty Service Station, Key West, Florida
Manager, Liberty Service Station, Shreveport, Louisiana
Manager, Liberty Service Station, Memphis, Tennessee
Manager, Liberty Service Station, Butte, Montana
Manager, Liberty Service Station, Tucson, Arizona
Manager, Liberty Service Station, Evanston, Illinois

525. Alphabetic Speed Drill. Lesson 206: 5 to 10 copies of ¶D.

526. Perfect Speed Drill. Your best speed, striving for errorless typing.

Those men will do work just for us if we give them good pay.　　12

527. Alphabetic Production Letter. Type in block style, 1 copy to each of the 10 addresses given.

Gentlemen: If you have any literature on the subject of office　13
modernization, we shall appreciate your making that literature　27
available to us. We can use up to three copies of each piece. ¶ We are　40
now making plans for next year, at which time we contemplate mak-　53
ing certain major improvements in all our offices. These improve-　67
ments will involve new office layout, color and sound conditioning,　81
and purchase of new office equipment. ¶ It may be that you can　94
also put us in touch with other firms who can offer information　107
along these lines, in which case we shall be grateful for your assist-　121
ance. Yours very truly, Wendell C. Myron, Treasurer. P. S. If there　135
is a charge for your literature, please bill us in duplicate.　148

Seale Paint Company, Seale Building, Detroit 16, Michigan
Colgate Furniture Company, Pullman Building, Toledo 4, Ohio
Reade Furniture Company, Reade Square, Gary 4, Indiana
Block Paint Company, Block Building, St. Louis 6, Missouri
The Bristol Company, Bristol Corners, Denver 7, Colorado
Appley Insulation Company, Appley Building, Seattle 12, Washington
Meredith Supply Company, Towne Building, Kansas City 4, Missouri
Perry Furniture Company, Crane Building, Trenton 8, New Jersey
The Martin Corporation, Martin Building, Toledo 4, Ohio
Watson & Mann, Leland Building, Flint 6, Michigan

LESSON 211

528. Typing Style Recall. Type 1 copy.

On June 16, 1954, between 3 p.m. and 4:30 p.m. we held our meeting with Elder & Elder at 48 East 17 Street (Conference Room #21). Thirty more (25%) than the 120 expected attended, paying $3 to $5.50, plus 35 cents for literature. "It was indeed a 'surprise' showing," writes Mr. French, "and we are happy it was such a well-attended meeting."

529. Alphabetic Speed Drill for 5-Minute Timed Writing.

	W·A·M	
	1m	5m

A

	1m	5m
If you have ever traveled in a foreign country whose language you	14	3
did not speak, you know the strange feeling you experienced when	27	5
you found it difficult to request even your simplest needs, such as	40	8
ordering a meal or asking directions to a popular avenue. There you	54	11
were in the midst of civilized persons like yourself, persons with	68	14
whom you had need to speak and with whom you would have liked	81	16
to exchange ideas, and yet you were just as helpless as if you were	94	19
a person with no language.	99	20

B

You realized quickly the great importance of language, and maybe	14	23
you even arrived at the thought that it is the source of our laws and	28	25
government, of the literature of the world and knowledge of the	41	28
ages, just as it is the basis of all human relationships and of all our	55	31
social and business activities. But of course you live among people	69	34
who speak your language, and you express yourself well enough to	83	36
be understood in carrying on the everyday routine of living.	95	39

C

But there is a difference between that and expressing yourself well	14	42
enough to make the most of yourself on your job, speaking and	27	44
writing quickly, and well enough to influence others, to inspire their	41	47
respect and friendship, and well enough to sell your ideas. Perhaps	55	50
you did not go to college. Perhaps you did go but missed many	68	52
courses that you should have taken. In either case, you realize	81	55
language is of vital importance to you.	89	57

D

Undoubtedly you have very often wished you could just fill this gap	14	59
in your education and acquire this extra knowledge necessary to	27	62
business and social success. Now your wish can be fulfilled. Our	40	65
language editor has made it a vital part of his work to bring to-	54	68
gether a fine library of five volumes. It was his great hope that the	68	70
price of these prized volumes might be made so low that no one need	81	73
be denied their help and inspiration.	88	74

530. Perfect Speed Drill. Your best speed, striving for errorless typing.

Those men will do work just for us if we give them good pay.   12

531. Alphabetic Speed Drill. Lesson 211: 5 to 10 copies of ¶A, then ¶B.

LESSON 213

532. Addressing Drill. Type 3 envelopes or index cards for each of the following names and addresses.

Mr. John V. McCabe, Apex Studio, New Haven 2, Connecticut
Mr. N. V. Bullard, Bullard Photo Shop, Stamford 6, Connecticut
Mr. C. C. Romer, Romer Art Studio, Orange 3, New Jersey
Mr. O. N. Backer, Regal Art Studio, Montclair 9, New Jersey
Mr. B. B. Grail, Grail Studios, Hartsdale 2, New York
Mr. J. V. Whyte, Lee Commercial Photographers, White Plains 3, New York
Mr. A. E. Newman, Newman Art Studio, Providence 2, Rhode Island
Mr. R. F. Weyer, The Crane Studio, Lynbrook 8, New York
Mr. T. G. Dunn, Dunn & Dunn, Yonkers 11, New York
Mr. S. N. Ambert, Seal Photograph Company, Pearl River 4, New York
Seale Paint Company, Seale Building, Detroit 16, Michigan
Reade Furniture Company, Reade Square, Gary 4, Indiana

533. Alphabetic Speed Drill. Lesson 211: 5 to 10 copies of ¶C.

LESSON 214

534. Billing Drill. On the duplicated billheads that will be supplied, type the 8 copies of the following bill needed for the 8 addresses given. Set tabular stops according to the printed columns on the billhead.

Chemical Car Window Cleaner at $5 Doz.

Liberty Service Station, Macon 2, Georgia
    Invoice No. 3614, Order No. 6263, Quantity: 8 Doz.
Liberty Service Station, Warren 7, Pennsylvania
    Invoice No. 3615, Order No. 9832, Quantity: 5 Doz.
Liberty Service Station, Redwood City 4, California
    Invoice No. 3616, Order No. 1352, Quantity: 5 Doz.
Liberty Service Station, Elizabeth 3, New Jersey
    Invoice No. 3617, Order No. 7324, Quantity: 4 Doz.

Liberty Service Station, Key West 1, Florida
    Invoice No. 3618, Order No. 1875, Quantity: 10 Doz.
Liberty Service Station, Shreveport 7, Louisiana
    Invoice No. 3619, Order No. 3219, Quantity: 8 Doz.
Liberty Service Station, Memphis 8, Tennessee
    Invoice No. 3620, Order No. 9324, Quantity: 5 Doz.
Liberty Service Station, Butte 6, Montana
    Invoice No. 3621, Order No. 5437, Quantity: 6 Doz.

535. Alphabetic Speed Drill. Lesson 211: 5 to 10 copies of ¶D.

LESSON 215

536. Perfect Speed Drill. Your best speed, striving for errorless typing.

Those men will do work just for us if we give them good pay.   12

537. Alphabetic Production Letter. Type in semiblock style, 1 copy to each of the 6 addresses given.

Dear Mr.——: We are returning the list of delinquent accounts taken   13
from your last trial balance. Will you please indicate the status of   27
each as of the first of this month and return the list to us immediately.   41
This includes the accounts showing large balances as well as the   54
longer list showing small balances. ¶ There are probably a number   67
of accounts that require correspondence, and apparently we have   80
received no papers to turn over to our collection department. If there   94
are any accounts on the attached list that should have the immediate   108
attention of our collection department, please see that we are sup-   122
plied with all papers and itemized statements in duplicate in each   135
instance. ¶ We will have an extensive drive on collections this   148
month, including all large balances as well as all small balances, and   162
collection letters will be mailed for the firms we represent in the   176
order in which each firm's list reaches us. Sincerely yours, C. W.   189
Barker, Collection Manager   195

Mr. G. F. Lincoln, Treasurer, Stewart Sales Company, Omaha 8, Nebraska
Mrs. V. R. Asher, Treasurer, Kenneth & Brown, Waterloo 4, Iowa
Mr. S. T. Vale, Treasurer, Burke Clothing Company, Norfolk 3, Virginia
Miss N. R. Bradle, Treasurer, Peck Supply Company, Erie 7, Pennsylvania
Mr. G. G. Chester, Treasurer, Blanding & Frey, El Paso 12, Texas
Mr. Owen G. Grant, Treasurer, Burns Offset Company, Tacoma 6, Wash-
    ington.

LESSON 216

538. Typing Style Recall. Type 1 copy.

This remittance of $120.90 represents $120 for the bill and 90 cents for delivery. Deliver the machine after May 14, 1954, any time between 9 a.m. and 5:30 p.m. at our Crowell & Lester Building address, 160 West 60 Street (Department #3021). Six of your products have been demonstrated to our 112 people. "We want well-tested products that are '100% dependable,'" they agree, "and not those that have been only half tested."

539. Alphabetic Speed Drill for 5-Minute Timed Writing.

	W·A·M	
	1m	5m

A

	1m	5m
If it were possible for us to visit you personally, or for you to come	14	3
to the school so that we might talk to you about becoming a writer,	27	5
our very first thought would be to express our congratulations. For	41	8
in considering the field of writing as your vocation or life work, you	55	11
will quickly recognize it as not only one of the most profitable but	69	14
also one of the most interesting jobs open to you today. There is no	82	16
calling that brings richer rewards or satisfaction in life than writing.	96	19

B

	1m	5m
Few other fields can possibly open up such opportunities as you can	14	22
expect in this work, whether you consider it as a life work, as a source	27	25
of added income, as an aid in home building, or as a means of ac-	40	28
quiring some other aim. It does not matter whether you live in the	53	30
city or country, whether you have gone through high school and	67	33
college or not, or what your age is; if you want to realize a better	80	36
position in life, we say to you frankly, just become a writer.	93	38

C

	1m	5m
Today and tomorrow, writers will be needed. You can prepare now	13	41
for that opportunity by looking ahead and studying in your spare	27	44
time and letting us help you as we have helped so many others. One	40	46
advantage of learning to write is that one can often expect to earn	53	49
while he is learning. As a quick start, we invite you to join the	66	51
contest we are sponsoring for a large food company. Here is an	79	54
opportunity for you to test your ability and realize some profit.	91	56

D

	1m	5m
Compose a letter in which you tell us five new and tasty methods of	14	59
preparing cereal. There is no limit to the length of the letter you	27	61
may write; it may be either a short one or a long one. The letters will	41	64
be judged for prizes solely on their interest quality and the clearness	55	67
with which they explain the five new methods. You may submit as	68	70
many entries as you wish. All entries should be mailed to me person-	82	72
ally. There is nothing that you have to buy to enter this contest.	95	75

LESSON 217

540. Perfect Speed Drill. Your best speed, striving for errorless typing.

Those men will do work just for us if we give them good pay.   12

541. Alphabetic Speed Drill. Lesson 216: 5 to 10 copies of ¶A, then ¶B.

LESSON 218

542. Centering Drill. Set up the following title page attractively on a full sheet, 8½″ x 11″.

CURRENT TRENDS IN BUSINESS ADMINISTRATIVE PLANNING

E. Walter Ferndale
Chairman
National Committee on Business Methods

Comments on the report of the National Committee on Business Methods, which surveyed the operation of more than 350 business firms around the country.

Published by
The National Association of Business Officials
Chicago

543. Alphabetic Speed Drill. Lesson 216: 5 to 10 copies of ¶C.

LESSON 219

544. Manuscript Typing Drill. Type 1 copy of the following page of manuscript, corrected as indicated.

545. Alphabetic Speed Drill. Lesson 216: 5 to 10 copies of ¶D.

The plight of many of our member firms is reflected in
the findings of the national committee that studied the current
situation. The report,[1] released a few weeks ago, shows that
most firms are handicapped by ~~partisan~~ politics and lack of
control over finances, while at the same time they are trying
to meet ~~surging~~ *more & more urgent* demands for service.

Typical Findings

The report shows how a chairman can ~~hamstring~~ *hold up* the board
by use of the veto power. It also describes the haphazard
evolution of certain departments, a situation ~~paralleled~~ *found* in
many firms. For example, the committee found the office
overloaded with the administration of programs, which takes the
time of approximately 35% of the present staff. Said the report:

> It would appear that the shortage of personnel was
> particularly acute in the outlying areas and that
> there was a critical and immediate need for additional
> services in research, planning, and transportation.

The Association ~~currently~~ *at this time* offers only the part-time services
of the director of guidance in this field. The failure to provide
adequately for this service is causing a substantial loss. "In
terms of sound business practice," says the report, "organizations
in many states have more divisions than are desirable."[2]

---

[1]"A Report on Current Trends in Business Administrative
Planning," 1950, National Committee on Business Methods.
[2]The Committee, on page 12 of its report, lists 18 states
in this category.

LESSON 220

546. Perfect Speed Drill. Your best speed, striving for errorless typing.

Those men will do work just for us if we give them good pay.   12

547. Alphabetic Production Letter. On the interoffice letterhead form that will be supplied to you, type 1 copy of the letter below to each of the 6 addresses given.

TO   —
FROM   General Manager
SUBJECT   Recall of Type 101 Tires
DATE   —

Continued experimentation has brought to light that the new Type   14
101 tires recently released are defective in that the rubber does not   27
seem to age properly. There have been some evidences that the   39
newly developed tire will harden and crack. For that reason, the   53
policy has been put into effect to recall the limited number of tires   67
sold to date. ¶ It is recommended that your office quickly contact   80
all dealer outlets that have stocked this tire and recall the shipment,   94
giving explanation for this action. Offer in place of Type 101 the   108
traditional Type 100, which is similar in all respects except that it   122
utilizes the older, time-proven manufacturing processes. ¶ Should   136
any dealer prefer not to stock type 100, then offer to take the   149
defective tires with the understanding that full credit will be given   163
the dealer. ¶ It is unfortunate that each branch has to take on   177
this extra job, but you will agree that this is the best course, looking   191
at the picture from the long range sales point of view. T. A. Worth-   205
ington   206

Manager, Boston Office
Manager, St. Louis Office
Manager, Houston Office
Manager, Seattle Office
Manager, San Francisco Office
Manager, Chicago Office

548. Typing Style Recall. Type 1 copy.

"I just read 'The Little Mountain,'" says Bill, "and it is worth considering for this year's gift." In his letter, dated August 24, 1954, he mentions a bookdealer at 63 East 78 Street (Parrot & Smith, Counter #7) where budget-cover editions are available at 60 cents, $1, and $2.25, plus 1% tax. Eighty order blanks can be picked up any day at 9:30 a.m. for some of the 125 members.

549. Alphabetic Speed Drill for 5-Minute Timed Writing.

	W·A·M	
	1m	5m

A

	1m	5m
They submit all their important books to us quite ahead of printing,	14	3
and every month we choose one outstanding book for you. You next	27	5
receive a carefully written description of this book in advance of	41	8
publication. If you decide from analyzing this report that it is a	55	11
book you think you would not enjoy, you send back the form we	68	14
provide, telling us you want no book, or you want some other book.	81	16
This system enables you to keep any unwanted book from coming.	93	19

B

	1m	5m
You do not pay any yearly price as for a magazine. You just pay the	13	21
special low price for each selection. This is almost always lower than	27	24
the retail price. As an example of the saving, note how many of the	41	27
books listed here are sold below retail. A bill is mailed to you	54	30
with each book you indicate you want under the system outlined	68	32
above, and these bills are all you pay as a member, except for a	81	35
small charge added to cover postage and mailing to your zone.	94	38

C

	1m	5m
For many years our selections have invariably been among the most	14	41
interesting and important books published. And, last but not least,	28	43
you get and read particular new books, which you are anxious not to	42	46
miss but which you frequently just fail to read. We send you these	56	49
in a special binding. Our organization does this because thousands	69	52
of readers have requested that we offer our regular monthly book	83	54
supplements in a more permanent and durable binding.	94	57

D

	1m	5m
Reserve your copy of this volume and increase the pleasures of the	14	59
hours you spend in reading. Here, in this one volume, are the best of	27	62
the important books with which you will want to be familiar. They	41	65
are the books that you will read again and again. What is more,	54	67
next year's books will be attractive in appearance. They will be	67	70
printed in a beautiful style of type with gold stamping on the	80	73
cover. The books will be bound in a strong cover.	90	75

LESSON 222

550. Perfect Speed Drill. Your best speed, striving for errorless typing.

Those men will do work just for us if we give them good pay.   12

551. Alphabetic Speed Drill. Lesson 221: 5 to 10 copies of ¶A, then ¶B.

LESSON 223

552. Addressing Drill. Type 3 envelopes or index cards for each of the following names and addresses.

The Martin Corporation, Martin Building, Toledo 4, Ohio
Watson & Mann, Leland Building, Flint 6, Michigan
Mr. G. F. Lincoln, Treasurer, Stewart Sales Company, Omaha 8, Nebraska
Mrs. V. R. Asher, Treasurer, Kenneth & Brown, Waterloo 4, Iowa
Mrs. S. T. Vale, Treasurer, Burke Clothing Company, Norfolk 3, Virginia
Miss N. R. Bradle, Treasurer, Peck Supply Company, Erie 7, Pennsylvania
Mr. G. G. Chester, Treasurer, Blanding & Frey, El Paso 12, Texas
Mr. R. W. Eldon, Treasurer, Foley Supply Company, Utica 9, New York
Mr. P. C. Lindner, Manager, Sweeney & Sons, Inc., Helena 2, Montana
Miss R. E. Taylor, Manager, Ward Office Supply Company, Boise 12, Idaho

553. Alphabetic Speed Drill. Lesson 221: 5 to 10 copies of ¶C.

LESSON 224

554. Tabulation Drill. Set up the following tabulation attractively.

WORLD MOTION PICTURE THEATERS

Region	No. Theaters	No. Seats
Europe	52,344	24,062,799
United States	18,351	11,796,072
South America	4,994	3,302,529
Far East	3,523	2,368,675
Middle East	2,676	1,583,425
South Pacific	2,268	1,687,460
Mexico	1,952	1,720,185
Canada	1,695	874,094
Africa	1,281	784,818

555. Alphabetic Speed Drill. Lesson 221: 5 to 10 copies of ¶D.

556. Perfect Speed Drill. Your best speed, striving for errorless typing.

Those men will do work just for us if we give them good pay.   12

557. Alphabetic Production Letter. Type in block style, 1 copy to each of the 10 addresses given.

Attention of the President Gentlemen: May we have an appoint-   13
ment with you to discuss all the possibilities of cutting costs and   26
increasing production in your plants? The improvement of plant   39
methods has been our business for the past quarter century, and   52
our work, as you may know, has. been with some of the largest   64
organizations in the country. ¶ When we call, we shall be glad to   77
show you just what we have done in companies and exactly what   90
improvements have resulted. Because of your competitive field, this   104
information should be of interest to you. ¶ Please use the enclosed   118
envelope when letting us know when we may call. Very truly yours,   131
R. F. DEWEY COMPANY, G. M. Connolly, Director of Research   143

Sperry Brass Company, 26 Ferry Street, Dayton 8, Ohio
Reed & Company, 42 Reed Avenue, Scranton 2, Pennsylvania
Condon & Condon, 16 Tulsa Street, Reading 6, Pennsylvania
White & Company, 46 Anne Street, Baltimore 7, Maryland
The Merry Company, Inc., Wheeling 9, West Virginia
Triangle Metal Company, 8 Garth Road, Canton 6, Ohio
Powell Stamping Company, Powell Square, Camden 2, New Jersey
Ritchie Machine Company, Ritchie Building, Toledo 8, Ohio
Gaines & Company, Gaines Terminal, Trenton 4, New Jersey
French & Crosse, Riggs Building, Newark 8, New Jersey

558. Typing Style Recall. Type 1 copy.

"If you want service that has country-wide acceptance," most experienced travelers will tell you, "take the 'Falcon' route." Sixteen special trains are run by 180 experienced railroaders. Attend the Travel Fair and luncheon on June 6, 1954, between 9:30 a.m. and 2 p.m. in the Homer & Burns Building, 34 South 71 Street (Suite #632). Single tickets will be 80 cents, books of tickets at $3.50 and $5, plus 10% tax.

559. Alphabetic Speed Drill for 5-Minute Timed Writing.

	W·A·M	
	1m	5m

A

One great advantage recognized in business as a career is the	14	3
chance for advancement it offers to every earnest person. There are	28	6
many attractive jobs in the different fields of business open to	41	8
thoroughly competent students. Graduates have quickly risen	54	11
to be office managers, court reporters, and even officers of large	67	13
companies around the country. Many of our other students and	80	16
graduates, some of whose letters are reproduced in this book, are	93	19
earning extremely good incomes.	99	20

B

Many of our graduates own businesses where the field is just wide	14	23
open with opportunities for men and women. Incomes like those	27	25
expressed here, and even more, are frequent, as their letters show.	40	28
As the last point, and not the least among the rewards of a business	53	30
career, are those prized satisfactions for which every person longs,	66	33
the deepening and broadening knowledge, the development of	79	36
greater understanding of life, and tact in dealing with people.	92	39

C

Far above the rewards of position and income that come to our	13	41
graduates is the broader and happier life they enjoy and that you	26	43
can expect to be yours also. Our advice, based on long experience,	39	46
is to decide as soon as you possibly can and get into the field without	53	49
delay. During the many years that our school has been serving this	67	51
city, we have seen thousands of young people take positions in	80	54
business organizations and rise quickly to important places.	93	57

D

We also, unfortunately, know of many thousands of young people	13	59
who have entered business with no business preparation and who	27	62
have just remained in very small jobs for the rest of their lives. The	41	65
businessman expects his employees to be well trained when they	54	67
leave school. He realizes, of course, that he will have to train new	67	70
employees in the special duties that apply to his business. He has	81	73
no time, however, to devote to teaching beginners.	91	75

LESSON 227

560. Perfect Speed Drill. Your best speed, striving for errorless typing.

Those men will do work just for us if we give them good pay.   12

561. Alphabetic Speed Drill. Lesson 226: 5 to 10 copies of ¶A, then ¶B.

LESSON 228

562. Centering Drill. Set up the following list of officers attractively on a full sheet, 8½″ x 11″.

NATIONAL ASSOCIATION OF BUSINESS OFFICIALS
District Officers
EASTERN DISTRICT

Chairman. . . . . W. A. Forsyth
Vice-Chairman. . . . . O. M. Condon
Secretary-Treasurer. . . . .(Miss) E. V. Claire

CENTRAL DISTRICT

Chairman. . . . . .J. C. Ogden
Vice-Chairman. . . . . .A. R. Porter
Secretary-Treasurer. . . . .(Mrs.) G. L. Robinson

WESTERN DISTRICT

Chairman . . . . .C. G. Schaefer
Vice-Chairman. . . . . .D. V. Walker
Secretary-Treasurer. . . . .(Mrs.) N. O. Jansen

563. Alphabetic Speed Drill. Lesson 226: 5 to 10 copies of ¶C.

LESSON 229

564. Telegram Drill. On the telegram blank forms that will be supplied to you, type 1 copy of the night letter below to each of the 10 addresses listed.

Our methods engineer traveling your territory. Will call within week to discuss possible production problems your plant and offer services.

> G. M. Connolly
> R. F. Dewey Company

President, Sperry Brass Company, 26 Ferry Street, Dayton, Ohio
President, Reed & Company, 42 Reed Avenue, Scranton, Pennsylvania
President, Condon & Condon, 16 Tulsa Street, Reading, Pennsylvania

President, White & Company, 46 Anne Street, Baltimore, Maryland
President, The Merry Company, Inc., Wheeling, West Virginia
President, Triangle Metal Company, 8 Garth Road, Canton, Ohio
President, Powell Stamping Company, Powell Square, Camden, New Jersey
President, Ritchie Machine Company, Ritchie Building, Toledo, Ohio
President, Gaines & Company, Gaines Terminal, Trenton, New Jersey
President, French & Crosse, Riggs Building, Newark, New Jersey

565. Alphabetic Speed Drill. Lesson 226: 5 to 10 copies of ¶D.

LESSON 230

566. Perfect Speed Drill. Your best speed, striving for errorless typing.

Those men will do work just for us if we give them good pay.   12

567. Alphabetic Production Letter. Type in semiblock style, 1 copy to each
of the 10 addresses given.

Dear Mr.——: Thank you for your recent letter requesting samples   14
and information about our new decorator wallpapers. In addition to   28
the regular catalog, we are sending you a special supplement showing   42
our latest developments in waterproof papers. This literature should   56
reach you within the next ten days, but if it should not, please let us   70
know without delay. ¶ These wallpapers are carried by leading   83
stores around the country, and the name of the dealer organization   97
nearest you is listed on the catalog cover. They will be glad to answer   111
any questions, and if you wish, assist you in the job of selecting the   125
papers best suited to your needs. Yours very truly, **ROYAL &**   138
SCOTT COMPANY, James H. Wilson, Sales Service Division   150

Mr. T. J. Burke, 33 Elm Street, Phoenix 2, Arizona
Mrs. O. W. Landon, 46 Oak Avenue, Paterson 4, New Jersey
Mrs. G. S. Simmons, 39 Poplar Road, Utica 8, New York
Mr. N. A. Coles, 89 Locust Drive, Lowell 12, Massachusetts
Mrs. G. E. Hanley, 56 Maple Avenue, San Diego 7, California
Miss Anne G. Helm, 23 Beach Court, Seattle 8, Washington
Mrs. T. S. Barker, 82 Peach Drive, Atlanta 7, Georgia
Mr. S. S. Haines, 38 Cherry Lane, Urbana 4, Illinois
Mrs. K. R. Wilson, 77 Pine Road, Rutland 8, Vermont
Mr. G. S. Gimble, 65 Walnut Avenue, Boise 6, Idaho

LESSON 231

568. Typing Style Recall. Type 1 copy.

On November 8, 1954, we remitted $8.75 to Hamden & Colher to cover bills for 75 cents and $8. The check (#2795) was addressed to your office at 24 West 66 Road and mailed between 10 a.m. and 2:30 p.m. Three losses have resulted out of 920 such payments this year. "This is a well-maintained system," says our treasurer, "as the 'record' will show."

569. Alphabetic Speed Drill for 5-Minute Timed Writing.

W·A·M
1m 5m

A

It was in just this land that history was made by the pioneers, that   14   3
gallant race of men who carved out a new type of adventure while   27   5
they were developing a great and mighty industry. It was on the   40   8
wide ranges and the rolling plains and in the deep valleys of the ex-   53   11
tensive land that this new race of men lifted the quiet business of   67   13
the ancient cowherd to a position of daring and color. These were   80   16
a group of riding men who played their dazzling part in history.   93   19

B

By their deeds, those men quickly carved a new chapter in the story   14   21
of our country. So great was the influence of the early industry,   27   24
and the men who made that industry possible, on the civilization   40   27
which followed the pioneers, that today it affects almost every   54   29
phase of life in the state. Wherever the visitor may choose to go, he   68   32
can expect to hear the clink of spurs or the tap of boots. The more   81   35
hardy traveler may like to spend a few days on a real ranch.   93   37

C

On a real ranch, barbed wire fences are few and far between, cattle   13   40
are still raised in the same manner as they were by the early day   26   42
ranchers, and there is still a glad, free life for those who grow tired   39   45
of motor cars and the noises of the city. The flavor of the old days   52   48
still prevails in this amazing land, as well as the hospitality which   66   50
made the land famous. Once you settle down in this atmosphere,   80   53
you will quickly forget the existence of the busy cities.   93   56

D

Your card makes it amazingly easy for you to take advantage of all   13   59
the conveniences that air travel offers. You simply telephone our   27   61
nearest office and they will reserve a seat on the flight you desire.   40   64
All you have to do is to give your name and the number of the card.   53   67
You can then obtain your ticket by presenting your card at our   66   69
office or at the airport. You just sign a receipt, and your ticket will   80   72
be issued and charged to your travel expense account. No cash is   93   75
required.   95   75

LESSON 232

570. Perfect Speed Drill. Your best speed, striving for errorless typing.

Those men will do work just for us if we give them good pay. 12

571. Alphabetic Speed Drill. Lesson 231: 5 to 10 copies of ¶A, then ¶B.

LESSON 233

572. Addressing Drill. Type 3 envelopes or index cards for each of the following names and addresses.

Sperry Brass Company, 26 Ferry Street, Dayton 8, Ohio
Reed & Company, 42 Reed Avenue, Scranton 2, Pennsylvania
Condon & Condon, 16 Tulsa Street, Reading 6, Pennsylvania
White & Company, 46 Anne Street, Baltimore 7, Maryland
The Merry Company, Inc., Wheeling 9, West Virginia
Triangle Metal Company, 8 Garth Road, Canton 6, Ohio
Powell Stamping Company, Powell Square, Camden 2, New Jersey
Ritchie Machine Company, Ritchie Building, Toledo 8, Ohio
Gaines & Company, Gaines Terminal, Trenton 4, New Jersey
French & Crosse, Riggs Building, Newark 8, New Jersey

573. Alphabetic Speed Drill. Lesson 231: 5 to 10 copies of ¶C.

LESSON 234

574. Tabulation Drill. Set up the following tabulation attractively.

UNIVERSITIES WITH LARGEST ENROLLMENTS

Name	City	State	Organized	Students
City College	New York	N. Y.	1847	48,150
New York University	New York	N. Y.	1831	43,200
University of California	Berkeley	Cal.	1868	42,100
University of Illinois	Urbana	Ill.	1868	28,600
Columbia University	New York	N. Y.	1754	27,650
University of Minnesota	Minneapolis	Minn.	1851	26,100
University of Pittsburgh	Pittsburgh	Pa.	1787	25,800
Boston University	Boston	Mass.	1839	21,700
University of Wisconsin	Madison	Wisc.	1848	20,900
Ohio State University	Columbus	Ohio	1873	20,800

575. Alphabetic Speed Drill. Lesson 231: 5 to 10 copies of ¶D.

576. Perfect Speed Drill. Your best speed, striving for errorless typing.

Those men will do work just for us if we give them good pay.   12

577. Alphabetic Production Letter. Type in block style, 1 copy to each of the 5 addresses given.

Dear Mr.——: So many students have written us to say that they   14
simply cannot afford the monthly tuition installments under present   28
conditions that we have worked out a plan to enable serious and   41
qualified students to enroll at more easily budgeted rates. ¶ It is   54
our intention to accept a limited number of students under a plan   67
that will permit payment of relatively small monthly installments.   81
Students who find it necessary to come in under this plan will be   94
treated exactly as if they had enrolled under the regular plan. ¶ This   107
new reduced rate plan will permit students of limited income to   121
enroll without committing themselves to monthly payments that   134
they cannot afford. Here is an example of how payments can be made: 147

Amount Due	No. Payments	
		151
$200	10	153
400	15	154
600	20	155

¶ There will be no carrying charge or other added expense for   168
students who make use of this plan. It will be necessary only to   182
establish reliability and seriousness of purpose with the registrar.   196
¶ Just as soon as your application is approved, your enrollment   209
will go through without delay. Yours truly, BAKER INSTITUTE,   222
W. M. Alden, Registrar   227

Mr. R. S. Brown, 121 Water Street, Evanston 3, Illinois
Mr. T. G. Knoll, 87 Earl Road, Oak Park 4, Illinois
Miss A. Conley, 46 Bay Street, Gary 6, Indiana
Mr. W. Turner, 68 Main Street, Indianapolis 12, Indiana
Miss F. Harper, 37 Deer Drive, Springfield 7, Illinois

578. Typing Style Recall. Type 1 copy.

They went to the Clarke & Stone store at 548 North 22 Terrace on May 7, 1954, from 11 a.m. to 2:30 p.m. and examined the model (Model #41) but found it priced at $8.50 and $10, with parts kits at 60 cents. Thirty parts are in the kit, with 75 in the large kit, which saves 20% in cost. "Even if the well-made machine is higher than expected," Jim says, "it is well suited for our 'rush' jobs."

579. Alphabetic Speed Drill for 5-Minute Timed Writing.

	W·A·M	
	1m	5m

A

	1m	5m
These represent a unique form of saving with members. After your	13	3
first purchase, with every book you buy from among those chosen,	27	5
you receive a prize book as a dividend. These are highly useful	40	8
books like those offered here, sometimes important current books,	54	11
sometimes fine editions of great books that you want to live with	68	14
all your life. This member type of saving is very similar, you will	82	16
notice, to that extended by any firm that deals with books.	92	18

B

	1m	5m
This is just one striking example of the savings made possible by	13	21
large quantity buying. Members never have to take the book	26	24
selection, but so many want it each month that large editions can	39	26
be printed all at one time. The great saving in costs that results is	52	29
utilized to reduce the price of the book to each and every member,	65	32
and in any case, to set a fund aside for a dividend. As it grows, this	78	34
fund is invested in books; it is all used to buy other books.	91	37

C

	1m	5m
The books mentioned are the dividends you earn and receive as a	13	40
member. Because books are earned by members, instead of cash, the	26	42
value of what members get is magnified many times over. Frequent-	39	45
ly you may just buy our selection on the outside, in bookstores or	51	47
from other book dealers, not knowing it is one of our dividends,	64	50
and pay more for the book. It is more reasonable to buy that book	76	52
through us. You benefit because these prize books are picked for	89	55
you, and because you receive them without extra cost.	99	57

D

	1m	5m
If you are too busy to read the important new books in full but	13	59
want to be familiar with what they contain, we suggest that you	26	62
quickly join the great number of people who have solved their	39	65
reading problem. You can now get the vital content of several	52	67
leading books each month summarized in a new kind of reading ser-	65	70
vice that makes possible a great saving of time and money for its	78	72
readers. We now invite you to share the extra privileges that these	90	75
people enjoy.		

LESSON 237

580. Perfect Speed Drill. Your best speed, striving for errorless typing.

Those men will do work just for us if we give them good pay.   12

581. Alphabetic Speed Drill. Lesson 236: 5 to 10 copies of ¶A, then ¶B.

LESSON 238

582. Centering Drill. Set up the following announcement attractively on a full sheet, 8½″ x 11″.

FREE FILM SHOWING
"Highlights of a World Tour"
Wednesday, June 3, 1954
5 o'clock
Civic Auditorium

This will be the first showing of the unusually interesting scenes recorded on film by the Natural Museum Travel Society on its recent world-wide tour. This group of experienced travelers covered more than 35,000 miles in 14 months, visiting some of the most remote corners of the globe. Here is an opportunity to see something truly educational and, at the same time, entertaining.

OPEN TO ALL!

583. Alphabetic Speed Drill. Lesson 236: 5 to 10 copies of ¶C.

LESSON 239

584. Manuscript Typing Drill. Type 1 copy of the following page of manuscript, corrected as indicated.

585. Alphabetic Speed Drill. Lesson 236: 5 to 10 copies of ¶D.

BUSINESS

More and more, management is showing increasing interest in adopting scientific ideas for the ~~office~~ *business* office. It is being proved every day that this scientific approach makes for greater worker morale, improved working conditions, and therefore increased ~~productivity~~ *production*.

The Importance of Color

Lighting engineers have ~~shown~~ *been able to prove* that the light reflectance[1] factor of colors used in office equipment plays an important part in eye-comfort. Regardless of other surroundings, if light reflectance factors are wrong, office workers suffer from unnecessary eye-fatigue. Tired eyes, strained eyes, and headaches resulting from such strains *are bound to cause* ~~create~~ office friction, errors, and slow work.

In studying the effect of light reflection and the psychology of color on actual production, one company recently completed an exhaustive *and most interesting* experiment. The effect on 100 clerical employees of properly colored walls and ceilings, together with proper lighting, was studied over a two-year period. In spite of more detail in the work which had to be added during this period, substantial increases in output resulted.

[1] *a term used by lighting engineers to describe the amount of light reflected by a given surface.*

586. Perfect Speed Drill. Your best speed, striving for errorless typing.

Those men will do work just for us if we give them good pay.   12

587. Alphabetic Production Letter. Type in semiblock style, 1 copy to each of the 3 addresses given.

Dear Mr.——: About ten days ago we sent you a booklet describing   14
our course in salesmanship. If you did not receive it, we should be   27
pleased to send a duplicate out at once. ¶ If you did, you probably   40
have been delaying your reply because you are doubtful that we can   54
help you. It is only natural that you should be hesitant. You are   68
considering an investment of time and money which may alter your   81
entire life. ¶ Success in selling can mean everything to you: freedom   95
from shop or office routine, financial independence, ability to travel,   109
to mix with successful, congenial people who share your inter-   123
ests. ¶ Yet you have no way of knowing for sure that you can   136
attain success or that we can help you. You may be asking yourself   149
if you can ever succeed at selling. ¶ The best way for us to help you   162
answer those questions is perhaps to quote a letter from a graduate   176
who, not too long ago, felt just as you feel now, hesitant, quite   189
doubtful, inclined to put off making the first step.   200

> I have not written you before as I wanted to know my fate on   212
> my first selling job. Last week I received a commission check   224
> for $200. This speaks for itself, I think, regarding the training   237
> which your school gives its students. I can truthfully state that   250
> without the course it would never have occurred to me to sell.   262

Yes, we can teach selling, and we have helped people like you to   276
realize real success. But the first decision is yours. You must make   289
up your mind if we are to help you. ¶ Stop and consider now where   302
you will be a year from today. Will you still be hoping and still be   315
telling yourself that some day you will try selling? Or will you be   329
enjoying the fruits of creative selling, knowing the daily joy of put-   343
ting your own ideas to work, experiencing independence, the little   357
extra things that make life worth while? ¶ You can do it. Nor do   370
you need to aim first at the very top. There are thousands of places   384
where new salesmen can earn real cash for their efforts. ¶ Change   397
that "some day" to "today." Fill out the enclosed application form   411
and send it along to us now, while your thoughts are fresh. And tell   424
yourself: "A year from today, I'll be selling." Sincerely yours, John   438
T. Herron, Business Manager   444

Mr. Owen F. Kling, 48 Willard Street, Dallas 7, Texas
Mr. G. R. Phillips, 92 James Avenue, Buffalo 14, New York
Mr. K. D. Hainge, 67 Pacific Street, San Mateo 2, California

588. Typing Style Recall. Type 1 copy.

The Baxter & Greene store at 479 East 68 Road is featuring the power tool you wanted (Model #21) at $14.95 and $20. Sixty polishing wheels are 60 cents and a package of 120 may be had at a saving of 15%. A special demonstration is planned for October 8, 1954, between the hours of 10 a.m. and 2:30 p.m. "This particular model," said Mr. Greene, "will give you an 'extra-fine' finish."

589. Alphabetic Speed Drill for 5-Minute Timed Writing.

	W·A·M	
	1m	5m

A

When an employee in our organization is assigned more than one	13	3
duty, it is important not to assign him low responsibility jobs along	27	5
with high responsibility jobs. As soon as this is done, the employee	41	8
will lower his estimation of the whole job to the level of the most	55	11
menial duty he performs. If there is any doubt as to the truth of	68	14
this statement, just pick out one of your employees with quite a	81	16
high job and give him the assignment of dusting office furniture	94	19
every day.	96	19

B

Every job has its standard of performance. These standards may	13	22
take the form of a blueprint, a written statement of the job require-	27	25
ments, or merely a talk between the boss and the employee. In any	41	27
case, the employee wants to know what the standards are, and he is	54	30
entitled to know. These standards must be given to the employee	68	33
as a guide in doing his work, not kept a secret by the boss to be	81	35
referred to only when the job is not going as he expected it.	93	38

C

When authority and responsibility fail to balance, bad manage-	13	40
ment will be the result. For every single duty, or part of a duty,	27	43
within the framework of an organization there is the corresponding	41	46
authority to get it done. Reduced to simple terms, for every unit of	54	49
responsibility in an organization, there is required a unit of author-	68	51
ity. The balance between authority and responsibility is extremely	82	54
delicate. A correct and even balance must always be maintained.	95	57

D

There are several reasons for setting up a method of reporting back.	14	59
It permits delegation of responsibility to the employee without any	27	62
abdication on the part of the boss. These reports should take what-	41	65
ever form, and be made as often as and in whatever detail, the	54	68
nature of the work may require to give the boss complete but	67	70
passive control of the operation of his organization. In the absence	81	73
of such controls, you will almost surely find the executive checking	94	76
on the job.	97	77

LESSON 242

590. Perfect Speed Drill. Your best speed, striving for errorless typing.

They will just have to sign the pay forms for the good work.   12

591. Alphabetic Speed Drill. Lesson 241: 5 to 10 copies of ¶A, then ¶B.

LESSON 243

592. Addressing Drill. Type 3 envelopes or index cards for each of the following names and addresses.

Miss Anne G. Helm, 23 Beech Court, Seattle 8, Washington
Mrs. T. S. Barker, 82 Peach Drive, Atlanta 7, Georgia
Mrs. S. S. Haines, 38 Cherry Lane, Urbana 4, Illinois
Mrs. K. B. Wilson, 77 Pine Road, Rutland 8, Vermont
Mr. G. S. Gimble, 65 Walnut Avenue, Boise 6, Idaho
Mr. R. S. Brown, 121 Water Street, Evanston 3, Illinois
Mr. T. G. Knoll, 87 Earl Road, Oak Park 4, Illinois
Miss A. Conley, 46 Bay Street, Gary 6, Indiana
Mr. W. Turner, 68 Main Street, Indianapolis 12, Indiana
Miss F. Harper, 37 Deer Drive, Springfield 7, Illinois

593. Alphabetic Speed Drill. Lesson 241: 5 to 10 copies of ¶C.

LESSON 244

594. Tabulation Drill. Set up the following tabulation attractively.

LIST OF ACCOUNTS RECEIVABLE

January 1, 1954

Name	City & State	Account No.	Due
L. J. Carney	Oakland, California	2632	$1,202.40
Baylor & Baylor	Dallas, Texas	2423	806.29
F. J. Thompson	Denver, Colorado	2907	921.40
Crestwood Company	Boise, Idaho	3704	166.77
Hale & Landis	Des Moines, Iowa	3402	388.40
R. T. Stevenson	St. Joseph, Missouri	2163	2,664.50
John D. Meyers	Cincinnati, Ohio	1642	800.50
Maaske & Sons	Atlanta, Georgia	1973	702.70

595. Alphabetic Speed Drill. Lesson 241: 5 to 10 copies of ¶D.

596. Perfect Speed Drill. Your best speed, striving for errorless typing.

They will just have to sign the pay forms for the good work.   12

597. Alphabetic Production Letter. Type in block style, 1 copy to each of the 10 addresses given.

Dear Mr.——: The long-awaited improved sweepers are quickly   14
coming off the assembly line and shipments will soon begin on back   27
orders, among which will be your order. ¶ The new sweepers will   40
sell at exactly the same price as the current model, as shown on the   54
attached price list. However, we still have a good supply of the   68
older model, which has always been a good seller, and it will be   81
available to our dealer organizations at a 25% cut in cost. You may   95
credit this discount on any old models you may still have in stock,   109
or if you wish, just return that stock to us for full credit. Very truly   122
yours, B. W. Remington, Dealer Sales   130

Mr. C. V. Weston, Manager, Macon Furniture Company, Macon 2, Georgia
Mr. W. S. Doyle, Manager, Dale Appliance Company, Albany 6, New York
Mr. F. J. Sands, Manager, Sands Furniture Store, Omaha 7, Nebraska
Mr. S. S. Bruff, Bruff Department Store, Flint 7, Michigan
Mr. J. S. Handy, Buyer, The Ritchie Store, Long Beach 12, California
Mr. D. V. Graham, Manager, Park Street Store, San Antonio 9, Texas
Mr. T. H. Henry, King Furniture Company, Camden 7, New Jersey
Mr. R. W. Fowler, Fowler & Sons, Duluth 12, Minnesota
Mr. J. C. Wallace, Buyer, Dorr Appliance Company, Memphis 6, Tennessee
Mr. L. D. Acken, Adams Appliance Company, New Bedford 2, Massachusetts

598. Typing Style Recall. Type 1 copy.

Thirty new machines ranging in price from $35 to $79.50 have been ordered by Hammond & Company, 465 North 82 Street (Room #318) for their 150 employees and they expect delivery on September 29, 1954, between 8 a.m. and 4:30 p.m. "All 'efficiency-minded' employees," said the manager, "will appreciate that with a time saving of 15% on these machines, they can earn from 75 cents to $1 an hour more."

599. Alphabetic Speed Drill for 5-Minute Timed Writing.

	W·A·M	
	1m	5m

A

	1m	5m
An employee is entitled to know that he will receive orders from	14	3
only one person. This does not quite mean that others in the organ-	28	6
ization are forbidden to have contact with the employee in such	41	8
matters as securing or exchanging business information, but it does	55	11
mean everybody should not be permitted to give orders to the	69	14
worker. All orders should filter through one boss. Confusion is only	83	17
part of the story. There are several sound reasons for having one boss.	97	19

B

One should not get the mistaken idea that there are just a few things	14	22
an employee is entitled to expect from his boss. We doubt whether	27	25
there has ever been a count, and we doubt further whether a count	41	27
would accomplish any end result. We do know that a great bulk of	55	30
things that an employee is entitled to expect from his boss revolve	69	33
around a few very fundamental management principles. Properly	82	36
understood, these principles can serve as guides to more smoothly	95	39
running organizations.	99	40

C

These involve such things as conflicting orders, the scheduling of	14	43
work, even workloads, and, very important in the mind of the	27	45
employee, getting credit for work done. We realize that sometimes	40	48
it may appear difficult to operate in this fashion, but the boss who	54	51
does will be well repaid in better work and more satisfied employees.	67	53
Too frequently a job will consist of the uninteresting and routine	80	56
phases of the next higher job.	86	57

D

Many an employee has left his job to take another at lower pay	13	60
merely because he was unhappy about having no definite job as-	26	63
signed to him. Assigning whole segments of work is the quicker way	40	66
to broader horizons, greater interest, and a greater probability of	54	69
success in a job. At times it may appear difficult to assign whole	67	71
segments of work. It may even call for some sacrifice on the part of	81	74
the boss. But the end will justify any extra effort required.	93	77

LESSON 247

600. Perfect Speed Drill. Your best speed, striving for errorless typing.

They will just have to sign the pay forms for the good work.   12

601. Alphabetic Speed Drill. Lesson 246: 5 to 10 copies of ¶A, then ¶B.

LESSON 248

602. Centering Drill. Set up the following title page attractively on a full sheet, 8½″ x 11″.

NOISE vs. QUIET IN THE OFFICE
Baxter O. Browne
Consultant on Office Efficiency
Browne & Seeley
New York

A brief explanation of the effects of noise and quiet on general office morale, efficiency, and productivity.

Distributed by
THE JOHNSON & ELLINGTON COMPANY
New York   Chicago   San Francisco

603. Alphabetic Speed Drill. Lesson 246: 5 to 10 copies of ¶C.

LESSON 249

604. Manuscript Typing Drill. Type 1 copy of the following page of manuscript, corrected as indicated.

605. Alphabetic Speed Drill. Lesson 246: 5 to 10 copies of ¶D.

The detrimental effect of noise upon the nervous system is well documented by the medical profession and by research *much* among office and industrial ~~workers~~ *personnel.* Dr. Henry O. Backer states, "Noise lowers efficiency by interfering with concentration. It increases nervous tension and induces fatigue."[1]

An acoustical ceiling ~~does~~ *will do* away with much of the reverberation of sound in a room by absorbing a high percentage of the sound waves striking the ceiling.

Amount of Sound Absorption

Amount of sound absorption varies according to the frequency or pitch of sound, the method of application or mounting, and the thickness *of the tile used as well as its weight* ~~and weight of the tile~~. It also varies according to the diameter, depth, and spacing of the perforations, and with the composition or density of the material.

Production engineers are in agreement on the values of quiet on the job. H. E. Merton has wisely stated:[2]

> The processes of office production are often their own worst enemies in that the noise they generate causes worker fatigue which, in turn, leads to careless work, errors, and reduced output.

An acoustical ceiling, by quieting noise, can help to bring about a reduction in spoilage and *in the number of* accidents.

---

[1]Dr. Henry O. Backer, Quiet Pays Dividends, Baltimore, Smithson Publishing Company, 1951.
[2]H. E. Merton, "The Case for Acoustics," Engineering Journal, 12:151-152, January, 1953.

606. Perfect Speed Drill. Your best speed, striving for errorless typing.

They will just have to sign the pay forms for the good work.　　　12

607. Alphabetic Production Letter. Type in semiblock style, 1 copy to each of the 10 addresses given.

Dear Mr.——: Thank you for extending us the privilege of demon-　14
strating our machines for boxing small parts. You and your associates　28
made us feel right at home and it was a pleasure to work with you　41
under those conditions. ¶ The model you selected will be left on　55
trial for as long as you wish, and any mechanical servicing that may　69
be needed will be attended to by our local organization. They will　83
arrange to have a man drop in once a day to see that the machine is　96
adjusted properly and to answer any questions that may arise in　109
your shipping department. ¶ When you are satisfied that the test is　123
completed, just send the enclosed return card. Yours very truly,　137
ATLAS MACHINE COMPANY, J. H. Baylor, Chief Engineer　149

Mr. C. K. Waverly, Comptroller, Coe Motors, Lansing 3, Michigan
Mr. B. F. Warren, Jr., Treasurer, Plaza Tool Company, Toledo 4, Ohio
Mr. L. W. Baron, White & Sons, Inc., Reading 7, Pennsylvania
Mr. R. C. Forster, York Machine Company, Evansville 14, Indiana
Mr. John C. Lewis, Davis & Sargeant, Inc., Wilmington 9, Delaware
Mr. G. N. Richmond, Royal Die Company, Elizabeth 10, New Jersey
Mr. A. E. Corbett, Corbett Tool Company, Utica 15, New York
Mr. L. A. Layman, Robbins & Cramer, Inc., Allentown 13, New Jersey
Mr. G. F. Bauman, Treasurer, The Flint Company, Bridgeport 6, Connecticut
Mr. S. H. Braun, Chief Engineer, Gay Tool Company, Lynn 2, Massachusetts

608. Typing Style Recall. Type 1 copy.

On September 1, 1954, our sales department will move to our new offices in the Rogers & Sloan Building, 467 West 28 Drive (Room #591). Fifty people, 10% more than now, will handle book orders from 9:30 a.m. to 5 p.m. Many of our books will be reduced to $1.75 and $2, with some selling as low as 90 cents. "This new arrangement," says the manager, "will surely be welcomed by the 'book-minded' public."

609. Alphabetic Speed Drill for 5-Minute Timed Writing.

	W·A·M	
	1m	5m

A

	1m	5m
Some prize errors can be made by the executive who becomes fired	14	3
with enthusiasm for culling out unnecessary activities and then ends	28	6
up spending more time and energy trying to find answers to questions	42	8
in the incomplete and insufficient details that are available after the	56	11
general housecleaning is over. Before one undertakes a program of	70	14
simplified office activities, it is recommended that a clear under-	84	17
standing of the term be had.	90	19

B

	1m	5m
Records and reports are developed to meet present demands for	13	22
information and data. These same records and reports also meet	26	24
future requirements for statistical and historical data. Before any	40	27
report or record is discontinued, a careful check should be made of	54	30
its ultimate use. A company in your city dropped considerable	68	33
operating detail and other subordinate analyses and in consequence	81	35
saved about six man hours per month in the accounting department.	94	38

C

	1m	5m
In the preliminary survey there was a failure to check all depart-	13	41
ments which used the report. The executive, operating, and account-	26	43
ing departments were interrogated concerning the reduction in	39	46
contents of the report and their approval was obtained. Had the	52	48
budget department just been checked, it would have been quickly	65	51
discovered that once each year this department prepared a detailed	79	54
past experience record, which was used in determining trends for	93	57
future estimates.	96	58

D

	1m	5m
This is but one out of hundreds of examples illustrating the pitfalls	14	60
of simplification. Present demands for information must be carefully	28	63
scrutinized and screened and the requirements of the future must	41	65
also be minutely appraised, to avoid the discontinuance of data	54	68
which will subsequently be required. We must make a distinction	67	70
between desirable information and required information. Much of	81	73
the information I have seen recorded in various offices is desirable.	95	76

LESSON 252

610. Perfect Speed Drill. Your best speed, striving for errorless typing.

They will just have to sign the pay forms for the good work.   12

611. Alphabetic Speed Drill. Lesson 251: 5 to 10 copies of ¶A, then ¶B.

LESSON 253

612. Addressing Drill. Type 3 envelopes or index cards for each of the following names and addresses.

Mr. C. V. Weston, Manager, Macon Furniture Company, Macon 2, Georgia
Mr. W. S. Doyle, Manager, Dale Appliance Company, Albany 6, New York
Mr. F. J. Sands, Manager, Sands Furniture Store, Omaha 7, Nebraska
Mr. S. S. Bruff, Bruff Department Store, Flint 7, Michigan
Mr. J. S. Handy, Buyer, The Ritchie Store, Long Beach 12, California
Mr. D. V. Graham, Manager, Park Street Store, San Antonio 9, Texas
Mr. R. W. Fowler, Fowler & Sons, Duluth 12, Minnesota
Mr. J. C. Wallace, Buyer, Dorr Appliance Company, Memphis 6, Tennessee
Mr. C. K. Waverly, Comptroller, Coe Motors, Lansing 3, Michigan
Mr. L. W. Baron, White & Sons, Inc., Reading 7, Pennsylvania

613. Alphabetic Speed Drill. Lesson 251: 5 to 10 copies of ¶C.

LESSON 254

614. Tabulation Drill. Set up the following tabulation attractively.

POPULATION OF BIGGEST U. S. CITIES

Rank	City	1950	1940	1930
1	New York	7,841,023	7,454,995	6,930,446
2	Chicago	3,631,835	3,396,808	3,376,438
3	Philadelphia	2,057,210	1,931,334	1,950,961
4	Los Angeles	1,954,036	1,504,277	1,238,048
5	Detroit	1,837,613	1,623,452	1,568,662
6	Baltimore	939,865	859,100	804,874
7	Cleveland	909,546	878,336	900,429
8	St. Louis	852,253	816,048	821,960
9	Washington	792,234	663,091	486,869
10	Boston	788,552	770,816	781,188

615. Alphabetic Speed Drill. Lesson 251: 5 to 10 copies of ¶D.

616. Perfect Speed Drill. Your best speed, striving for errorless typing.

They will just have to sign the pay forms for the good work.   12

617. Alphabetic Production Letter. Type in block style, 1 copy to each of the 6 addresses given.

Dear Mr.——: Princeton tools are designed to help you get the most   14
in profit from the time spent in your shop, to help you accomplish   28
in minutes what might take hours with the usual hand tools. And   42
they are built to industrial standards of accuracy and efficiency to   56
give you professional workmanship on any project you undertake,   70
from furniture and equipment repairs to fine cabinet work. ¶ You   84
will find out a lot about the tools by reading the enclosed specifica-   96
tions and features that are important to you in your plant work,   109
but to appreciate the sturdiness and precision construction you   122
need to see the tools and put some on production tests in your plant.   136
¶ Our representative will be in your area within the next few weeks.   150
He will be glad to call and discuss this with you and will quote some   163
amazingly low prices. Sincerely yours, **C. H. Treet**, Sales Manager   176

Plant Manager, J. Willis & Sons, Waterbury 8, Connecticut
Plant Manager, C. V. Burgess Company, Syracuse 2, New York
Plant Manager, Camden Pencil Company, Nashville 9, Tennessee
Plant Manager, Grant Manufacturing Company, Denver 7, Colorado
Plant Manager, French Desk Company, Portland 14, Oregon
Plant Manager, Turner Tool Company, Houston 8, Texas

LESSON 256

618. Typing Style Recall. Type 1 copy.

Mr. Phillips writes that he expects more than 150 to attend the sales meeting scheduled for November 18, 1954, at the Glenn & Cary Building, 476 East 59 Road (Conference Room #4), between 11 a.m. and 3:30 p.m. Eighty can be accommodated for lunch and will pay $1 to $1.50, plus 25 cents tip and 2% for tax. "I feel sure," says Mr. Phillips, "that many of our 'shop-tested' suggestions will be well received."

619. Alphabetic Speed Drill for 5-Minute Timed Writing.

		W·A·M	
		1m	5m

A

	1m	5m
A department store, realizing that routine correspondence was	14	3
requiring considerable time and space for indexing and filing, decided	28	6
to retain no correspondence of a purely routine, courtesy nature.	42	8
There would be no record of complaints, thank-you letters, and	56	11
general information letters, once they had been answered and prop-	69	14
erly handled. Only a few times were they inconvenienced by having	83	17
no record of previous letters, thus having to request the information.	96	19

B

	1m	5m
There was a time when many office managers thought of microfilm-	14	22
ing only in respect to storage materials. Several midwest organiza-	28	24
tions have all current file material of lasting value filmed each day	42	27
before it goes into the files so that they are building up their films	56	30
currently. When this material is ready for storage, there is no	70	33
confusion and delay. The films have already been prepared and	83	35
indexed. Instead of transferring the material, it is quickly destroyed.	97	38

C

	1m	5m
A machine is as fast as the operator, but the potential capacity of	14	41
most mechanized operations is next to unlimited. A properly en-	28	44
gineered machine is more accurate in its operation on a consistent	42	47
basis than is a manual operation. The shorter work week places an	56	49
additional requirement on speed, on being able to process a greater	70	52
volume of work in a shorter period of time. Increased demands of	84	55
management for information just emphasized further simplicity.	96	57

D

	1m	5m
Time and speed are related. A financial report prepared six weeks	13	60
after the books are closed loses some of its value because of the time	27	63
factor. Corrective action, if required, is delayed too long beyond the	41	66
point of action if control reports are delayed. Probably the most	55	69
common area for work simplification is in arrangement. A process	68	71
analysis of the operations followed in completing paper work will	82	74
emphasize quite a few things.	88	75

LESSON 257

620. Perfect Speed Drill. Your best speed, striving for errorless typing.

They will just have to sign the pay forms for the good work.　　12

621. Alphabetic Speed Drill. Lesson 256: 5 to 10 copies of ¶A, then ¶B.

LESSON 258

622. Centering Drill. Set up the following table of contents attractively.

Noise vs. Quiet in the Office

CONTENTS

Section		Page
I	The Characteristics of Sound	1
II	The Effect of Noise	3
III	The Effect of Quiet	5
IV	Sound-Reducing Ideas	6
V	Acoustic Ceilings	8
VI	Installation	11
VII	Maintenance	14
VIII	Cost	19
IX	Other Qualities	22
X	Typical Installations	27

623. Alphabetic Speed Drill. Lesson 256: 5 to 10 copies of ¶C.

LESSON 259

624. Telegram Drill. On the telegram blank forms that will be supplied to you, type 1 copy of the full rate telegram below to each of the 10 addresses listed.

Can send 50 Model #321 sweepers at half current price for immediate clearance. Wire order.

B. W. Remington

Mr. C. V. Weston, Macon Furniture Company, Macon, Georgia
Mr. W. S. Doyle, Dale Appliance Company, Albany, New York
Mr. F. J. Sands, Sands Furniture Store, Omaha, Nebraska
Mr. S. S. Bruff, Bruff Department Store, Flint, Michigan
Mr. J. S. Handy, The Ritchie Store, Long Beach, California

185

Mr. D. V. Graham, Park Street Store, San Antonio, Texas

Mr. L. D. Acken, Adams Appliance Company, New Bedford, Massachusetts

Mr. T. H. Henry, King Furniture Company, Camden, New Jersey

Mr. R. W. Fowler, Fowler & Sons, Duluth, Minnesota

Mr. J. C. Wallace, Door Appliance Company, Memphis, Tennessee

625. Alphabetic Speed Drill. Lesson 256: 5 to 10 copies of ¶D.

LESSON 260

626. Perfect Speed Drill. Your best speed, striving for errorless typing.

They will just have to sign the pay forms for the good work.   12

627. Alphabetic Production Letter. On the interoffice letterhead form that will be supplied to you, type 1 copy of the letter below to each of the 6 addresses listed.

```
TO        —
FROM      Manager of Pricing
SUBJECT   New Price List
DATE      —
```

Enclosed is a copy of the new price list, covering all cotton goods, to   14
go into effect the first of next year. All orders taken the remainder   28
of this year, even those marked for delivery in January of next year,   42
will be billed at the present prices. However, orders taken this year   56
for delivery after January 31 of next year will have to be billed at the   70
new prices. ¶ You will note that generally prices have increased   83
throughout the line, but there are quite a few exceptions. In a number   97
of cases prices remain the same, and in some cases there is even a   110
slight decrease. ¶ You will also note that the format of the price   123
book is completely changed, also that there is a new discount policy.   137
These changes will necessitate some formal instruction of the field   150
organization. For that reason, a representative of my office will call   164
on your branch just before the end of this year, at which time he   177
will explain the new price book to your men in one or two meetings.   191
R. S. MacGarvey   194

Manager, Denver Office   Manager, Portland Office
Manager, New Orleans Office   Manager, Baltimore Office
Manager, Chicago Office   Manager, Providence Office

628. Typing Style Recall. Type 1 copy.

"If you want a 'sure-fire' method for increasing sales," Mr. Lane says, "read the new booklet on display at our office in the Hall & Rand Building, 327 North 84 Drive (Room #561)." Published on August 1, 1954, the booklet is on sale from 10 a.m. to 4:30 p.m. Eighty cents is the special price, while quantity orders of more than 120 may be had at a saving of 15%. Bookstore prices will be 90 cents to $1 or $1.25.

629. Alphabetic Speed Drill for 5-Minute Timed Writing.

	W·A·M 1m	5m

A

When office work had to be done the hard way, no new task was	13	3
added without thorough consideration of its necessity. Now modern	27	5
machines, equipment, and supplies make it so easy to carry on an	41	8
office project that we tend to minimize the importance of explaining	55	11
the need for it, and office costs rise steadily year after year. Economy	69	14
begins when a project is still in the suggestion stage, whether the	83	17
question is a major or a minor addition to the work required.	94	19

B

One of our representatives just passed on a friendly tip from a friend	14	22
who had heard a group of our customers discussing among them-	26	24
selves that we should get away from the idea of seeking to save	39	27
paper by using two sides of a letterhead in letters of more than one	53	29
page. This has brought up a very interesting question, which I feel is	67	32
worth explaining to our readers. In the first place, we realize the	81	35
two-sided letter was adopted during the war as an economy.	93	37

C

Like many other lessons we learned in the war, perhaps this is one	13	40
which could just as easily be carried over into the post-war period	27	43
to some advantage. First, let me explain that our recognized practice	41	46
of using the second side of a letter has not been continued quite so	55	49
much with the idea of saving one sheet of paper, as because we	68	52
have found it a decided advantage in our filing. The fact that it is	82	54
more economical has something to do with it, but it is not the	95	57
deciding factor.	98	57

D

Here are just a few of the points which we consider favor a two-sided	13	59
letter. When letters are typed on two sheets, they come in the mail	27	62
and sometimes separate on the mail desk. Next, they then have to be	42	65
clipped, pinned, or stapled together; otherwise they have the habit of	56	67
becoming misplaced. The second sheet, which frequently has no	70	70
heading on it, is difficult to match up with its original if separated.	83	73
With a one-sheet letter there is only one sheet of paper to handle.	96	75

630. Perfect Speed Drill. Your best speed, striving for errorless typing.

They will just have to sign the pay forms for the good work. 12

631. Alphabetic Speed Drill. Lesson 261: 5 to 10 copies of ¶A, then ¶B.

LESSON 263

632. Addressing Drill. Type 3 envelopes or index cards for each of the following names and addresses.

Mr. R. C. Forster, York Machine Company, Evansville 14, Indiana
Mr. John C. Lewis, Davis & Sargeant, Inc., Wilmington 9, Delaware
Mr. G. N. Richmond, Royal Die Company, Elizabeth 10, New Jersey
Mr. A. E. Corbett, Corbett Tool Company, Utica 15, New York
Mr. L. A. Layman, Robbins & Cramer, Inc., Allentown 13, New Jersey
Plant Manager, J. Willis & Sons, Waterbury 8, Connecticut
Plant Manager, C. V. Burgess Company, Syracuse 2, New York
Plant Manager, Camden Pencil Company, Nashville 9, Tennessee
Plant Manager, Grant Manufacturing Company, Denver 7, Colorado
Plant Manager, French Desk Company, Portland 14, Oregon
Plant Manager, Turner Tool Company, Houston 8, Texas

633. Alphabetic Speed Drill. Lesson 261: 5 to 10 copies of ¶C.

LESSON 264

634. Billing Drill. On the duplicated billheads that will be supplied, type the 10 copies of the following bill needed for the 10 addresses given. Set tabular stops according to the printed columns on the billhead.

Packaging Machine #25 at $550
Packaging Twine #14 at $5 Doz.

Coe Motor Company, Lansing 3, Michigan
    Invoice No. 7902, Order No. 2210, Quantity: 1 #25, 5 Doz. #14
The Flint Company, Bridgeport 6, Connecticut
    Invoice No. 7903, Order No. 1345, Quantity: 1 #25, 5 Doz. #14
Plaza Manufacturing Company, Toledo 4, Ohio
    Invoice No. 7904, Order No. 1984, Quantity: 1 #25, 5 Doz. #14
Gay Tool Company, Fall River 2, Massachusetts
    Invoice No. 7905, Order No. 1463, Quantity: 1 #25, 6 Doz. #14
White & Sons, Inc., Reading 7, Pennsylvania
    Invoice No. 7906, Order No. 4357, Quantity: 1 #25, 8 Doz. #14

York Machine Company, Evansville 14, Indiana
     Invoice No. 7907, Order No. 9438, Quantity: 1 #25, 6 Doz. #14
Davis & Sargeant, Inc., Wilmington 9, Delaware
     Invoice No. 7908, Order No. 8435, Quantity: 1 #25, 8 Doz. #14
Royal Die Company, Elizabeth 10, New Jersey
     Invoice No. 7909, Order No. 4538, Quantity: 1 #25, 5 Doz. #14
Corbett Tool Company, Utica 15, New York
     Invoice No. 7910, Order No. 3526, Quantity: 1 #25, 5 Doz. #14
Robbins & Cramer, Inc., Allentown 13, New Jersey
     Invoice No. 7911, Order No. 4537, Quantity: 1 #25, 5 Doz. #14

635. Alphabetic Speed Drill. Lesson 261: 5 to 10 copies of ¶D.

LESSON 265

636. Perfect Speed Drill. Your best speed, striving for errorless typing.

They will just have to sign the pay forms for the good work.   12

637. Alphabetic Production Letter. Type in semiblock style, 1 copy to each
of the 10 addresses given.

Dear Mr.——: Thank you for your request for information about   13
sound conditioning in offices. We do have some very helpful litera- 27
ture on the subject in the form of an excellent booklet, which we   41
have mailed to you under another cover. ¶ Many organizations have   54
written us, after receiving "Practical Sound Conditioning," stating 68
that the information proved invaluable to them in their planning.   81
And many more have written, stating how much they had gained in   94
efficiency through the use of our products. ¶ Our representative   107
will call in just a few days to answer any questions and to give you 121
any price information you may wish. Yours very truly, JONES &   134
CONDON, INC., G. G. Smithson, Sales Department   143

Mr. R. W. Bowman, Wiley, Smith & Sons, Chester 29, Pennsylvania
Mrs. V. E. Baker, Carr Publishing Company, Elizabeth 8, New Jersey
Mr. W. C. Damuth, Treasurer, Ward Press, San Diego 4, California
Mr. E. G. Goodyear, Guaranty Insurance Company, Seattle 6, Washington
Mr. H. L. Green, Gulf Electric Company, Kansas City 9, Missouri
Miss G. W. Patton, Hill & Gibbs, 78 Ferry Street, Cincinnati 7, Ohio
Mrs. G. M. Walter, President, Searle Distributors, Champaign 2, Illinois
Mr. F. C. Hill, Holland Clothing Company, Birmingham 7, Alabama
Mr. M. S. Russell, General Brick Company, Worcester 18, Massachusetts
Mr. S. G. Winslow, Treasurer, Globe Company, Salt Lake City 7, Utah

LESSON 266

638. Typing Style Recall. Type 1 copy.

We were at the Randall & Cross store at 524 East 76 Road between 9 a.m. and 11:30 p.m. on September 9, 1954, and inspected their new machines (Model #28) priced at $12.50 and $15, with color refills at 80 cents a package. Fifty units are in the small package and 175 in the large, the latter now priced to save 20%. "This 'first-rate' machine," said Cross, "is a fine addition to your office."

639. Alphabetic Speed Drill for 5-Minute Timed Writing.

	W·A·M	
	1m	5m

A

	1m	5m
It is easy to permit your interest to follow any one of a dozen	13	3
thoughts about the questions involved, but the single one to which	26	5
we direct your attention is that the department head and the office	40	8
manager should have had available a proper measure of the work	54	11
burden in that section by means of a control of forms consumption,	67	13
and of examining this measure of work burden in relation to the job	81	16
of processing the same form in other sections or departments.	93	19

B

	1m	5m
Just two forms were used by one individual, prepared by hand. One	14	21
was the daily assembly of information, and the other the monthly	27	24
summary thereof. Only a small number of these forms were used	40	27
each year and the total cost of forms was nominal. The problem was	54	29
so small it hardly justified the attention of the busy office manager.	68	32
But not so the inquiring analyst. The problem was analyzed and it	81	35
was revealed that exactly three times as many of the summary	94	37
forms were being used.	98	38

C

	1m	5m
The information recorded was confidential and the work was done	14	41
by a trusted employee, many years with the firm and now quite	27	44
along in years. For these reasons his working methods had been	39	46
inviolable. The office manager had been in the firm less than half as	52	48
long. No one knew just how many forms he used, or why, because	65	51
there was no organized way for management to see exactly what	79	54
was going on, yet it could have been obtained by a forms control	92	57
program.	94	57

D

	1m	5m
This company has just recently arranged for a blanket handling of	14	60
all its forms by a printer as a simple way of disposing of a problem	27	62
generally regarded as a nuisance. Not only is the total forms pur-	41	65
chasing nominal, but the number of forms to be purchased is large,	54	68
causing the whole matter to become something of a sizeable problem.	68	71
Yet we have seen the excellent results of such a technique ten and	82	73
fifteen years later.	86	74

LESSON 267

640. Perfect Speed Drill. Your best speed, striving for errorless typing.

They will just have to sign the pay forms for the good work.   12

641. Alphabetic Speed Drill. Lesson 266: 5 to 10 copies of ¶A, then ¶B.

LESSON 268

642. Centering Drill. Set up the following announcement attractively on a full sheet, 8½" x 11".

Important Change of Date

TELEPHONE COMPANY TOUR

Because of a conflict of dates the Telephone Company Tour will not be held as originally announced, on Thursday, April 22, 1954. Instead, the tour will be held exactly one week later. Those who had planned to go please make a note of the following information:

PLACE: Telephone Building Lobby
DATE: April 29, 1954
TIME: 4:30 p.m.

643. Alphabetic Speed Drill. Lesson 266: 5 to 10 copies of ¶C.

LESSON 269

644. Manuscript Typing Drill. Type 1 copy of the following page of manuscript, corrected as indicated.

645. Alphabetic Speed Drill. Lesson 266: 5 to 10 copies of ¶D.

Observations have shown that the closer the task being performed, the greater is the stress on the body. Much of one's time is devoted to close work--like reading, writing, drawing, and manipulative tasks. It is this type of work, which involves the greatest activity of the body's balancing nerves and muscles, *that is the most fatiguing.* ~~consequently the most fatigue.~~ Understandably, therefore, authorities place great emphasis on seeing and vision. O. L. Morton, who has done *more than one* a study along these lines, states:[1]

> When it is realized that vision or the reacting
> to brightness is everyone's main form of activity,
> we can appreciate the importance of *the* factors, *that*
> affect~~ing~~ eyesight.

Certain tasks require adjustment of both eyes to work at a definite distance from the material being read. The head and body must also adjust to support both eyes at a definite distance from the work, and hold them there.

What Educators Think *It is* ~~In~~ the opinion of a growing number of educators, "A moderately sloped surface provides the most efficient surface for reading, writing, and drawing, and a level plane provides the best surface for manipulative tasks."[2] Many feel that a slight slope should also be available. ~~for certain uses.~~

---

[1] O. L. Morton, Working Surfaces, Chicago, Cameron Hall Publishing Company, 1952.
[2] C. L. Matthews, "Work Without Strain," Journal Of Educational Research, 16:120, May, 1952.

646. Perfect Speed Drill. Your best speed, striving for errorless typing.

They will just have to sign the pay forms for the good work.   12

647. Alphabetic Production Letter. Type in block style, 1 copy to each of the 10 addresses given.

Dear Mr.——: We are considering the possibility of producing a film   14
showing the use of one of our unique products, and your studio has   27
been suggested as one that does that type of commercial filming.   41
¶ Can you have your representative call at his convenience to help   54
us analyze this project and advise us on a number of matters con-   67
cerning our plans? We are not sure, for example, whether motion or   80
sound slide film would be best for the job, and whether or not color   94
is advisable. ¶ Once the necessary information has been left with   107
us, it will be referred to our sales planning committee for further   121
study. Very truly yours, Owen V. Greeves, Vice-President.   P.S.   133
If you have any literature on this subject, please send it in advance   147
so we may review it.   151

Mr. P. D. Martins, Hadley Studios Building, Newark 14, New Jersey
Mr. R. S. Johnson, Kay Photographers, Inc., Jersey City 12, New Jersey
Mr. O. W. Lang, Lang Studio, New Brunswick 6, New Jersey
Mr. R. T. Huff, New Era Studio, 646 West Street, New York 7, New York
Mr. L. L. Carter, National Studios, Inc., Yonkers 12, New York
Mr. J. C. Koller, Koller Company, 199 South Street, New York 32, N. Y.
Mr. E. D. Hardy, 228 East 15 Street, New York 22, New York
Mr. G. G. Roland, Marcy Studios, 827 John Street, Newark 14, New Jersey
Mr. D. C. Wells, Metro Studio, 344 Rio Road, Paterson 7, New Jersey
Mr. H. F. Ahlers, Miller Studio, 62 Fifth Avenue, New York 10, New York

LESSON 271

648. Typing Style Recall. Type 1 copy.

Graham & Riggs will have a showing of their new fall line at 879 North 46 Avenue (Suite #253) on May 12, 1954, between 10 a.m. and 2:30 p.m. "This 'out-of-the-ordinary' showing," says Mr. Riggs, "will be a surprise to all." They expect about 450 people, almost 75% of those invited, to attend. Ten admission booths have been set up and tickets will sell at 75 cents, $1, and $1.50.

649. Alphabetic Speed Drill for 5-Minute Timed Writing.

		W·A·M	
		1m	5m
A	On reaching the filing department it is definitely an advantage to	14	3
	file one sheet instead of two. When the file clerk looks up a letter, she	28	6
	has only two sheets to bring out, one original and one sheet for the	41	8
	answer, assuming of course that they are both two sides. If typed on	55	11
	one side only, there would be four sheets to handle, with the possi-	68	14
	bility of one or more of the extra papers becoming dislodged in the	82	16
	process. The office manager is quick to recognize this advantage.	95	19
B	The filing space of most offices becomes extremely cramped and is	13	22
	often at a premium. Sometimes transfer space is even scarcer than	27	24
	the current filing space, and when correspondence is kept for five or	41	27
	seven years as the case may be, the old files become quite a sizeable	54	30
	problem. Therefore, as a matter of efficiency, right from the time	68	33
	the letter is received, through the handling in the various depart-	82	35
	ments, it seems the letter on two sides would prove advantageous.	95	38
C	Now let us analyze the situation and see if we can find some ad-	13	41
	vantages in the second sheet. Probably two sheets typed on just one	27	43
	side, when received in the office of a bank president or a large in-	40	46
	dustrialist, would carry a little extra prestige compared to a single	54	49
	sheet. But the composition of the letterhead, the grade of the paper	67	51
	used, and the wording of the letter itself are far more important than	80	54
	whether it is on one sheet or two. Probably the letter on two sheets	93	57
	does merit more prestige.	98	58
D	I just cannot think of any other advantages the letter on two sheets	14	60
	has over the single sheet. There may be others and doubtless	26	63
	there are. I have passed over quickly the matter of economy in the	39	65
	way of cost, but that might have some slight bearing in a firm	52	68
	sending out considerable correspondence. I do not think it would	65	71
	be enough to be a deciding factor. We have not continued to use this	79	74
	idea in order to save the cost of the extra sheet of paper. We sincerely	93	76
	recognize it to be the best.	99	77

LESSON 272

650. Perfect Speed Drill. Your best speed, striving for errorless typing.

They will just have to sign the pay forms for the good work.   12

651. Alphabetic Speed Drill. Lesson 271: 5 to 10 copies of ¶A, then ¶B.

LESSON 273

652. Addressing Drill. Type 3 envelopes or index cards for each of the following names and addresses.

Mr. W. Bowman, Wiley, Smith & Sons, Chester 29, Pennsylvania
Mrs. V. E. Baker, Carr Publishing Company, Elizabeth 8, New Jersey
Mr. W. C. Damuth, Treasurer, Ward Press, San Diego 4, California
Mr. E. G. Goodyear, Guaranty Insurance Company, Seattle 6, Washington
Mr. H. L. Green, Gulf Electric Company, Kansas City 9, Missouri
Miss G. W. Patton, Hill & Gibbs, 78 Ferry Street, Cincinnati 7, Ohio
Mr. S. G. Winslow, Treasurer, Globe Company, Salt Lake City 7, Utah
Mr. P. D. Martins, Hadley Studios Building, Newark 14, New Jersey
Mr. O. W. Lang, Lang Studio, New Brunswick 6, New Jersey

653. Alphabetic Speed Drill. Lesson 271: 5 to 10 copies of ¶C.

LESSON 274

654. Tabulation Drill. Set up the following tabulation attractively.

WORLD TELEPHONE STATISTICS

World Distribution of 66 Million Telephones

Country	Number	Country	Number
United States	39,490,000	Australia	905,107
United Kingdom	4,654,500	Switzerland	744,997
Canada	2,213,400	Argentina	651,082
France	2,108,140	Denmark	617,586
Germany	1,753,000	Netherlands	575,995
Sweden	1,450,478	Belgium	534,780
Japan	1,195,238	Spain	509,993
Italy	958,813	All other	7,637,000

655. Alphabetic Speed Drill. Lesson 271: 5 to 10 copies of ¶D.

195

656. Perfect Speed Drill. Your best speed, striving for errorless typing.

They will just have to sign the pay forms for the good work.   12

657. Alphabetic Production Letter. Type in semiblock style, 1 copy to each of the 5 addresses given.

Dear Mr.——: We are pleased to see that your construction work is   14
progressing rapidly. As one of the leading manufacturers of church,   28
school, and auditorium seating, we ask the privilege of serving you.   42
The enclosed set of interior views of some of the schools we have   55
furnished, exemplifies the high standard of our product. A local   68
representative will be pleased to conduct you to installations in your   82
area. ¶ Our factories cover many thousands of feet of floor space—   96
more than three city blocks, and our experience extends over more   110
than fifty years. We have the additional advantage of being a   124
subsidiary of one of the most substantial financial organizations in   138
the country. You can readily understand how such large facilities   151
enable us to maintain a standard of highest quality at the lowest   164
cost. ¶ We are enclosing a return card and if you will indicate your   177
approximate requirements and about when you expect to give con-   190
sideration to the question of furnishings, we shall be glad to plan   203
accordingly. You, of course, are incurring no obligation. Our service   217
is freely given and we shall be grateful for the opportunity of showing   231
you designs and samples of our workmanship so that you may judge   245
for yourself whether or not we merit your consideration. Yours truly,   259
V. T. Kimball, President.   264

Mr. W. S. Shaw, Shaw Screens, 37 Broad Street, Cleveland 8, Ohio
Mr. S. S. Marks, Ames Insurance, 822 West 28 Street, Columbus 22, Ohio
Mr. J. G. Muller, Mosler Mill, 227 North 17 Street, Wooster 17, Ohio
Mr. F. T. Millbank, Merrill & Sons, 320 Plaza Road, Elkhart 16, Indiana
Mr. Clyde V. Rogers, Bryant Company, 44 Park Avenue, St. Louis 16, Missouri

658. Typing Style Recall. Type 1 copy.

Thirty suites have recently been rented in the new Warner &
Phipps Building, 984 West 32 Street. We spoke to the renting manager (Room #7—open from 8:30 a.m. until 4 p.m.) and he states
they expect to be 100% rented by September 6, 1954. "All of our
250 suites," he said, "will incorporate 'space-saving' design." Space
rents from $65 to $98.50 a month, with dead storage at 80 cents.

659. Alphabetic Speed Drill for 5-Minute Timed Writing.

	W·A·M	
	1m	5m

A

It has been definitely established by research that personal appear-	14	3
ance gives no outward indication of personality qualities, intelli-	28	6
gence, or emotional stability. Take any organization of executives,	42	8
doctors, or salesmen as an example. Although these men are all	55	11
successful in their particular fields, they do not have any mannerisms	69	14
or appearance characteristics that we could think of as being common	83	17
to the entire group.	87	18

B

Unfortunately, most of us think that we have the ability to appraise	14	21
character and personality by a brief conversation with a man. This	28	24
is the recognized cause of most of the mistakes made in the selection	41	27
of key personnel. To insure against bad judgment in hiring, it is very	55	29
important that we choose the most unprejudiced people possible to	69	32
do the interviewing. Persons with a keen interest in people and with	83	35
a quiet understanding, plus experience.	91	37

C

The key to good interviewing is the ability to make the candidate	13	40
feel confident and thereby inspire him to talk about himself. Know-	27	43
ing the questions to ask in order to get the required information and	40	46
knowing how to interpret the data when it is revealed are also im-	54	48
portant factors. Interviewing men at the executive level for office	68	51
positions is often particularly difficult. When you hire a cost account-	82	54
ant, or other man, it is a test of your skill as an interviewer.	94	56

D

The following suggestions may be helpful the next time you are	13	59
selecting a man for an important position. If you can quickly forget	27	62
that he has impressed you favorably or unfavorably on first meeting,	41	65
and assume that you have absolutely no ability to size him up by	55	67
talking to him or by looking at him, you are off to a good start. Try	68	70
to make yourself judge him mostly on his past history and his atti-	81	73
tude towards work and towards life in general.	91	75

LESSON 277

660. Perfect Speed Drill. Your best speed, striving for errorless typing.

They will just have to sign the pay forms for the good work.　　12

661. Alphabetic Speed Drill. Lesson 276: 5 to 10 copies of ¶A, then ¶B.

LESSON 278

662. Centering Drill. Set up the following invitation attractively on a full sheet, 8½" x 11".

THE BUSINESS CLUB

requests the pleasure of your company
at its Annual Dinner Dance
Friday, December 17, 1954
at six-thirty o'clock
The Business Club Ballroom
22 Terrace Avenue

Dress Informal　　　　　　　　　　R.S.V.P.

663. Alphabetic Speed Drill. Lesson 276: 5 to 10 copies of ¶C.

LESSON 279

664. Billing Drill. On the duplicated billheads that will be supplied, type the 10 copies of the following bill needed for the 10 addresses given. Set tabular stops according to the printed columns on the billhead.

Model #321 Sweeper at $5
Model #322 Sweeper at $10

Mr. C. V. Weston, Macon Furniture Company, Macon 2, Georgia
　　Invoice No. 4451, Order No. 3296, Quantity: 50 #321, 10 #322
Mr. W. S. Doyle, Dale Appliance Company, Albany 6, New York
　　Invoice No. 4452, Order No. 7345, Quantity: 50 #321, 10 #322
Mr. F. J. Sands, Sands Furniture Store, Omaha 7, Nebraska
　　Invoice No. 4453, Order No. 9058, Quantity: 50 #321, 10 #322
Mr. S. S. Bruff, Bruff Department Store, Flint 7, Michigan
　　Invoice No. 4454, Order No. 0946, Quantity: 50 #321, 10 #322
Mr. J. S. Handy, The Ritchie Store, Long Beach 12, California
　　Invoice No. 4455, Order No. 8586, Quantity: 50 #321, 20 #322
Mr. D. V. Graham, Park Street Store, San Antonio 18, Texas
　　Invoice No. 4456, Order No. 9045, Quantity: 50 #321, 20 #322

Mr. L. D. Acken, Adams Appliance Company, New Bedford 2,
   Massachusetts
      Invoice No. 4457, Order No. 3468, Quantity: 50 #321, 20 #322
Mr. T. H. Henry, King Furniture Company, Camden 7, New Jersey
      Invoice No. 4458, Order No. 4839, Quantity: 50 #321, 20 #322
Mr. R. W. Fowler, Fowler & Sons, Duluth 12, Minnesota
      Invoice No. 4459, Order No. 3258, Quantity: 20 #321, 20 #322
Mr. J. C. Wallace, Dorr Appliance Company, Memphis 6, Tennessee
      Invoice No. 4460, Order No. 3857, Quantity: 20 #321, 20 #322

665. Alphabetic Speed Drill. Lesson 276: 5 to 10 copies of ¶D.

LESSON 280

666. Perfect Speed Drill. Your best speed, striving for errorless typing.

They will just have to sign the pay forms for the good work.   12

667. Alphabetic Production Letter. Type in block style, 1 copy to each of
the 3 addresses given.

Dear Mr.——: It has long been a financial axiom that the way to make   14
a fortune is to buy when the crowd is selling and sell when everybody   28
wants to buy. ¶ To some extent it has always been possible to apply   42
this theory to buying anything, including clothes. The way to pick   56
up a bargain, as many a retailer knows, is to wait for a factory over-   69
stock sale. Trouble is that sales and clearances usually come at the   83
end of a season and you may have to wait a whole year to realize   97
your bargain. ¶ Today, however, something new has been added by   111
this manufacturer. We have made it possible to buy in advance of   124
the season just as profitably as waiting for the end of it! It is done by   130
means of a pre-season discount that quickly builds our sales when   152
business is usually slow. In return it saves a whole lot of money for   165
our retailers. In other words, we invite you to pick out your winter   179
line now and have it delivered when you need it and pay for it at   192
that time. ¶ Here is how the plan works. Early this spring we made   205
a special big lot of new overcoats, topcoats, and convertibles. Today,   219
as a result, we undoubtedly have the greatest collection of coats in   233
this area. During the month of August only, we will offer special   247
groups of these wonderful coats at pre-season discounts. ¶ In this   260
special August event we are offering three groups of overcoats. The   274
following shows the regular and the special sale prices: 286

	Regular	Special	89
Group I	$80	$65	292
Group II	60	49	295
Group III	40	29	298

The first group is the most magnificent of all—a very special offering 312
of imported cashmere and lamb's wool overcoats. ¶ If you will come 325
in and select your overcoat line now, we will make any desired style 339
changes and then keep the stock for you in mothproof storage and 353
make delivery about October 1, but earlier or later if you prefer. And 367
we guarantee that these coats will not be available at these low 381
preseason prices after August 31. ¶ We think our suggestions make 394
good sense at any time, but particularly now when prices are firm, 408
and showing a tendency to advance. This letter is going to our 421
regular retailers only. We should like to suggest that you insure a 435
complete selection by ordering early. Sincerely yours, GRAY 447
TEXTILES, INC., John V. Ely, General Manager 456

Mr. C. V. Dean, President, Dean & Dean, Inc., Erie 4, Pennsylvania
Mr. G. C. West, President, Nestle Clothiers, Easton 6, Pennsylvania
Mr. A. M. Burns, President, The Empire Shop, Chester 4, Pennsylvania

668. Typing Style Recall. Type 1 copy.

On October 8, 1954, between 11:30 a.m. and 3 p.m. we held our monthly sales meeting in the Blaine & Williams offices, 692 South 47 Avenue (Conference Room #28). Twenty-five more, about 20%, than the expected 140 attended the meeting. Admission was $1.50 to $3, in addition to a tip of 50 cents. "Our sales force," said the manager, "has done a really 'man-sized' job."

669. Alphabetic Speed Drill for 5-Minute Timed Writing.

		W·A·M	
		1m	5m
A	The first crude office ever developed in ancient history must have	14	3
	had office management, although we could hardly recognize either	27	5
	the office or its management today. Everyone since that time with	40	8
	responsibilities for the office must have been interested in office	53	11
	management. By and large, all the term office management does is	66	13
	to recognize the groups of office services in the modern office, to	79	16
	classify its problems, to realize that there are good and bad solutions	92	18
	from the field of experience.	98	20
B	Our modern office is in a variety of forms and must meet a variety of	14	22
	situations. It may be a desk and chair in the corner of a small factory	27	25
	or in some branch sales office. It may encompass an enterprise of	40	28
	some public service with floors of offices. Some office services may be	54	30
	centralized and still have many other branch offices at the point of	68	33
	use. It has been pointed out also that the extra large office is just a	82	36
	collection of smaller offices.	88	37
C	We can hardly plan a piece of extended work without something in	14	40
	the way of a blueprint. It has always seemed to me that if we cannot	27	43
	draw a chart of our organization, the chances are that there is job	41	45
	confusion somewhere. Many an organization must function by	54	48
	tradition, and the channels of control are distorted by growth be-	67	51
	yond reason or simplicity. Whether we wish to circulate a chart or	81	53
	not, we can put down on paper the relationship of office service units	94	56
	to each other.	97	57
D	In office management we are usually talking about details, but we	14	59
	should maintain a proper perspective. In our interest for details and	28	62
	our belief in their importance, we may attempt to oversell executives	42	65
	on the details themselves. We cannot quite make the executive into a	56	68
	detailist. He should be in a position to take his details or just leave	70	71
	them alone. But he should have a proper respect for their value and	83	73
	cost, for this is the stuff his organization is made of.	94	76

LESSON 282

670. Perfect Speed Drill. Your best speed, striving for errorless typing.

They will just have to sign the pay forms for the good work.   12

671. Alphabetic Speed Drill. Lesson 281: 5 to 10 copies of ¶A, then ¶B.

LESSON 283

672. Addressing Drill. Type 5 envelopes or index cards for each of the following names and addresses.

Merrill & Sons, 320 Plaza Road, Elkhart 16, Indiana
Mr. C. V. Dean, President, Dean & Dean, Inc., Erie 4, Pennsylvania
Mr. G. C. West, President, Nestle Clothiers, Easton 6, Pennsylvania
Mr. A. M. Burns, President, The Empire Shop, Chester 4, Pennsylvania
Mr. R. F. Barber, President, Bell Supply Company, Muncie 4, Indiana
Mr. L. A. Keating, Keating Company, 42 Oak Drive, Utica 6, New York

673. Alphabetic Speed Drill. Lesson 281: 5 to 10 copies of ¶C.

LESSON 284

674. Tabulation Drill. Set up the following tabulation attractively.

FAMOUS PEAKS

Name	Location	Height in Feet
Mount Everest	Nepal-Tibet (Asia)	29,002
Mount Aconcagua	Argentina (S. A.)	22,835
Mount McKinley	Alaska (N. A.)	20,257
Kilimanjaro	Tanganyika (Africa)	19,587
Orizaba	Mexico (N. A.)	18,700
Mount Elbrus	Caucasus (Europe)	18,481
Mont Blanc	Alps (Europe)	15,781
Mount Whitney	California (N. A.)	14,495
Mount Ranier	Washington (N. A.)	14,408
Pikes Peak	Colorado (N. A.)	14,110

675. Alphabetic Speed Drill. Lesson 281: 5 to 10 copies of ¶D.

676. Perfect Speed Drill. Your best speed, striving for errorless typing.

They will just have to sign the pay forms for the good work. 12

677. Alphabetic Production Letter. Type in semiblock style, 1 copy to each of the 10 addresses given.

Dear Mr.——: For several years we have recognized the advisability 14
of introducing psychological tests in the hiring of sales personnel, but 28
we have not been successful in resolving the question of what type of 42
tests will give us the best results. ¶ We have been informed that 56
you have an excellent testing program, and we wonder if we may 69
impose on your kindness for assistance along this line. If you are at 82
liberty to say, can you tell us just what type of tests you have found 96
most satisfactory in hiring sales personnel, and where we may obtain 110
those tests? ¶ We shall indeed be grateful for any information you can 124
supply. Sincerely yours, Edgar C. Roe, Director of Sales Personnel 138

Mr. M. G. Hatton, Sales Training Director, Bradley Mills, Inc., Providence 8, Rhode Island

Mr. C. G. Stone, Director of Sales Training, Oxford Textile Company, Akron 7, Ohio

Mrs. M. A. Tucker, Personnel Director, Rose & Company, Oklahoma City 12, Oklahoma

Mr. G. W. Burke, Personnel Director, J. R. Royal, Inc., Los Angeles 22, California

Mr. W. A. Pine, Director of Personnel, Price & Company, Dallas 8, Texas

Mr. A. N. Sanger, Director of Sales Personnel, Parsons & Sons, San Francisco 8, California

Mr. N. C. Sharpe, Personnel Director, J. Hart Company, Boston 12, Massachusetts

Mr. V. T. Davis, Sales Training Director, Sheffield Mills, Utica 17, New York

Mr. T. W. Dolen, Director of Personnel, Shaw Industries, Inc., Hartford 8, Connecticut

Mr. T. J. Lamb, Director of Personnel, A. Smith Corporation, Pittsburgh 28, Pennsylvania

678. Typing Style Recall. Type 1 copy.

The Kent & Kramer showroom at 647 West 85 Lane (Suite #9) will be open for inspection on November 1, 1954, between 10 a.m. and 2:30 p.m. Their new quarters, with 25% more space, were rented at an increase of $1.50 to $2 per foot, plus 90 cents for the basement space. Thirty people were added to the staff, which now numbers 115. "Our increased facilities and 'grand-scale' arrangement," says Kent, "will be a pleasure to all."

679. Alphabetic Speed Drill for 5-Minute Timed Writing.

	W·A·M 1m	5m

A

	1m	5m
Surveys show that the chair is the most important single item of	14	3
office furniture because it not only controls the amount of work the	28	6
employee can do in a day on the job but also determines the ease	42	8
and comfort with which the work is done. Records kept by many	55	11
organizations prove this point and establish the fact that a proper	69	14
chair makes work easier and pleasanter because it permits the worker	83	17
to work effectively and to relax while sitting.	94	19

B

Rapid strides have been made since the war in the manufacture of	14	22
better office chairs, chairs exactly right for the job to be done. Chairs	28	24
that fit and are comfortable are replacing those that merely have a	42	27
handsome and impressive appearance. This accounts for the strong	55	30
trend toward adjustable office chairs, better known as posture chairs,	68	32
because conventional types of chairs do not quite fit all persons on	81	35
account of physical differences and do not provide proper sitting	94	38
comfort.	96	38

C

A common error in many offices is neglecting to adjust posture chairs	14	41
to fit the people using them. Regardless of the design of your posture	28	44
chairs, they are no better than conventional chairs unless they are	42	46
adjusted properly. Then again, it is well to recognize that the best	56	49
posture chair ever made cannot quite provide good posture by itself.	70	52
The office manager and his personnel are expected to know of the	84	55
great importance of sitting correctly.	92	56

D

A desk development of exceptional interest to the office manager is	14	59
the new conference desk with an overhang on both ends and the	27	62
back for knee room. When the meeting adjourns, it continues to	40	64
function as a most efficient executive desk. This new desk, of course,	54	67
eliminates the desk and table arrangements found in many organiza-	68	70
tions where meetings are part of the routine, and is deserving of great	82	73
popularity for its fine space-saving features alone.	93	75

LESSON 287

680. Perfect Speed Drill. Your best speed, striving for errorless typing.

They will just have to sign the pay forms for the good work.   12

681. Alphabetic Speed Drill. Lesson 286: 5 to 10 copies of ¶A, then ¶B.

LESSON 288

682. Centering Drill. Set up the following program attractively on a full sheet, 8½″ x 11″.

THE COMMUNITY CHEST ASSOCIATION
PROGRAM
Welcome
Harvey V. Spence
President, Valley Realty Associates

Outline of the Work
Ernest O. Keats
County Education Services Director

Address
"The Pride of the Community"
J. V. Sterling
President, County Community Chest

Closing Remarks
G. O. Cameronly
Secretary, The First National Bank

683. Alphabetic Speed Drill. Lesson 286: 5 to 10 copies of ¶C.

LESSON 289

684. Telegram Drill. On the telegram blank forms that will be supplied to you, type 1 copy of the night letter below to each of the 10 addresses listed.

Conference regarding possible film our products in ten days. Can you send representative with information before meeting?

Owen V. Greeves

Mr. P. D. Martins, Hadley Studios Building, Newark, New Jersey
Mr. R. S. Johnson, Kay Photographers, Inc., Jersey City, New Jersey
Mr. O. W. Lang, Lang Studio, New Brunswick, New Jersey
Mr. R. T. Huff, New Era Studio, 646 West Street, New York, N. Y.
Mr. L. L. Carter, National Studios, Inc., Yonkers, New York
Mr. J. C. Koller, Koller Company, 199 South Street, New York, New York
Mr. E. D. Hardy, 228 East 15 Street, New York, New York
Mr. G. G. Roland, Marcy Studios, 827 John Street, Newark, New Jersey
Mr. D. C. Wells, Metro Studio, 344 Rio Road, Paterson, New Jersey
Mr. H. F. Ahlers, Miller Studio, 62 Fifth Avenue, New York, New York

685. Alphabetic Speed Drill. Lesson 286: 5 to 10 copies of ¶D.

LESSON 290

686. Perfect Speed Drill. Your best speed, striving for errorless typing.

They will just have to sign the pay forms for the good work.   12

687. Alphabetic Production Letter. Type in block style, 1 copy to each of
the 10 addresses given.

Attention of General Sales Manager   7
Gentlemen: We have found from experience in our store that the   21
products which our salesmen can demonstrate with ease and con-   34
viction are the products that sell quickly. It is our intention, there-   48
fore, to make available to each store salesman the information he   62
will need to give an excellent demonstration of any of the appliances   76
we carry. ¶ Can you send literature or other aids that may be used   89
by us in this training program? We realize, of course, that the most   103
effective way for our men to learn would be to see a live demonstra-   117
tion themselves, but since this is not possible, literature will probably   131
do the job. Very truly yours, George C. Breck, Manager   142

Merrick Electric Company, Merrick Building, Birmingham 14, Alabama
Stone Appliance Company, Terminal Square, Flint 7, Michigan
Abbott Electric Corporation, 14 River Drive, St. Louis 18, Missouri
Scovell Manufacturing Company, Scovell Square, Stamford 17, Connecticut
Scott Appliances, Inc., Front Street, Philadelphia 6, Pennsylvania
Franklin Sales Corporation, Franklin Building, Chicago 17, Illinois
Webster Supply Company, Rand Building, Erie 14, Pennsylvania
Walker Electric Company, Warren Avenue, Baltimore 16, Maryland
Standard Appliance Company, Strong Building, Wilmington 6, Delaware
Thomas Manufacturing Company, Water Street, Buffalo 18, New York

688. Typing Style Recall. Type 1 copy.

We called on Taylor & Smythe at 468 South 72 Drive (Department #9) between 10:45 a.m. and 2 p.m. on July 5, 1954, and explained that we had received a return of 6% on the circulars. Two thousand circulars were mailed instead of 1,500, and they listed items from 90 cents to $59.50, with most averaging $15. "Our get-acquainted offer," we told Mr. Taylor, "has been a 'sellout.' "

689. Alphabetic Speed Drill for 5-Minute Timed Writing.

	1m	5m
A		
In our organization safety has become a fetish. A man habitually	14	3
leaving material where others could fall over it, with resulting	27	6
injuries, would be first warned and then expect to be discharged.	40	8
Nevertheless, I dare any one of you to go home and inspect the	53	11
cellar stairs. Invariably you will find that families have the habit of	66	13
putting at the top anything that is to go down and at the bottom	79	16
everything that is to be taken up. The practice saves steps but is the	92	18
direct cause of serious accidents.	99	20
B		
Inasmuch as it is not quite possible to discharge any members of a	14	23
family, if we wish to have the cellar stairs made safe we necessarily	28	25
must figure out some means whereby we can get the guilty persons	42	28
to want to change their own habits. All of which may sound like	56	31
working by indirection, but the inescapable necessity of obtaining	70	34
results in this manner just causes us to think and thereby develop	83	36
principles for quite excellent human relations.	93	38
C		
It is possible to learn many sterling principles of management the	13	41
same hard way around the home. Consider the delegation of au	26	44
thority, for example. Everyone knows it is quite stupid to do a job	40	47
that you can get someone else to do for you. Many a man is no	53	49
longer asked to fix or repair anything around the house, on the theory	67	52
that if he does, it will be infinitely worse after he has finished. At	81	55
least that is exactly the way things are in my home organization.	94	57
D		
Another principle one learns the hard way is never to expect appre-	14	59
ciation or gratitude. This is a sure way not to be disappointed. You	28	62
may even develop a helpful personal philosophy. If you get up in	42	65
the morning saying that everything is going to be grand, for example,	56	68
you soon discover that is one quick way of realizing a disappoint-	69	71
ment. If you just start out with the thought that everything is wrong	82	73
and is going to be in a mess all day, occasionally you may be sur-	95	76
prised and delighted.	99	77

LESSON 292

690. Perfect Speed Drill. Your best speed, striving for errorless typing.

They will just have to sign the pay forms for the good work.   12

691. Alphabetic Speed Drill. Lesson 291: 5 to 10 copies of ¶A, then ¶B.

LESSON 293

692. Addressing Drill. Type 5 envelopes or index cards for each of the following names and addresses.

Mr. M. G. Hatton, Sales Training Director, Bradley Mills, Inc., Providence 8, Rhode Island

Mr. C. G. Stone, Director of Sales Training, Oxford Textile Company, Akron 7, Ohio

Mrs. M. A. Tucker, Personnel Director, Rose & Company, Oklahoma City 12, Oklahoma

Mr. G. W. Burke, Personnel Director, J. R. Royal, Inc., Los Angeles 22, California

Mr. W. A. Pine, Director of Personnel, Price & Company, Dallas 8, Texas

Mr. A. N. Sanger, Director of Sales Personnel, Parsons & Sons, San Francisco 8, California

693. Alphabetic Speed Drill. Lesson 291: 5 to 10 copies of ¶C.

LESSON 294

694. Billing Drill. On the duplicated billheads that will be supplied, type the 10 copies of the following bill needed for the 10 addresses given. Set tabular stops according to the printed columns on the billhead.

Speed Printer #15 at $50
Speed Developer #44 at $25

Mr. John V. McCabe, Apex Studio, New Haven 2, Connecticut
    Invoice No. 2391, Order No. 8674, Quantity: 1 #15, 1 #44

Mr. N. V. Bullard, Bullard Photo Shop, Stamford 6, Connecticut
    Invoice No. 2392, Order No. 3847, Quantity: 1 #15, 1 #44

Mr. C. C. Romer, Romer Art Studio, Orange 4, New Jersey
    Invoice No. 2393, Order No. 3648, Quantity: 1 #15, 1 #44

Mr. O. N. Backer, Regal Art Studio, Montclair 9, New Jersey
    Invoice No. 2394, Order No. 5930, Quantity: 1 #15, 1 #44

Mr. B. B. Grail, Grail Studios, Hartsdale 2, New York
    Invoice No. 2395, Order No. 3469, Quantity: 1 #15, 1 # 44

Mr. J. V. Whyte, Lee Photographers, White Plains 3, New York
   Invoice No. 2396, Order No. 7564, Quantity: 1 #15, 1 #44

Mr. A. E. Newman, Newman Art Studio, Providence 2, Rhode Island
   Invoice No. 2397, Order No. 0934, Quantity: 1 #15, 1 #44

Mr. R. F. Weyer, The Crane Studio, Lynbrook 8, New York
   Invoice No. 2398, Order No. 9476, Quantity: 1 #15, 2 #44

Mr. T. G. Dunn, Dunn & Dunn, Yonkers 11, New York
   Invoice No. 2399, Order No. 2375, Quantity: 2 #15, 2 #44

Mr. S. N. Amberg, Seal Photograph Company, Pearl River 4, New York
   Invoice No. 2400, Order No. 0489, Quantity: 2 #15, 2 #44

695. Alphabetic Speed Drill. Lesson 291: 5 to 10 copies of ¶D.

LESSON 295

696. Perfect Speed Drill. Your best speed, striving for errorless typing.

They will just have to sign the pay forms for the good work.   12

697. Alphabetic Production Letter. Type in semiblock style, 1 copy to each of the 6 addresses given.

Dear Mr.——: The companies in the cities shown on the attached 14
sheet are using our film service and may adapt its use to their 28
branches around the country. As fast as the job is done in one loca- 41
tion, the equipment will be moved to the next branch office and 55
filming will be done. In other words, the equipment is to be con- 68
sidered mobile and not stationary. ¶ We will be advised when these 82
moves take place and in turn advise the interested dealers. Please 95
follow the branch offices in your zone and assist in any way possible. 109
Orders for the film to do these jobs will be cleared as quickly as 122
possible. ¶ Competition has some equipment in your areas and they 135
will undoubtedly be guarding their installations with plenty of 149
service and calls. We must be on the alert to keep contact with these 163
customers and be of real assistance to them in this large program. 177
Yours truly, C. W. Hood, General Manager 185

Mr. A. R. Marsh, Marsh Services, 366 John Street, Gary 8, Indiana
Mr. C. G. Mitchell, Millbank Company, 26 Lee Street, St. Paul 7, Minnesota
Mr. A. J. Collins, Collins Company, 246 Main, Denver 13, Colorado
Mr. Owen T. Adams, Ford & Sons, 22 Russell Square, Houston 14, Texas
Mr. F. T. Bray, Sun Machines Company, 36 Plaza Street, Newark 7, New Jersey
Mr. S. V. Johnston, Acme Service, 721 May Street, Portland 28, Maine

LESSON 296

698. Typing Style Recall. Type 1 copy.

"This ad-packed edition of 'The Stream,'" states the publisher, "should really produce income." The publication date has been set for July 15, 1954, and the book will be on sale at Lewis & Crane, 497 West 61 Street (Room #328), between 9 a.m. and 5:30 p.m. Ninety copies out of the 630 available have already been reserved, and will sell at 95 cents to $2, and $3.50 for the de luxe edition, plus 2% tax.

699. Alphabetic Speed Drill for 5-Minute Timed Writing.

	W·A·M
	1m 5m

A

	1m	5m
I remember gaping at the first queer automobile in our part of town.	14	3
Fifty years ago automobiles were as scarce as were television sets the	28	6
year you entered first grade. I was just past ten before I got a ride	42	8
in an auto. I remember when my mother had saved enough money	55	11
to buy a set of aluminum cooking utensils. It was one of the first	69	14
aluminum sets in our neighborhood. Visitors flocked in amazement	83	17
to hear my mother explain how she cooked with the pot and pan.	96	19

B

	1m	5m
Another big event in our house occurred when my dad brought home	14	22
a vacuum cleaner that was pumped by hand. Mother said he was out	27	25
of his head. She preferred a broom to pumping. But what excitement	41	27
a few years later when he appeared with a real prize, an electric	55	30
vacuum cleaner. Mother was just overjoyed. Dad announced that	68	33
the carpets and rugs would not even need to be beaten any more.	81	35
We boys whooped with delight, but Mother was unconvinced.	99	38

C

	1m	5m
Perhaps these memories and others may help you realize how	12	41
quickly your everyday life can change in a few years. For example,	25	44
when I was a boy there was no such thing as a five and ten store.	38	46
The chain store, even in big cities, was a man with a horse and	51	49
wagon. None of us had ever heard of a motor bus and no farm boy	64	52
had seen a tractor. Not for years would I hear music and voices	77	54
over a wireless, which later became known as radio.	89	57

D

	1m	5m
Those are some examples of the things that were happening in the	13	59
small corner of our country where I lived as a boy. Everywhere	26	62
across the land the builders of industries were at work. They were	40	65
driving quickly ahead, just as the builders are today, seeking new	54	67
ways to produce and distribute more and more goods and comforts	67	70
to more and more people. The discovery of atomic energy and the	80	73
advances in engineering and agriculture offer amazing opportunities.	93	76

210

LESSON 297

700. Perfect Speed Drill. Your best speed, striving for errorless typing.

They will just have to sign the pay forms for the good work.   12

701. Alphabetic Speed Drill. Lesson 296: 5 to 10 copies of ¶A, then ¶B.

LESSON 298

702. Centering Drill. Set up the following title page attractively on a full sheet, 8½" x 11".

A STUDY OF THE RELATIONSHIP BETWEEN GRADES
OBTAINED IN SKILL SUBJECTS AND SUCCESS ON
A JOB REQUIRING USE OF THOSE SKILL SUBJECTS
A Thesis
Presented to the
Faculty of the School of Education
University of Hamilton
In Partial Fulfillment of the
Requirements for the Degree
Master of Science in Education
By
Mary H. Leeds
August, 1954

703. Alphabetic Speed Drill. Lesson 296: 5 to 10 copies of ¶C.

LESSON 299

704. Manuscript Typing Drill. Type 1 copy of the following page of manuscript, corrected as indicated.

705. Alphabetic Speed Drill. Lesson 296: 5 to 10 copies of ¶D.

On any day when outdoor temperatures are below freezing, the large window area of the modern office is equivalent to a *solid* wall of ice. The interior walls and the air near them may be warm in the extreme, while the window or outside wall area is uncomfortably cold, *to say the least.* Unless--and until--the occupants near it are protected from this ice wall, there can be no such thing as body comfort To quote a well-known authority on heating:[1]

> Body surfaces near the cold wall are being robbed
> of their body heat and the discomfort is not
> remedied by simply raising the room air temperature.
> The whole case for a comfortable thermal environment
> cannot be rested upon room temperature alone.

How, then, do we achieve *this* ~~the second~~ requirement--protection from cold surfaces? Engineers *have been able to* do it by providing a blanket of warm air over the cold surfaces . . . by raising a thermal blanket between the cold window and the occupants of the room.

Heat Removal and Ventilation

It has long been an accepted fact that a heating and ventilating system, *if it is* ~~in order~~ to maintain a satisfactory thermal environment within a room, must possess the capacity to remove *and, when needed,* ~~as well as~~ to supply heat to the room. "Unusual as it may seem," says Dr. Winslow, "what is needed more frequently is cooling rather than heating capacity."

---

[1]R. C. Edison, "How To Heat Properly," The Engineers Digest, 14:148, March, 1951.

706. Perfect Speed Drill. Your best speed, striving for errorless typing.

They will just have to sign the pay forms for the good work.   12

707. Alphabetic Production Letter. On the interoffice letterhead form that will be supplied to you, type 1 copy of the letter below to each of the 6 addresses listed.

```
TO        —
FROM      Director of Sales Personnel
SUBJECT   Testing of Applicants
DATE      —
```

During the past sixteen months, this office has been working with the   14
local sales office on the matter of considering new sales applicants.   28
A series of tests was used as an experiment, and it was found that the   42
job of determining whether or not an applicant should be hired was   56
made immeasurably easier. Furthermore, time is beginning to show   70
that those who did well on the tests have better sales records than   84
those who were hired quickly, without benefit of testing. ¶ A set of   98
the tests used is enclosed, and a supply of them will follow within   111
the month. Hereafter, this battery of tests will be administered to   125
all sales applicants who are seriously being considered for positions.   138
No salesman should be hired who does not make a satisfactory score,   152
as explained in the instructions. Test results will bc mailed to this   166
office and analyzed. ¶ It is not intended that these tests replace the   179
interview step, but rather furnish a means to study further those who   193
are found acceptable in the interview. O. V. Bellingham   204

Branch Manager, Boston
Branch Manager, Atlanta
Branch Manager, New York
Branch Manager, Washington, D. C.
Branch Manager, Los Angeles
Branch Manager, St. Louis

708. Typing Style Recall. Type 1 copy.

On August 15, 1954, our sales department in the Brent & Wood Building, 278 North 92 Street (Section #46), will increase its space about 20%. Thirty employees will work from 8 a.m. to 4:30 p.m. to handle the expected 450 daily customers, and will be paid from 75 cents an hour to $1.30, with specially trained workers receiving $2. "With these 'scientific' working conditions," says the manager, "we expect to do a first-rate job."

709. Alphabetic Speed Drill for 5-Minute Timed Writing.

	W·A·M	
	1m	5m

A

	1m	5m
The colors of office furniture in general use in the early part of this	14	3
century were dark oak, dark red mahogany, and dark walnut,	26	5
because dark colors were most suitable for the dim light of those	40	8
times. In fact, dark colors in office furniture were recognized as a	54	11
mark of luxury and dignity. When metal office furniture was first	68	14
introduced, its sponsors naturally sought a color to go with the dark	81	16
wood furniture then in use, and olive green was selected as best	94	19
meeting this requirement.	99	20

B

	1m	5m
Due to improved office lighting, the trend for several years has been	14	23
towards brighter and more colorful offices. This transition from	27	25
darkness and the growing realization on the part of office manage-	41	28
ment of the extra value of planned lighting and color have produced	55	31
quite a strong trend towards new light finishes for both wood and	69	34
steel office furniture. It seems to be just a matter of time until the	83	36
dark woods will be forgotten.	89	38

C

	1m	5m
The two basic materials, wood and steel, have quite naturally di-	13	40
vided the office furniture industry into two camps, those who make	27	43
wood desks and those who make steel desks. But, paradoxically,	40	46
this has been good for the office furniture industry, because many of	54	48
the recent developments in the manufacture of both wood and steel	68	51
desks have undoubtedly resulted from the competitive maneuvers	81	54
of the organizations involved in this industry.	90	56

D

	1m	5m
The wood manufacturers contend that since wood is a natural	13	58
material, wood desks have a more friendly appeal and attractiveness,	27	61
like the furniture in your own home, and that wood is quiet to use	40	64
and extremely durable. The steel desk organizations contend that	54	67
steel is the better basic material for office desks because of extra	67	69
long life and low maintenance costs, and that steel finishes do not	81	72
mar easily and can just be refinished at low cost.	91	74

LESSON 302

710. Perfect Speed Drill. Your best speed, striving for errorless typing.

They will just have to sign the pay forms for the good work.   12

711. Alphabetic Speed Drill. Lesson 301: 5 to 10 copies of ¶A, then ¶B.

LESSON 303

712. Addressing Drill. Type 5 envelopes or index cards for each of the following names and addresses.

Franklin Sales Corporation, Franklin Building, Chicago 17, Illinois
Webster Supply Company, Rand Building, Erie 14, Pennsylvania
Walker Electric Company, Warren Avenue, Baltimore 16, Maryland
Thomas Manufacturing Company, Water Street, Buffalo 18, New York
Standard Appliance Company, Strong Building, Wilmington 6, Delaware
Mr. Owen T. Adams, Ford & Sons, 22 Russell Square, Houston 14, Texas
Mr. F. T. Bray, Sun Machines Company, 36 Plaza Street, Newark 7,
    New Jersey

713. Alphabetic Speed Drill. Lesson 301: 5 to 10 copies of ¶C.

LESSON 304

714. Tabulation Drill. Set up the following tabulation attractively.

JUDSON SUPPLY COMPANY

Salesman	Territory	Car Owned	Expenses	Sales
J. V. Tead	New England	Pontiac	$1,116	$28,493
H. R. Stacy	Northeast	Buick	1,206	26,466
D. W. Rowden	East	Chevrolet	987	30,909
J. J. Taylor	Southeast	Ford	1,632	25,850
G. C. Luke	North Central	Ford	866	22,700
G. C. Kenny	Central	Chevrolet	908	23,840
O. C. Fryer	South Central	DeSoto	1,472	29,900
R. J. Nolte	Northwest	Plymouth	1,309	31,006
M. D. Elliott	West	Dodge	1,119	27,644
H. W. Spence	Southwest	Chrysler	1,267	26,250

715. Alphabetic Speed Drill. Lesson 301: 5 to 10 copies of ¶D.

716. Perfect Speed Drill. Your best speed, striving for errorless typing.

They will just have to sign the pay forms for the good work.   12

717. Alphabetic Production Letter. Type in block style, 1 copy to each of the 10 addresses given.

Dear Mr.——: We have received so many requests from our dealers   14
for information on the proper demonstration of our products that we   28
have decided to go beyond the printing of literature on the subject.   42
¶ One of our special representatives will be touring your district   55
during the next month and he will call on you. His purpose will be   68
actually to demonstrate before you and your sales help how the   81
machines are to be sold. He will also leave with you sales literature   95
that can be used during a customer demonstration. ¶ We know you   108
will be pleased with the service, for our records show that improved   122
demonstrations will help you realize increased sales. Yours very   136
truly, E. M. Sterling, Sales Promotion Manager   144

Mr. John V. Trainor, Home Appliance Company, Atlanta 2, Georgia
Mr. S. S. Waymer, Waymer & Sons, Inc., Greensboro 6, North Carolina
Mr. J. J. Ascher, Cole Company, Richmond 8, Virginia
Mr. O. M. Borden, Crystal Furnishings, Inc., San Antonio 14, Texas
Mr. Robert C. Ullman, Century Department Store, Omaha 6, Nebraska
Mr. J. O. Cahill, Cahill Brothers, Inc., Phoenix 7, Arizona
Mr. L. L. Newman, Newman & Sons, San Diego 7, California
Mr. C. B. Bristol, Bristol Brothers, Tacoma 13, Washington
Mr. G. M. Dewey, Dewey Store, Minneapolis 12, Minnesota
Mr. W. H. Perry, Peet Appliance Company, St. Joseph 6, Missouri

718. Typing Style Recall. Type 1 copy.

Twenty of the 150 books ordered on August 17, 1954, have just been delivered to us in the Smith & Reynolds Building, 489 East 26 Avenue (Division #317). The remainder will follow tomorrow between 10:30 a.m. and 3 p.m. These books have been billed at 60 cents and $1, total billing $112.50, less a discount of 10%. "Our 'set' policy," said your clerk, "is to allow slightly larger discounts on large-volume orders."

719. Alphabetic Speed Drill for 5-Minute Timed Writing.

		W·A·M	
		1m	5m
A			
After having a brief friendly chat with the applicant, you might ask		14	3
him to give you a resume of his work experience, starting with his		27	5
very first job. When he has finished his story, ask him a few questions		41	8
about his past jobs. Find out something about his early work history.		55	11
Find out if he helped earn his spending money in school and college,		69	14
and thereby learned habits of hard work from the beginning. Also if		83	17
he has the ambition that provides him with the motivation to work.		97	19
B			
Next, ask him to tell you about his school experience. Learn if he was		14	22
a good student, if he ever stood first in his class, or if he ever failed a		28	25
term. Did he participate in school activities, thereby developing		41	28
social skills and the ability to co-operate with others, or did he just		54	30
indulge in solitary activities, such as reading or tinkering with types		68	33
of machinery? If so, he may have acquired tendencies which prevent		81	36
him from working effectively with people.		89	38
C			
Next, try exploring the area of his social, economic, physical, and		13	40
spiritual life, or any field of his past activity that gives some clear		27	43
insight into the development of his attitudes, personality, and		40	46
character. When you have finished a complete survey of his history,		54	49
you will probably have changed your mind several times about his		68	51
suitability for the job. This will convince you of the futility of trying		82	54
to size men up quickly from their appearance and from a casual		95	57
conversation.		98	58
D			
Sometimes it will be simple for you to make a decision regarding the		14	60
candidate's suitability. Often, however, the data that you are able		28	63
to get concerning him will be both positive and negative. In these		41	66
instances, making a decision will be more difficult. Such cases call		55	68
for a deeper type of job interview, which can only be made by some-		68	71
one with formal training in the field of psychology and with long		82	74
experience and practice in the technique of interviewing.		94	76

LESSON 307

720. Perfect Speed Drill. Your best speed, striving for errorless typing.

They will just have to sign the pay forms for the good work.   12

721. Alphabetic Speed Drill. Lesson 306: 5 to 10 copies of ¶A, then ¶B.

LESSON 308

722. Centering Drill. Set up the following announcement attractively on a full sheet, 8½" x 11".

CAMERA CLUB MEETING

TIME
Friday, January 15, 1954, 4 p.m.

PLACE
Conference Room

ATTENDANCE
Old members and prospective new members

This is the first meeting of the new year for the Camera Club and we want to be sure to get 100% attendance of old members as well as a large turnout of prospective new members. Bring along any friends who may be interested in any phase of photography. Also any particularly interesting photographs that may be shown and discussed at the meeting.

723. Alphabetic Speed Drill. Lesson 306: 5 to 10 copies of ¶C.

LESSON 309

724. Telegram Drill. On the telegram blank forms that will be supplied to you, type 1 copy of the night letter below to each of the 10 addresses listed.

Representative will call within week to review with your sales staff latest demonstration our machines.

E. M. Sterling

Mr. John V. Trainor, Home Appliances, Charleston, South Carolina

Mr. S. S. Waymer, Waymer & Sons, Inc., Greensboro, North Carolina

Mr. J. J. Ascher, Cole Company, Richmond, Virginia

Mr. O. M. Borden, Crystal Furnishings, Inc., San Antonio, Texas

Mr. Robert C. Ullman, Century Department Store, Omaha, Nebraska

Mr. J. O. Cahill, Cahill Brothers, Inc., Phoenix, Arizona

Mr. L. L. Newman, Newman & Sons, San Diego, California

Mr. C. B. Bristol, Bristol Brothers, Tacoma, Washington

Mr. G. M. Dewey, Dewey Store, Minneapolis, Minnesota

Mr. W. H. Perry, Peet Appliance Company, St. Joseph, Missouri

725. Alphabetic Speed Drill. Lesson 306: 5 to 10 copies of ¶D.

LESSON 310

726. Perfect Speed Drill. Your best speed, striving for errorless typing.

They will just have to sign the pay forms for the good work.   12

727. Alphabetic Production Letter. Type in semiblock style, 1 copy to each of the 10 addresses given.

Dear Mr.——: You will find enclosed a copy of a unique booklet,   14
"Landscaping Guide," which is being introduced to you at this time   28
as a suggested aid for increasing your landscaping business. ¶ In   41
quantity lots, this amazing little booklet will cost you just a few   55
cents, yet it can be the means of creating interest in landscape im-   69
provement among all your prospective customers. It will provoke   83
inquiries and will also lead to requests for suggested plans. ¶ The   97
prices given on the enclosed sheet include the cost of imprinting your   111
name on the front cover of every booklet. Order your supply now, in   125
time to encourage your customers to start planting next spring. Very   139
truly yours, T. A. Ellsworth, Vice President.   148

Mr. P. S. Johnston, Johnston Nursery, Painted Post 2, New York

Mr. G. W. Leslie, Scarsdale Nursery, Clinton 3, Michigan

Mr. W. C. Hamilton, Hamilton Nurseries, Inc., Princeton 6, New Jersey

Mr. W. L. Crosley, Evergreen Nursery, Lakeview 4, Ohio

Mr. P. M. Downey, Poplar Nurseries, Whitefish 3, Montana

Mr. O. W. Bigelow, Bigelow Landscaping Company, Natchez 3, Mississippi

Mr. D. D. Ritter, Allstate Nurseries, Columbia 6, Missouri

Mr. S. T. Burnham, Burnham Nursery, Saratoga Springs 7, New York

Mr. G. C. Nichols, Bullard Nurseries, Mineola 6, New York

Mr. A. R. Romer, Southern Nurseries, Inc., New Orleans 9, Louisiana

LESSON 311

728. Typing Style Recall. Type 1 copy.

On July 8, 1954, from 11 a.m. to 4:30 p.m. the Wilson & Adams Company will have an exhibition of modern equipment at 576 West 58 Drive (Display Room #4). Eighty new machines will be exhibited to about 650 people, who will pay 90 cents, $1.50, and $2 for various types of admissions, with an additional 15% for tax. "This new eye-catching equipment," says Mr. Adams, "should be a 'must' on your list."

729. Alphabetic Speed Drill for 5-Minute Timed Writing.

	W·A·M	
	1m	5m

A

	1m	5m
The employee who dismisses a new or revised procedure as just	13	3
some more red tape errs in not grasping its important news value.	26	5
He fails to understand that it is an example of healthy progress, a	40	8
sign that his organization is alive, changing, and advancing. A feeling	54	11
of satisfaction can come from the knowledge that he has cast his lot	67	13
with a concern that makes quick adjustments to changing conditions.	81	16
This can mean that his job is that much more secure.	92	18

B

	1m	5m
Management has quite a responsibility, too, in encouraging the	14	21
employee to change his attitude. Office procedures should be ex-	27	24
plained and then presented in such a manner that they will be re-	41	27
ceived as news, will be interesting to read. A guiding objective	54	29
should be to reach the happy day when the staff will actually look	67	32
forward to getting copies of these new releases, with the feeling that	81	35
the bulletins contain vital information about their team and about	95	37
their jobs.	97	38

C

	1m	5m
People working close to the firing line have a good understanding	13	40
of the problems involved in their daily routine activities. It is quite	27	43
necessary to have the benefit of their opinions. At the same time,	41	46
nearness to basic problems sometimes reduces the ability to analyze	55	49
correctly their relative importance and their magnitude so far as the	69	52
company as a whole is concerned. They might exaggerate less im-	82	54
portant features just because they themselves are directly concerned.	96	57

D

	1m	5m
The number and the complexity of these procedures will vary with	14	60
the type and the size of the company. Where there is quite a small	28	63
office force, procedures can usually be passed on orally. But when	42	65
dealing with a larger or more highly diversified situation, the rules	56	68
of the game, the ways and means of doing business, will have to be	69	71
defined, written down, and worked into a procedure manual. This	82	73
manual will be helpful to new employees.	90	75

LESSON 312

730. Perfect Speed Drill. Your best speed, striving for errorless typing.

They will just have to sign the pay forms for the good work.　　12

731. Alphabetic Speed Drill. Lesson 311: 5 to 10 copies of ¶A, then ¶B.

LESSON 313

732. Addressing Drill. Type 5 envelopes or index cards for each of the following names and addresses.

Mr. C. B. Bristol, Bristol Brothers, Tacoma 13, Washington
Mr. G. M. Dewey, Dewey Store, Minneapolis 12, Minnesota
Mr. W. H. Perry, Peet Appliance Company, St. Joseph 6, Missouri
Mr. P. S. Johnston, Johnston Nursery, Painted Post 2, New York
Mr. G. W. Leslie, Scarsdale Nursery, Clinton 3, Michigan
Mr. W. C. Hamilton, Hamilton Nurseries, Inc., Princeton 6, New Jersey
Mr. W. L. Crosley, Evergreen Nursery, Lakeview 4, Ohio
Mr. P. M. Downey, Poplar Nurseries, Whitefish 3, Montana

733. Alphabetic Speed Drill. Lesson 311: 5 to 10 copies of ¶C.

LESSON 314

734. Tabulation Drill. Set up the following tabulation attractively on a full sheet, 8½″ x 11″.

WORLD'S HIGHEST WATERFALLS

Name	Location	Continent	Height in Feet
Angel	Venezuela	South America	3,212
Tugela	Natal	Africa	2,810
Kukenaan	Venezuela	South America	2,000
Southerland	New Zealand	Islands	1,904
Ribbon	California	North America	1,616
King George VI	British Guiana	South America	1,600
Yosemite	California	North America	1,430
Gavarnie	France	Europe	1,385
Takkakaw	British Columbia	North America	1,200
Wollomombie	New South Wales	Australia	1,100

735. Alphabetic Speed Drill. Lesson 311: 5 to 10 copies of ¶D.

736. Perfect Speed Drill. Your best speed, striving for errorless typing.

They will just have to sign the pay forms for the good work. 12

737. Alphabetic Production Letter. Type in block style, 1 copy to each of the 5 addresses given.

Dear——: Subject: Safekeeping of Securities. The treasurer of a 15
leading industrial corporation has recently issued a circular letter 29
addressed to the stockholders in reply to numerous requests received 43
for the issuance of duplicate stock certificates to replace those lost, 57
stolen, or destroyed. He calls attention to the fact that in a majority 71
of cases reasonable care would have prevented the loss of the certifi- 85
cates, and then declares the conditions under which duplicates will 98
be issued by his corporation. To quote from his letter: 109

> The stockholder must advertise the loss in a local paper once 122
> a week for three weeks. Then he must furnish bond of an 134
> approved Surety Company for double the par or market 145
> value of the lost certificate. The cost of the bond and the 157
> expense of advertising must be borne by the owner. 167

¶ Our bank maintains safe deposit vaults in all its buildings. It is 180
prepared to offer the highest type of safe deposit protection and 194
service. Boxes for your valuables may be rented annually at nominal 208
rates, depending on the size of the box selected. We also provide 222
storage space at reasonable rates, based on the size of the container 235
stored and its declared valuation, for the storage of bulky articles 248
too large to be placed in a safe deposit box. ¶ All inquiries either 261
by mail or telephone will receive immediate attention. Very truly 274
yours, FIRST NATIONAL BANK, R. V. Little, Treasurer 285

Mr. P. J. Richards, 34 High Road, San Francisco 16, California
Mrs. O. V. Merrill, 162 Poplar Street, San Francisco 12, California
Mr. O. L. Wilson, 486 South Boulevard, San Francisco 22, California
Mr. James R. Ruby, 367 Racine, San Francisco 27, California
Mr. G. M. Cullen, 425 Pacific Avenue, San Francisco 19, California

TYPING APPLICATIONS REVIEW

The 5 lessons that follow provide a comprehensive
review of the important applications of typing.
The review covers:

Typing Style Recall
Alphabetic Speed Drill for
   5-Minute Timed Writing
Block Style Letter
Semiblock Style Letter
Two-page Letter
Addressing
Telegrams
Centering
Tabulation
Billing
Manuscript
Rough Draft
Title Page
Table of Contents
Announcement
Invitation
Program

738. Typing Style Recall. Type 1 copy.

"A wonderful improvement," states the director, "for the 'globe-trotting' public." New airline offices will be opened in the Clark & Dunn Terminal at 347 Park Drive (Level #2) on December 1, 1954. Twenty employees will sell tickets between 8:30 a.m. and 5 p.m., and it is expected that customers will increase to about 750 daily, a 15% increase. Luncheon will run from 85 cents to $1.75 and should account for about $500 daily.

739. Alphabetic Speed Drill for 5-Minute Timed Writing.

	W·A·M 1m	5m

A

	1m	5m
It is the responsibility of the executive to see that the philosophy of	14	3
simplification permeates the organization under his leadership.	27	5
Every short cut, every new gadget for improvement, every adapta-	41	8
tion of every form of equipment to the job is part of this philosophy.	55	11
When the paper work is great, the tools of work simplification	68	14
should be applied. There is no mystery about these tools in the	81	16
office. I have on my desk several manuals used for teaching them.	94	19

B

	1m	5m
We must recognize the effect of work conditions on morale and	13	21
production. We have become color conscious in the last few years.	26	23
Quite some time ago I viewed a new machine that was uncovered	39	26
to the public with some acclaim. There were a few new attractive	53	29
gadgets on it, but the major changes were in streamlined design and	67	32
color. A gleaming black machine had given place to de luxe grey	81	34
with crackle finish, more attractive in the eyes of the typist but also	94	36
without glare in her eyes.	99	37

C

	1m	5m
For the most part, as an ideal, we have galloped over the horizon. We	14	40
have had too many fine executives who have shown a better brand of	28	42
fine leadership by progressive organizations. You must agree with	42	45
me, however, that there are influences to develop complexes of the	56	48
prima donna in office managers. Those whose jobs and advancement	70	51
depend upon us are all about, and they concur in our decisions and	83	53
wisdom. They may anticipate our needs before we quite know them.	95	56

D

	1m	5m
In this office one thing in office services is more important than	13	59
anything else. You can not expect any progress without it. It under-	27	62
lies any and all progress in your organization. Office management	41	64
requires the backing of top management. If top management is	54	67
indifferent to the job of office management, you will make indifferent	68	70
progress. It must appreciate the importance of office management	82	73
in reducing costs and also in increasing efficiency.	92	75

740. Billing Drill. On the duplicated billheads that will be supplied, type the 6 copies of the following bill needed for the 6 addresses given. Set tabular stops according to the printed columns on the billhead.

Landscaping Guide at $2 Doz.

Mr. P. S. Johnston, Johnston Nursery, Painted Post 2, New York
Invoice No. 3427, Order No. 7549, Quantity: 5 Doz.

Mr. G. W. Leslie, Scarsdale Nursery, Clinton 3, Michigan
Invoice No. 3428, Order No. 4738, Quantity: 5 Doz.

Mr. W. L. Crosley, Evergreen Nursery, Lakeview 4, Ohio
Invoice No. 3429, Order No. 4830, Quantity: 6 Doz.

Mr. O. W. Bigelow, Bigelow Landscaping Company, Natchez 3, Mississippi
Invoice No. 3430, Order No. 9846, Quantity: 10 Doz.

Mr. D. D. Ritter, Allstate Nurseries, Columbia 6, Missouri
Invoice No. 3431, Order No. 4358, Quantity: 40 Doz.

Mr. G. C. Nichols, Bullard Nurseries, Mineola 6, New York
Invoice No. 3432, Order No. 8946, Quantity: 50 Doz.

741. Telegram Drill. On the telegram blank forms that will be supplied to you, type 1 copy of the following night letter to each of the 6 addresses given in ¶740, above.

Now filling your order for Landscaping Guides. Send at once exact copy for cover page imprint.

T. A. Ellsworth

742. Tabulation Drill. Set up the following tabulation attractively on a full sheet, 8½" x 11".

SALE OF LANDSCAPING GUIDES
By Quarters

Region	First	Second	Third	Fourth
East	12,000	17,000	11,500	12,500
Midwest	13,500	18,000	12,300	14,600
West	9,600	12,400	11,300	12,200
South	8,700	9,500	10,200	11,400

743. Title Page Drill. Set up the following title page attractively on a full sheet, 8½″ x 11″.

PRESENT-DAY LIGHTING STANDARDS
C. Oliver Wendley
Ellers Office Management Institute
Chicago

A report on the standards advised for today by the authorities on office illumination.

Distributed by
Williams Lighting Corporation
New York   Los Angeles

744. Table of Contents Drill. Set up the following table of contents attractively on a full sheet.

Present-Day Lighting Standards

CONTENTS

Section		Page
I	The Office of 1890	1
II	The Office of 1920	6
III	The Office of Today	12
IV	Determining Adequate Illumination	15
V	Determining Proper Type of Fixture	18

745. Manuscript Typing Drill. Type 1 copy of the following manuscript, corrected as indicated.

The standards ~~advised~~ *that are promoted* for today by illuminating engineers are many times as high as those endorsed yesterday. These new standards, *however,* are not the product of any specific investigation.

Current Trend Not New

To turn for a moment to another trend, namely, bilateral lighting, one should ~~remember~~ *bear in mind* that there is nothing new about it. In the last century, Germany adopted bilateral lighting, window glass surface in the rooms to equal one fifth the floor area, walls and ceilings with high coefficients of reflection, and the elimination of glare.

These ideas reached America at the end of the nineteenth century. At that time, school ~~population~~ *enrollment* was increasing rapidly, and larger schoolhouses were being built in *the larger* cities. In the words of J. O. Benton:[1]

> The most desirable orientation of classrooms was southeast, east, southwest, and south, though north lighting was accepted for laboratories and art rooms.

North Lighting New

The demand for north lighting for elementary school *classrooms* is of recent origin. The main cause is the activity program, *which* has been promoted to an exceptional degree. J. C. Carr *says,*[2] "As the activity program spread and grew in the cities, the classroom unit evolved, for rural conditions went along with it."

---

[1]J. O. Benton, Trends In School Lighting, Milwaukee, Riveredge Publishing Company, 1952.

[2]J. C. Carr, "More Light In Our Classrooms," School Journal 22:38-39. September, 1953.

746. Invitation Typing Drill. Set up the following invitation attractively on a full sheet, 8½″x11″.

BARTON BROTHERS COMPANY

cordially invites you to attend
a private sale
and a lecture on the fascinating history of rugmaking
by a noted authority on the subject
John V. Raymond
Friday, January 28, 1954
at two o'clock

747. Program Typing Drill. Set up the following program attractively on a full sheet.

Barton Brothers Company

PROGRAM

Greetings
J. Oscar Strandler
Barton Brothers Company President

Lecture
John V. Raymond
"The Art of Rug Design"

Refreshments
Chinese Tea Room

Private Sale

748. Announcement Typing Drill. Set up the following sale announcement on a full sheet.

Barton Brothers Company
SPECIAL PRIVATE SALE
Rugs

Winston 9x12 (Regularly $250)	$198
Royale 9x12 (Regularly $198)	$160

Chairs

Moderns (Regularly $150)	$109
Wing (Regularly $135)	$100
Barrel Back (Regularly $135)	$100

Sofas

Moderns (Regularly $220)	$159
Lawson (Regularly $190)	$142

749. Alphabetic Production Letter. Type 1 copy to each of the 2 addresses given, the first in block style, the second in semiblock style.

Dear Mr.——: We are glad to enclose copies of reports describing | 14
our product and reproductions of a few testimonials indicating its | 28
general approval by nationally known individuals and concerns who | 42
have put it to the test and are using it in actual service. ¶ Puroil | 56
invariably proves in service that it actually saves many times its cost | 69
in reducing costs of fuel and lubrication, decreased overhead and | 83
repair bills, and in improved efficiency of operation. In many lubri- | 97
cation problems it has been proved that only Puroil could overcome | 111
conditions that had been considered insurmountable and that had | 125
perplexed lubrication engineers. ¶ Whether you are interested in | 138
Puroil for a fleet of automobiles or for use in heavy machinery, it | 152
can be used with economy and success in practically all problems of | 165
lubrication—wherevre oil is used, be it a giant turbine, or the tiniest | 179
electric motor. ¶ Engineers of the highest reputation endorse our | 192
product, exacting university chemists and engineers have put it | 205
through every test and approve it without qualification. ¶ Puroil | 218
is what chemists and engineers call a pure oil product. By that they | 222
mean that it contains extreme lubricating qualities that are not | 236
found in ordinary commercial oils. However, it is much more than a | 250
lubricant. It not only thoroughly and completely covers all metal | 263
surfaces in the motor with a film of lubrication, which sticks to the | 277
metal and is therefore ready at all times to supply lubricity and to | 290
prevent excessive wear; it also is a corrosion preventive product. | 304
You undoubtedly know that acids are created in the crankcase of a | 317
motor through the ordinary operation. The alloy metals used in | 331
most of the up-to-date motors are easily affected by these acids. | 344
Corrosion results, and replacements and repairs are necessary. Puroil | 358
adheres to the metal, and it prevents these materials from reaching | 372
the metal and thus prevents corrosion. ¶ If you have any particularly | 386
vexing lubrication problem, we will be more than pleased to advise | 400
you how our product may be best used in its solution. An engineer | 413
from our organization will call if you will just return the enclosed | 427
card. Yours truly, PUROIL COMPANY, T. G. Smithson, President. | 441

1. Mr. W. C. Burney, Chief Engineer, Gilbert Motors, Inc., 16 Front Street, Dearborn 16, Michigan
2. Mr. T. C. Donaldson, Director of Research, Hunter Engineering Company, 36 Bay Street, San Francisco 19, California

750. Addressing Drill. Type an envelope and 2 index cards for each of the 2 addresses given above.

REFERENCE SECTION

Appreciation and grateful acknowledgment are extended to the following companies who generously permitted the use of illustrative material in this book: Remington Rand Inc., Royal Typewriter Company, Inc., Underwood Corporation, L C Smith & Corona Typewriters Inc, International Business Machines Corporation, Standard Register Company, American Automatic Typewriter Company, The Western Union Telegraph Company.

REFERENCE SECTION

Contents

General Products Company
100 GRAND CENTRAL AVENUE
NEW YORK 10, N. Y.

July 6, 1954

●r. D. W. Taylor
438 West 76 Street
Newark 20, New Jersey

Dear Mr. Taylor:

During the past few months we have had so many calls
for our current price list that at the present time
we find that our stock is completely out of that
item, even though our order this year was for twice
as many booklets as we ordered last year.

We realize your urgent need for the material and
have asked our printer to send you a supply of them
by express just as quickly as the first copies are
off the press, and to follow that with a second
shipment later if the entire supply is not sent in
the first shipment.

Very truly yours,

John A. Student

JAS:J

R-1. BLOCK STYLE LETTER
(*Letter Placement Guide*)

Use this illustration as a guide for learning proper letter placement. The lower dot shows the approximate starting point for a *short* letter, such as this letter, the middle dot for a *medium-length* letter, the top dot for a *long* letter.

General Products Company
100 GRAND CENTRAL AVENUE
NEW YORK 10, N. Y.

June 15, 1954

Mr. T. V. Alexander, President
Leland Foundry
Gary 7, Indiana

Dear Mr. Alexander:

Thank you for your request for information concerning office lighting. Due to an unforeseen demand, our present supply of our professional bulletin on this subject has been exhausted. Our printers, however, have promised us a delivery of additional copies within the next few days, and as soon as the booklet is received, we shall send you one in the mails.

In the meantime, you may find the attached catalog folder of interest. It analyzes and pictures each type of office lighting fixture we manufacture and explains where it fits in the office situation.

Our lighting fixtures are found in the offices and plants of leading manufacturers throughout the country. If you are looking for scientific lighting which will make for greater efficiency of office workers, our products are an excellent choice.

If we may be of further service to you, please write us and we shall be glad to furnish you with whatever additional information you may wish.

Yours very truly,

GENERAL PRODUCTS COMPANY

L. E. Zook
Chief Engineer

LEZ:J

R-2. SEMIBLOCK

Medium-length letter showing placement of addressee's title and placement of company name in signature.

General Products Company
100 GRAND CENTRAL AVENUE
NEW YORK 10, N. Y.

March 14, 1954

Mrs. G. C. Glacer
75 North Street
Camden 13, New Jersey

Dear Mrs. Glacer:

Subject: Writing Aptitude

Your inquiry is very much appreciated, since we are anxious to place in the hands of everyone who is seriously interested in writing full information about our training program and service.

We hope you will pardon this form letter. We wish it were possible to avoid generalities and get right down immediately to a discussion of your particular situation, but of course we cannot do that at this stage.

You may have never attempted to write a line for publication, yet feel that with proper guidance you could succeed in some branch of writing. Or perhaps you have been writing for a long time and are seeking a way to improve so that your work will sell more regularly and bring higher prices.

In either case, if you have the necessary natural talent and are willing to do your part, our service will help you surely and quickly to reach the goal you have set for yourself. Our students have successfully sold the following:

Magazine articles   437
Short stories   298
Newspaper columns   137
Radio scripts   212

So that we may learn more definitely where you stand and then reach a decision as to what we may be able to do to be of help to you, our faculty has devised the writing aptitude test enclosed. If you will answer the test questions to the best of your ability, as directed in the printed instructions, we shall report to you frankly just what the future may hold for you as a writer.

Sincerely yours,

E. J. Kendall

EJK:j
Enc.
cc: Mr. A. E. Elson

R-3. FULL BLOCK

Long letter showing placement of "Subject" line, tabulation within letter, enclosure and carbon copy notations.

General Products Company
100 GRAND CENTRAL AVENUE
NEW YORK 10, N. Y.

September 15, 1954

National Supply Corporation
630 Wilshire Boulevard
Los Angeles 22, California

Attention of Personnel Director

Gentlemen:

Here are several copies of a personality quiz with sealed key submitted for consideration within your organization. The quiz will be more interesting to you and your employees if the key is not opened until all those designated to take the quiz have filled in all the answers. Then break the seal, check the answers against the key, and figure the ratings.

But what is more important than those scores is the fact that the teaching of proper office behavior should be part of your company office training program. We all recognize the importance of employees' getting along with each other, using tact in their dealings with your customers, answering the telephone courteously. More than that, we think you will agree that a good personality is a priceless asset in any business office and that it plays an important part in the success of a business.

Because of the importance of this subject, we are sending you, also, an exciting little booklet which tells how one of the country's best known office management consultants developed a fascinating new way to cover the subject of office behavior in an employee training course. Dr. Beal's right and wrong method is as intriguing as a quiz program, as clear and easy to understand as red traffic lights. It teaches by simply presenting actual business situations.

Just note what the personnel director of a large insurance company says about the method:

If there is any doubt in the mind of a personnel director about the value of such a course in a company training program, that doubt will be eliminated after a few trial sessions.

And now to save the best until the last, you are extended a special invitation to become a member of our Personnel Directors Club. As such, you are entitled to receive library copies of all training materials published for office employees. If you will write us, signifying your intention to become a member, we will send you as a start your library copy of our course described in the booklet.

R-4. INDENTED

Two-page letter showing placement of "Attention" line and quotation within letter.

National Supply Corporation, September 15, 1954, page 2.

We should like you to look over that course and judge for yourself its potential value to your company. Then, if you decide to order sufficient materials for your training classes, you will receive the benefit of the discount allowed on quantity orders.

We are asking our representative, Mr. Brown, to stop in and see if he can be of some service to you.

Very truly yours,

J. R. Phillips
Research Director

JRP:j

P. S. If you need more copies of the personality quiz, just say how many copies you will need and we will send them at once.

R-5. SECOND PAGE

Showing placement of heading for second page and postscript.

General Products Company
100 GRAND CENTRAL AVENUE
NEW YORK 10, N.Y.

January 30, 1954.

Miss L. C. Adams,
Croton Coal Company,
674 West 26 Avenue,
Pittsburgh 30, Pennsylvania.

Dear Miss Adams:

We certainly appreciate your inquiry regarding our newest product, and we wish it were possible to sell you one of our de luxe office models as we know your office has an excellent application for that machine.

As with all our products, we like to feel sure that the improvement has no flaws; so we are now in the process of placing a number of machines on jobs in various offices. Although machines marked for testing in your zone have now been placed, we can arrange, in view of your interest, to place one in your office if you so desire.

Very truly yours,

O. R. Williams
Standards Department

ORR:j

R-6. CLOSE PUNCTUATION

Showing use of punctuation after date and in the inside address.

General Products Company
100 GRAND CENTRAL AVENUE
NEW YORK 10, N.Y.

June 23, 1954

Mr. John W. McCabe
Apex Studio
New Haven 2, Connecticut

This office has planned an unusual display of some commercial photography equipment that we feel will be of interest to you and your associates. Please accept the two enclosed invitations with our most sincere compliments.

The purpose of the exhibit is to introduce methods and equipment that cut costs for organizations such as yours, which we know are continually striving to give greater service to their customers with the greatest economy.

We look forward to seeing you at the exhibit. If you desire additional invitation cards, we will be happy to send them.

W. R. CRANE

R-7. NOMA SIMPLIFIED

Style proposed by National Office Management Association. Salutation and complimentary close are omitted.

General Products Company
100 GRAND CENTRAL AVENUE
NEW YORK 10, N.Y.

August 12, 1954

Manager
Liberty Service Station
Macon 2, Georgia

Dear Sir:

We are glad to note from your repeat orders that you have done so well with the line of our handy utility kit which you introduced just recently. We are about to announce an amazing new product, a chemical car window cleaner, and we feel quite sure this will be another good seller in your line of auto supplies.

Within the next few days you will receive an initial supply of samples which you may wish to distribute among your favorite customers as a quick means of introducing the product.

We are attaching our price list and will be happy to send your first shipment on consignment.

Very truly yours,

William R. Bates

WRB:j

R-8. HANGING INDENTION

Sometimes used in advertising letters, which are printed, but rarely for ordinary correspondence.

General Products Company
INTEROFFICE CORRESPONDENCE

TO   Branch Manager, Chicago
FROM   General Sales Manager
SUBJECT Hiring of Sales Personnel
DATE   January 16, 1954

After much study it has been decided that the hiring of sales personnel should be decentralized by the first of next year. At this time, no further papers of applicants need be processed through the home office. Each branch manager will have the complete authority to hire according to the standards he sets for his office.

While our centralized plan seemed to offer certain advantages, such as uniformity of standards, it was felt that the branch manager could not fairly be held responsible for the operation of his unit unless he completely controlled the selection of his personnel. Complete detailed instructions regarding the new policy will reach you from the personnel department.

T. R. CALLAN

TRC:j

R-9. INTEROFFICE

Designed to save time in typing and reading. Salutation and complimentary close are omitted.

501 Park Drive
Euclid 4, Ohio
July 16, 1954

The Jewel Electric Company
342 South Main Street
Euclid 8, Ohio

Attention of Personnel Director

Gentlemen:

May I have the privilege of an interview to
discuss my qualifications for a secretarial position
in your company? The attached personal data sheet
will give you the details of my training background
and experience.

Although my actual experience has been limited
to summer work, you will note I have had the benefit
of very extensive training in secretarial work, which
has helped me gain an above-average skill in both
shorthand and typing.

Please use the enclosed envelope to let me know
when I may call.

Very truly yours,

Mary C. Burns

R-10. PERSONAL BUSINESS

Showing placement of writer's address.

May 15, 1954

Dear George:

As you know, the club members appointed me a
committee of one to look into the possible purchase
of new furniture when we redecorate the club next
fall. Although I have almost three months to get
some good ideas, I am quite sure that is not going
to be too long a time for the job.

You know a lot more about furniture than I do,
and I was wondering if you have time to go with me
one day on a tour of furniture shops. We could set
the date at your best convenience. I realize how
busy you are but hope you may have a free day to
give me some of your good ideas.

Sincerely,

R-11. PERSONAL

Showing omission of inside address.

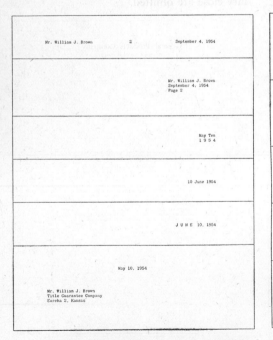

Mr. William J. Brown   2   September 4, 1954

Mr. William J. Brown
September 4, 1954
Page 2

May Ten
1 9 5 4

10 June 1954

J U N E 10, 1954

May 10, 1954

Mr. William J. Brown
Title Guarantee Company
Eureka 2, Kansas

R-12. CORRESPONDENCE STYLE NOTES

Variations in headings for second page of a
letter, and in style for date.

Mr. Robert E. Jones, Editor
Warwick Publishing Company
25 Fifth Avenue
New York 6, New York

Dear Mr. Jones:

Subject: Publicity Releases

Mr. Robert E. Jones
Editor, Warwick Publishing Company
25 Fifth Avenue
New York 6, New York

Dear Mr. Jones:

SUBJECT: Publicity Releases

Martin Tool Company
121 Fourth Avenue
Portland 2, Oregon

ATTENTION: Mr S. T. Norton

Gentlemen:

Martin Tool Company
121 Fourth Avenue
Portland 2, Oregon

Attention of Mr. S. T. Norton

Gentlemen:

Very truly yours,

THE MERRY COMPANY

Boyd L. Warren
Treasurer

R-13. CORRESPONDENCE STYLE NOTES

Variations in placement of addressee title,
"Attention" line, "Subject" line, style for company signature.

General Products Company
100 GRAND CENTRAL AVENUE
NEW YORK 10, N. Y.

Mr. T. L. Remington
National Shipping Company
201 Water Street
Baltimore 2, Maryland

General Products Company
100 GRAND CENTRAL AVENUE
NEW YORK 10, N. Y.

Mrs. N. A. Avery
2874 Maple Avenue
Salt Lake City 4, Utah

General Products Company
100 GRAND CENTRAL AVENUE
NEW YORK 10, N Y

Wyatt Manufacturing Company
37 Fowler Drive
Detroit 16, Michigan

Attention of Mr. C V. Kling

General Products Company
100 GRAND CENTRAL AVENUE
NEW YORK 10, N Y

Mrs N. A. Avery

2874 Maple Avenue

Salt Lake City 4 Utah

R-14. ENVELOPE ADDRESSES

Showing various styles used for address on small (No. 6) and large (No. 10) envelopes. First line of address is placed in approximate vertical and horizontal center of envelope.

L. G. Martin
6 Poplar Place
Fairlawn 2, Ohio

R-15. PERSONAL ENVELOPE

Mr. P. R. Griswold
645 Allen Boulevard
Santa Barbara 6, California

R-16. POSTAL CARD

Mrs. William J. Thomas
543 Plains Avenue
New Orleans 5, Louisiana

Mr. T. T. Lodge
Clary Products Company
16 Ridge Road
Omaha 9, Nebraska

R-17. INDEX (5x3) CARD

General Products Company
100 GRAND CENTRAL AVENUE
NEW YORK 10, N.Y.

Manager
Liberty Service Station
Erie 5, Pennsylvania

General Products Company
100 GRAND CENTRAL AVENUE
NEW YORK 10, N.Y.

Manager
Liberty Service Station
Canton 7, Ohio

General Products Company
100 GRAND CENTRAL AVENUE
NEW YORK 10, N.Y.

Manager
Liberty Service Station
Emporia 3, Kansas

General Products Company
100 GRAND CENTRAL AVENUE
NEW YORK 10, N.Y.

Manager
Liberty Service Station
Macon 2, Georgia

R-18. LABELS

WESTERN UNION

W. P. MARSHALL, PRESIDENT

December 12, 1954

Manager
Liberty Service Station
Warren, Pennsylvania

Advise decision regarding possible sale handy car utility kits.
New shipment received. Can send one hundred on consignment.

Edward A. Race

R-19. TELEGRAM

Charge to the account of Bickstorm, Dunnelly Inc. $

WESTERN UNION
INTERNATIONAL COMMUNICATIONS
CABLEGRAM

W. P. MARSHALL PRESIDENT

Send the following message subject to the conditions, rules and regulations of The Western Union Telegraph Company set forth in its tariffs on file with the Federal Communications Commission:

February 15 19 54

To_____ BICKDUN

```
TO OBTAIN FAST AND
ACCURATE SERVICE
INSERT
via W.U. Cables
```

LONDON (ENGLAND) Via   W.U. CABLES

HIJON ACKLN GHONE YENPE

R-20. CABLEGRAM (IN CODE)

Code is often used to cut down number of words and cost. The above message reads: "Before you accept, get offer including freight. Medium grades free of primage. 1,000 tons per month."

IMPROVEMENTS FOR THE OFFICE

More and more, management is showing increasing interest in adopting scientific ideas for the office. It is being proved every day that this scientific approach indeed makes for greater worker morale, improved working conditions, and therefore increased productivity.

The Importance of Color

Lighting engineers have shown that the light reflectance[1] factor of colors used in office equipment plays an important part in eye-comfort. Regardless of other surroundings, if light reflectance factors are wrong, office workers suffer from unnecessary eye-fatigue. Tired eyes, strained eyes, and headaches resulting from such strains create office friction, errors, and slow work.

In studying the effect of light reflection and the psychology of color on actual production, one company recently completed an exhaustive experiment. The effect of properly colored walls and ceilings together with proper lighting on 100 clerical employees was studied over a two-year period. In spite of more detail in the work which had to be added during this period, substantial increases in output resulted.

This finding means greater dollars-and-cents returns for the payroll dollar from lighting and color selection alone.

---

[1]Light reflectance is a term used by lighting engineers to describe the amount of light reflected by a given surface.

R-21. MANUSCRIPT
(First Page)
Showing main heading, side headings, footnote.

2

They do not reflect the considerable additional benefits in reduced absenteeism, improved morale, and more accurate work. The company's report summarizes:

> On the basis of the evidence, it is fair to state that in this operation, better lighting, painting and vision resulted in a definite increase in production; and that if the nature of the task remained the same in both years, it would have been substantially greater than the observed increase of 5.5%.

Straight-Line Production

Every departure from straight-line production wastes motion, and causes delay. For example, the sales manager who demands that every incoming order be routed directly to his private office from the mail clerk probably causes delays in filling orders—and increases the cost of handling them. He might keep in touch just as well by seeing a copy of the order after it is written up. J. C. Hanley, one of the early advocates of office-to-office layout, has always emphasized, "The straight-line principle applies to small offices as well as large ones."[2]

There is usually one source record around which the entire office layout may be built. In an insurance office it is an application for insurance. In an employment office it may be an application for a job. The application may be different, but the principle remains the same.

---

[2]J. C. Hanley, Increasing Office Production, Cincinnati, Wilson Publishing Company, 1950.

MANUSCRIPT
(Second Page)
Showing short and long quotations, page numbering, footnote.

```
CENTER  HEADING

CENTER  HEADING

CENTER HEADING

CENTER HEADING

Center Heading

Center Heading


Center  Heading
```

R-22. CENTER HEADINGS

Side Heading

    The above is an example of a separate line side head.
It is one of several types of side headings used in the
typing of manuscripts, reports, theses, and other copy

    Side Heading. This is known as a run-in side heading
and is often used to set off the main points of a subject
in the typing of manuscripts, reports, and similar copy.

    This is known as a marginal side heading, which
Side
Heading may also be used in setting off the main points
    of a manuscript, report, thesis, or other copy

Here is another type of side heading. It is known as the
inserted side heading It is not as commonly used as the
    other types of side headings, mostly because it
Side
Heading requires more time and care for proper placement.
In order to use this type of side head, paragraphs should
be long enough to allow two or more lines above and below

R-23. SIDE HEADINGS

    Material has been written along these lines by Jones[2]
and Kramer.[3] who are. without doubt, two of the leaders in
----
    [2]Boyd L Jones, Studies on Radio. Boston. Wallington
Publishing Company, 1949

    [3]John R Kramer, "Radio of the Future," Radio Annual,
22:146-148 March 1950
----
this rapidly growing field Although other material has
been published on this subject it does not have the same

R-24. FOOTNOTE (STYLE FOR PRINTER)

THE MARKET FOR WRITERS

C O N T E N T S

R-25. TABLE OF CONTENTS

B I B L I O G R A P H Y

Dulles, Samuel W. Big Opportunities. New York: Wise and Lake Publishing Company, 1950.

Hainge, George W. Selling More and More. Philadelphia: Quaker Press, 1947.

Jackson, Thomas F. Success in Selling. Boston: Troy Publishing Company, 1948

Johnson, W. C. "A Salesman's Salesman," Selling and Success, Vol. 22 (April, 1951), 174-176.

Watkins, George B. Top Sellers of America. New York: Tremont Publishing Company, 1948.

Wilson, Frank B. Making Your Quota. New York: Lee Publishing Company, 1951.

Zeltner, Oscar V. Don't Sell Yourself Short. Boston: Brown and Gaines Publishing Company, 1950.

R-26. BIBLIOGRAPHY

R-27. INDEX (WITH LEADERS)

R-28. INDEX (WITHOUT LEADERS)

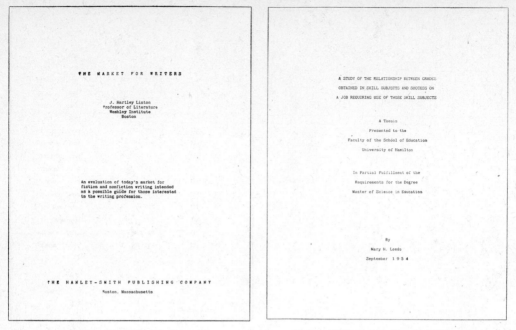

THE MARKET FOR WRITERS

J. Hartley Linton
Professor of Literature
Wembley Institute
Boston

An evaluation of today's market for
fiction and nonfiction writing intended
as a possible guide for those interested
in the writing profession.

THE HANLEY-SMITH PUBLISHING COMPANY
Boston, Massachusetts

A STUDY OF THE RELATIONSHIP BETWEEN GRADES
OBTAINED IN SKILL SUBJECTS AND SUCCESS ON
A JOB REQUIRING USE OF THOSE SKILL SUBJECTS

A Thesis

Presented to the

Faculty of the School of Education

University of Hamilton

In Partial Fulfillment of the

Requirements for the Degree

Master of Science in Education

By

Mary H. Leeds

September 1 9 5 4

R-29. TITLE PAGE

R-30. TITLE PAGE OF THESIS

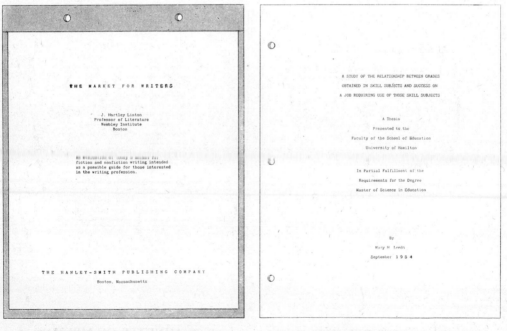

THE MARKET FOR WRITERS

J. Hartley Linton
Professor of Literature
Wembley Institute
Boston

An evaluation of today's market for
fiction and nonfiction writing intended
as a possible guide for those interested
in the writing profession.

THE HANLEY-SMITH PUBLISHING COMPANY
Boston, Massachusetts

A STUDY OF THE RELATIONSHIP BETWEEN GRADES
OBTAINED IN SKILL SUBJECTS AND SUCCESS ON
A JOB REQUIRING USE OF THOSE SKILL SUBJECTS

A Thesis

Presented to the

Faculty of the School of Education

University of Hamilton

In Partial Fulfillment of the

Requirements for the Degree

Master of Science in Education

By

Mary H. Leeds

September 1 9 5 4

R-31. END BOUND MANUSCRIPT

R-32. SIDE BOUND MANUSCRIPT

RANEY MANUFACTURING COMPANY EMPLOYEE CLUB

Board of Directors

I. Organization

  A. Employee representatives

    1. Number of representatives

    2. Method of selection

      a. Appointment

      b. Election

        (1) Spring period

          (a) January election (held the first
              Tuesday after the first Monday)

          (b) April election (held the first
              Tuesday after the first Monday)

        (2) Fall period

          (a) September election (held the first
              Tuesday after the first Monday)

          (b) November election (held the first
              Tuesday after the first Monday)

    3. Method of handling resignations

  B. Management representatives

    1. Number of representatives

    2. Method of selection

II. Purpose

III. Responsibilities

R-33. OUTLINE

1	I	17	XVII	600	DC
2	II	18	XVIII	700	DCC
3	III	19	XIX	800	DCCC
4	IV	20	XX	900	CM
5	V	30	XXX	1,000	M
6	VI	40	XL	1950	MCML
7	VII	50	L	1951	MCMLI
8	VIII	60	LX	1952	MCMLII
9	IX	70	LXX	1953	MCMLIII
10	X	80	LXXX	1954	MCMLIV
11	XI	90	XC	1955	MCMLV
12	XII	100	C	1956	MCMLVI
13	XIII	200	CC	1957	MCMLVII
14	XIV	300	CCC	1958	MCMLVIII
15	XV	400	CD	1959	MCMLIX
16	XVI	500	D	1960	MCMLX

R-34. ROMAN NUMERALS

NEWS FAIRCHILD STADIUM • NEW YORK

SIX FAIRCHILD SYMPHONY CONCERTS STARTING JUNE 8

* * *

Complete Performance of Verdi's 'Requiem'

For First Offering of Series

Six concerts of Robert Mantle and the Fairchild Symphony Orchestra will be offered on Saturday afternoons from June 8 to July 15

The first program will start at 6:30 p.m., and the remaining concerts at 6:45 p.m. All will continue until approximately 8:30 p.m.

The concerts will be sponsored by the Fairchild Corporation in commemoration of that company's 50th Anniversary this year

Commenting on the Fairchild Corporation sponsorship, Mr William Killen, business manager of the Musical Arts Institute, said, "The manner in which the commercial aspect is to be left in the background in this series fits in perfectly with the nature of the musical program."

Each of the concerts will be played as a benefit, as was done two years ago

R-35. NEWS RELEASE

MINUTES OF REGULAR MEETING

Raney Manufacturing Company Employee Club

August 2, 1954

The regular meeting of the Raney Manufacturing Company Employee Club was held on August 2, 1954. President John R Martins presided

The meeting was called to order by the president, and the minutes of the previous meeting were read.

The treasurer reported a balance of $3,245 to the credit of the club, $165.50 more than on this date last year

The Boat Ride Committee chairman reported that the new steamer Valley Stream has been chartered for the annual boat ride to be held on September 28 this year. The cost will be $1,075 for the boat, plus $175 for a band and $350 for prizes

Mr L. Joseph moved that free books of amusement ride tickets be purchased and distributed to all children under age 12 who attend the boat ride. The approximate cost of enough books of tickets for these children will be $200. The motion was seconded and carried. Mr Joseph was appointed to head a committee to purchase and distribute the amusement tickets.

Miss Mary Myers moved that the dance ordinarily held just before Thanksgiving be held this year just before Christmas in conjunction with the annual Christmas party. The motion was seconded and carried.

A motion for adjournment was seconded and carried

T R SMITH, Secretary

R-36. MINUTES OF MEETING

R-37. ANNOUNCEMENT

R-38. INVITATION

R-39. PROGRAM

R-40. MENU

```
*********************************************

X X X X X X X X X X X X X X X X X X X X X X

xoxoxoxoxoxoxoxoxoxoxoxoxoxoxoxoxoxoxoxoxox

///////////////////////////////////////////

: : : : : : : : : : : : : : : : : : : : : :

o o o o o o o o o o o o o o o o o o o o o o

$ $ $ $ $ $ $ $ $ $ $ $ $ $ $ $ $ $ $ $ $ $

& & & & & & & & & & & & & & & & & & & & & &
```

R-41. BORDER DESIGNS

~~typing~~ typewriter	Substitute	new the ˄ book	Insert
t(y)ping	Substitute	¶	New paragraph
typingg	Remove	No ¶	Do not paragraph
Typing	Small t	⑤	Spell out
typing	Capital t	one ˄ time	Insert hyphen
typing○	Change to period	up ‿ town	Close up
in|typing	Insert space	men(s)	Transpose
typing○	Delete	#	Insert space

R-42. PROFESSIONAL PROOFREADER'S MARKS

R-43. TYPING STYLE POINTS

(As given in the text, beginning with Lesson 50)

1. The comma is always written inside the quotation mark.
2. The period is always written inside the quotation mark.
3. A quotation within a quotation is set off by single quotation marks.
4. Spell out numbers starting a sentence.
5. Write clock time in figures, using a colon between hour and minutes; write a.m. and p.m.
6. Amounts of money, both dollars and cents, are written in figures.
7. Even amounts of dollars are written without the decimal point and ciphers.
8. Amounts under $1 are written in figures with the word *cents* spelled out.
9. In street addresses or dates, omit *rd, th, st*.
10. Hyphenate most compound adjectives preceding a noun. (Exception: adjectives formed with *ly* words—"a newly formed club.")

OTHER TYPING STYLE POINTS

11. The semicolon and colon are written outside the quotation mark.
12. The question mark and exclamation point are written inside the quotation mark if they belong to the quoted part; outside if they belong to the entire sentence.
13. Spell out numbers below 100 when they stand alone in a sentence.
14. Spell out a numbered street when the number is less than ten.
15. In legal documents, amounts are usually spelled out as well as written in figures.
16. In a date, a comma is used to separate the month or day from the year; in sentences, a comma also follows the year.
17. The oblique mark is used for forming fractions not found on the typewriter keyboard.
18. Use figures for units of measure or weight.
19. Write percentages in figures.
20. Use the % sign after figures in statistical work; otherwise, write *per cent*.

Typing a Stencil

Complete instructions for cutting stencils come with each package of stencils, but it is worth emphasizing these important points.

1. *Type a rough draft.* When time permits, in the duplicating of important work, first type a rough draft, just as the finished copy is to appear. This draft will make for faster copying and better placement on the stencil.

2. *Clean the typewriter keys.* Clean the typewriter keys thoroughly with a stiff brush.

3. *Move the ribbon selector.* Move the ribbon selector to the neutral, or white, position.

4. *Type the stencil.* Strike the keys with a uniform, staccato touch. Use less force on the letters *o, c, e,* the *period* and *comma;* strike the letters *w* and *m* with more force. These precautions are not necessary when using an electric typewriter because of the automatic, even stroke.

5. *Correct errors.* Using a single vertical stroke of the brush for each character, apply a thin but complete coat of correction fluid. Allow a minute for drying, then strike over with a little lighter than normal touch.

Typing a Direct Process Master

1. *Clean the typewriter keys.* Clean thoroughly, using a stiff brush.

2. *Use a medium hard platen.* Use a medium hard platen, or use a stiff backing sheet.

3. *Insert the master.* Insert the master in the machine so that the typing will be on the plain, uncarbonized sheet.

4. *Type the master.* Use a strong, staccato touch, as uniform as possible. These precautions are not necessary when using an electric typewriter because of the automatic, even stroke.

5. *Correct errors.* Finish typing the entire master. Then take out of the typewriter and remove the deposit of ink on the reverse side with a soft eraser. Place a small piece of fresh carbon behind the section to be corrected, re-insert in machine, and strike over the necessary characters.

R-45. BILL

General Products Company
100 GRAND CENTRAL AVENUE
NEW YORK 10, N. Y.

Life and Casualty Insurance
1540 Brewster Avenue
Cincinnati 6, Ohio

DATE: May 22, 1954
INVOICE NO. 3247

Quantity	Description	Unit Price	Amount	Total
1	Rollo Duplicator	125 00	125 00	
1	Rollo Service Kit	25 00	25 00	150 00

R-45. BILL

R-46. CREDIT MEMO

CREDIT MEMORANDUM

General Products Company
100 GRAND CENTRAL AVENUE
NEW YORK 10, N. Y.

The White Company
Des Moines 11, Iowa

DATE: April 6, 1954
INVOICE NO. 2951
ORDER NO. 3758

We CREDIT your account as follows:

Quantity	Description	Unit Price	Amount	Total
5 Doz	Leatherette Schoolbags #42	5 00	25 00	25 00

R-46. CREDIT MEMO

R-47. PURCHASE ORDER

PURCHASE ORDER

General Products Company, 100 GRAND CENTRAL AVENUE, NEW YORK 10, N.Y.

TO: Marlin Box Company
403 East 117 Avenue
Freeport 4, L. I., N. Y.

ORDER NO. 2375
DATE: August 1, 1954
FOR DEPT: Shipping

DELIVER TO: Warehouse, 317 Varick Street, New York 14, N. Y.

SHIP BY: Island Trucking Company   DELIVER: At Once

Quantity	Item No.	Description	Price	Total
300	3285	Standard Packing Crates	1 00	300 00
80	1754	Auto-Mailers	50	40 00
				340 00

PER: J. M. Walsh

R-47. PURCHASE ORDER

R-48. STATEMENT

STATEMENT

General Products Company, 100 GRAND CENTRAL AVENUE, NEW YORK 10, N.Y.

October 1, 1954

Mr. C. H. Watkins
Watkins Supply Company
312 Macon Street
Richmond 4, Virginia

DATE	DEBITS	CREDITS	BALANCE
9/1	162 14		
9/6	34 54		
9/14	60 17		
9/18	13 44		
9/20		84 45	
9/24		13 90	
			171 94

R-48. STATEMENT

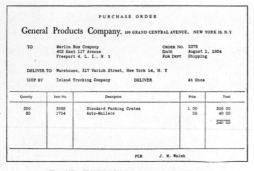

R-49. STRAIGHT BILL OF LADING

UNIFORM STRAIGHT BILL OF LADING — Original — Not Negotiable

THE NEW YORK CENTRAL RAILROAD COMPANY

Electric Supply Company
Dallas   Texas

John Murray Manufacturing Company
Black Rock, New York

	DESCRIPTION OF ARTICLES, SPECIAL MARKS, AND EXCEPTIONS					
100	Boxes Air Coolers & Fans					

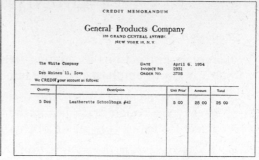

R-50. ORDER BILL OF LADING

UNIFORM ORDER BILL OF LADING
ORIGINAL

Shipper's No.
Agent's No.

THE NEW YORK CENTRAL RAILROAD COMPANY

RECEIVED, subject to the classifications and tariffs in effect on the date of the issue of this Bill of Lading.

Buffalo, New York   September 19, 1956

from Machine & Tool Works, Buffalo 1, New York

Consigned to ORDER OF Machine & Tool Works
Destination Albuquerque   State of New Mexico   County of
Notify K. O. Manufacturing Company
At Albuquerque   State of New Mexico   County of
Route
Delivering Carrier   Car Initial   Car No.

No. Packages	DESCRIPTION OF ARTICLES, SPECIAL MARKS AND EXCEPTIONS	*WEIGHT (Subject to Correction)	CLASS OR RATE	CHECK COLUMN	
1	Shears 1/S on Skids NBN				

Machine & Tool Works   Shipper
Per John S. Jones   Per
Permanent post-office address of shipper

R-50. ORDER BILL OF LADING

REYNOLDS SHOE COMPANY

Balance Sheet

December 31, 1955

R-51. BALANCE SHEET

A S S E T S

Cash...$31,854.35

Accounts Receivable......................... 3,845.22

Merchandise Inventory....................... 9,352.67

Equipment................................... 8,489.85

Total Assets................................$53,542.09

L I A B I L I T I E S

Accounts Payable............................$ 4,758.93

Notes Payable............................... 1,342.78

Total Liabilities...........................$ 6,101.71

P R O P R I E T O R S H I P

Capital, January 1, 1954....................$40,549.83

Net Profit.................................. 6,890.55

Capital, December 31, 1955.................. 47,440.38

Total Liabilities and Proprietorship........$53,542.09

HARTLEY & LEEMAN PAINT COMPANY

Profit and Loss Statement

Period Ending June 30, 1954

Sales.......................................$12,324.65

Deduct Cost of Merchandise Sold:

    Merchandise Inventory Dec. 31, 1953......$ 9,486.85

    Purchases................................ 3,859.75

    Merchandise Available for Sale..........$13,346.60

    Merchandise Inventory June 30, 1954...... 8,342.79

    Cost of Merchandise Sold................. 5,003.81

Gross Profit on Sales.......................$ 7,320.84

Deduct Expenses:

    Selling Expense..........................$ 2,645.78

    Rent.....................................   832.34

    Heat and Light...........................   178.67

    Equipment Depreciation...................   312.97

Total Expenses.............................. 3,969.76

Net Profit..................................$ 3,351.08

R-52. PROFIT AND LOSS
STATEMENT

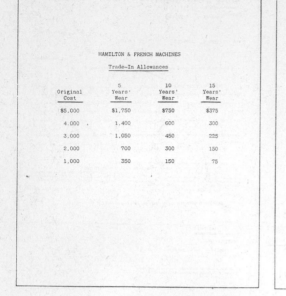

HAMILTON & FRENCH MACHINES

Trade-In Allowances

Original Cost	5 Years' Wear	10 Years' Wear	15 Years' Wear
$5,000	$1,750	$750	$375
4,000	1,400	600	300
3,000	1,050	450	225
2,000	700	300	150
1,000	350	150	75

R-53. TABULATION

Long column headings.

WILLIAMSON & CONNOLLY COMPANY

Prices of Leeds Rugs

SIZE	SPECIAL BRAND			SUPERIOR BRAND		
	Rose	Brown	Green	Rose	Brown	Green
9 X 12	$120	$125	$130	$150	$155	$160
10 X 14	150	155	160	180	185	190
12 X 15	180	185	190	210	215	220
15 X 18	210	215	220	240	245	250
18 X 21	240	245	250	270	275	280

R-54. TABULATION

Braced column headings.

HAMILTON & FRENCH MACHINES

Trade-In Allowances

Original Cost	5 Years' Wear	10 Years' Wear	15 Years' Wear
$5,000	$1,750	$750	$375
4,000	1,400	600	300
3,000	1,050	450	225
2,000	700	300	150
1,000	350	150	75

R-55. RULED TABULATION

Ruled on typewriter.

WILLIAMSON & CONNOLLY COMPANY

Prices of Leeds Rugs

SIZE	SPECIAL BRAND			SUPERIOR BRAND		
	Rose	Brown	Green	Rose	Brown	Green
9 X 12	$120	$125	$130	$150	$155	$160
10 X 14	150	155	160	180	185	190
12 X 15	180	185	190	210	215	220
15 X 18	210	215	220	240	245	250
18 X 21	240	245	250	270	275	280

R-56. RULED TABULATION

Ruled by hand.

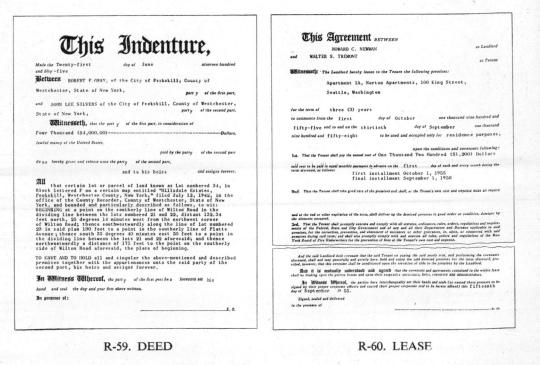

Know all Men by these Presents,

THAT I, LEONARD A. PERRY, of 376 Pleasantville Avenue, Brooklyn,
Kings County, State of New York.

of the first part, for and in consideration of the sum of Six Hundred Dollars————
————————————($600.00) Dollars, lawful money of the United States
to me in hand paid, at or before the ensealing and delivery of these presents by

William G. MacAvoy, of 879 Tremont Avenue, Brooklyn, Kings County,
State of New York.

of the second part, the receipt whereof is hereby acknowledged have bargained and sold, and by
these presents do sell grant and convey unto the said party of the second part, his
executors, administrators, successors and assigns one Hamilton All-Electric Kitchen
unit, Model Z-13475, Layout Pattern SW, consisting of six floor
cabinets and six wall cabinets, one complete double sink unit, and
one Hamilton Dishwasher.

To have and to hold the same unto the said party of the second part, his
executors, administrators, successors and assigns forever. AND I do for him and his heirs,
executors and administrators, covenant and agree, to and with the said party of the second
part, to warrant and defend the sale of the aforesaid Hamilton All-Electric Kitchen unit

hereby sold unto the said party of the second part, his executors, administrators, successors and assigns, against all and every person and persons whomsoever.

IN WITNESS WHEREOF, the part y of the first part ha s set his hand and
seal or caused these presents to be signed by its proper corporate officers and caused its proper corporate
seal to be hereto affixed, the fifth day of December 196 5

Signed, Sealed and Delivered }
in the Presence of

R-57. BILL OF SALE

This Mortgage, made the fourteenth day of October

nineteen hundred and fifty-five,
Between WARREN G. HELMFORD

, the mortgagor,

and CLAYTON W. LANSDALE

, the mortgagee.

Witnesseth, that to secure the payment of an indebtedness in the sum of

THREE THOUSAND DOLLARS ($3,000.00)————————————dollars,
lawful money of the United States, to be paid on the first day of January
nineteen hundred and sixty with interest thereon to be computed from this date
at the rate of five
per centum per annum, and to be paid annually on the first of January

according to a certain bond or obligation bearing even date herewith, the mortgagor hereby mortgages to the
mortgagee the two story dwelling located at 7346 Wingate Avenue, in the
city of Chicago, Cook County, State of Illinois.

And the mortgagor covenants with the mortgagee as follows:
1. That the mortgagor will pay the indebtedness as hereinbefore provided.
2. That the mortgagor will keep the premises insured against loss by fire for the ben-
efit of the mortgagee; that he will assign and deliver the policies to the mortgagee; and that he will reimburse
the mortgagee for any premiums paid for insurance made by the mortgagee on the mortgagor's default in so
insuring the buildings or in so assigning and delivering the policies.
3. That no building on the premises shall be removed or demolished without the consent of the mortgagee.

In Witness Whereof, this mortgage has been duly executed by the mortgagor.

In presence of:

ILLINOIS
STATE OF ILLINOIS }ss.:
COUNTY OF COOK
On the 14th day of October 19 55
before me came Warren G. Helmsford

to me known to be the individual described in, and who
executed the foregoing instrument, and acknowledged that
he executed the same.

R-58. MORTGAGE

This Indenture,

Made the Twenty-first day of June nineteen hundred
and fifty-five
Between ROBERT F. GRAY, of the City of Peekskill, County of
Westchester, State of New York, party of the first part,
and JOHN LEE SILVERS of the City of Peekskill, County of Westchester,
State of New York, party of the second part,

Witnesseth, that the party of the first part, in consideration of

Four Thousand ($4,000.00)————————————Dollars,
lawful money of the United States,

paid by the party of the second part
do es hereby grant and release unto the party of the second part,

and to his heirs and assigns forever,

All that certain lot or parcel of land known as Lot numbered 34, in
Block lettered F on a certain map entitled "Hillsdale Estates,
Peekskill, Westchester County, New York," filed July 12, 1942, in the
office of the County Recorder, County of Westchester, State of New
York, and bounded and particularly described as follows, to wit:
BEGINNING at a point on the southerly line of Wilton Road in the
dividing line between the lots numbered 21 and 22, distant 132.34
feet north, 25 degrees 14 minutes west from the northwest corner
of Wilton Road; thence southwestwardly along the line of lot numbered
23 in said plan 180 feet to a point in the southerly line of Platte
Avenue; thence south 35 degrees 40 minutes east 50 feet to a point in
the dividing line between the lots 21 and 22 aforesaid; and thence
northeastwardly a distance of 175 feet to the point on the southerly
side of Wilton Road aforesaid, the place of beginning.

TO HAVE AND TO HOLD all and singular the above-mentioned and described
premises together with the appurtenances unto the said party of the
second part, his heirs and assigns forever,

In Witness Whereof, the party of the first part ha s hereunto set his

hand and seal the day and year first above written.

In presence of:

_____ L. S.

R-59. DEED

This Agreement BETWEEN

HOWARD C. NEWMAN as Landlord
and WALTER S. TREMONT as Tenant

Witnesseth: The Landlord hereby leases to the Tenant the following premises:

Apartment 1A, Norton Apartments, 100 King Street,
Seattle, Washington

for the term of three (3) years
to commence from the first day of October one thousand nine hundred and
fifty-five and to end on the thirtieth day of September one thousand
nine hundred and fifty-eight to be used and occupied only for residence purposes,

upon the conditions and covenants following:
1st. That the Tenant shall pay the annual rent of One Thousand and Two Hundred ($1,200) Dollars
said rent to be paid in equal monthly payments in advance on the first day of each and every month during the
term aforesaid, as follows: first installment October 1, 1955
final installment September 1, 1958

2nd. That the Tenant shall take good care of the premises and shall, at the Tenant's own cost and expense make all repairs

and at the end or other expiration of the term, shall deliver up the demised premises in good order or condition, damages by
the elements excepted.

3rd. That the Tenant shall promptly execute and comply with all statutes, ordinances, rules, orders, regulations and requirements of the Federal, State and City Government and of any and all their Departments and Bureaus applicable to said
premises, for the correction, prevention, and abatement of nuisances or other grievances, in, upon, or connected with said
premises during said term; and shall also promptly comply with and execute all rules, orders and regulations of the New
York Board of Fire Underwriters for the prevention of fires at the Tenant's own cost and expense.

And the said Landlord doth covenant that the said Tenant on paying the said yearly rent, and performing the covenants
aforesaid, shall and may peacefully and quietly have, hold and enjoy the said demised premises for the term aforesaid, provided, however, that this covenant shall be conditioned upon the retention of title to the premises by the Landlord.

And it is mutually understood and agreed that the covenants and agreements contained in the within lease
shall be binding upon the parties hereto and upon their respective successors, heirs, executors and administrators.

In Witness Whereof, the parties have interchangeably set their hands and seals (or caused these presents to be
signed by their proper corporate officers and caused their proper corporate seal to be hereto affixed) this fifteenth
day of September 19 55.

Signed, sealed and delivered
In the presence of

_____ L. S.

R-60. LEASE

R-61. WILL

I, MARTIN L. TUCKER

being of sound and disposing mind and memory, and considering the uncertainty of this life, do make, publish and declare this to be my last **Will and Testament** as follows, hereby revoking all other former Wills by me at any time made.

First, after my lawful debts are paid, I give
and bequeath all my property and estate, real as well as personal, which at the time of my death shall belong to me or be subject to my disposal by will, to my wife, Margaret Alice Tucker.

Second, I hereby nominate, constitute, and appoint as this my Last Will and Testament, and I hereby direct that she shall not be required to furnish bond for the faithful performance of her duties as such executrix in any jurisdiction.

In Witness Whereof, I have hereunto subscribed my name, and affixed my seal, the __nineteenth__ day of May __in the year one thousand nine hundred and forty-five.

Witnesses:

_____

_____

_____

Subscribed by _____ the Testat_____ named in the foregoing Will in the presence of each of us, and at the time of making such subscription, the above Instrument was declared by the said Testat__ to be __ last Will and Testament, and each of us, at the request of said Testat__ and in __ presence and in the presence of each other, signed out names as witnesses thereto.

_____ Residing

_____ Residing

_____ Residing

R-62 POWER OF ATTORNEY

Notice: The powers granted by this document are broad and sweeping. They are defined in New York General Business Law, Article 13, sections 222-234, which expressly permits the use of any other or different form of power of attorney desired by the parties concerned.

Know All Men by These Presents, which are intended to constitute a *GENERAL POWER OF ATTORNEY* pursuant to Article 13 of the New York General Business Law:

That I, EDWARD C. CONWAY, of 978 North Williams Street, Rainey, Locust County, Kansas,

do hereby appoint

HAROLD S. TRETHAWAY, of 235 Summit Avenue, Rainey, Locust County, Kansas

my attorney-in-fact TO ACT

First: in my name, place and stead in any way which I myself could do, if I were personally present, with respect to the following matters as each of them is defined in Article 13 of the New York General Business Law to the extent that I am permitted by law to act through an agent:

To strike out any subdivision the principal must draw a line through the text of that subdivision AND write his initials in the box opposite.

(A) real estate transactions; [ ]

(B) chattel and goods transactions; [ ]

(C) bond, share and commodity transactions; [ ]

(D) banking transactions; [ ]

(E) business operating transactions; [ ]

(F) insurance transactions; [ ]

(G) estate transactions; [ ]

(H) claims and litigation; [ ]

(I) personal relationships and affairs; [ ]

Second: with full and unqualified authority to delegate any or all of the foregoing powers to any person or persons whom my attorney(s)-in-fact shall select.

In Witness Whereof, I have hereunto signed my name and affixed my seal this fifth day of July, 19 54

_____(Seal)
(Signature of Principal)

STATE OF Kansas } ss.:
COUNTY OF Locust

On the fifth day of July in the year one thousand nine hundred and fifty-four before me personally came Edward C. Conway

to me known, and known to me to be the individual described in, and who executed the foregoing instrument, and he acknowledged to me that he executed the same.

R-63. PROXY

241—Proxy.
JULIUS BLUMBERG, INC., LAW BLANK PUBLISHERS
71 BROADWAY and 1 RECTOR ST., NEW YORK

Know all Men by these Presents,

That I, THOMAS L. ROGERS

do hereby constitute and appoint DANIEL W. GRAYSON

Attorney and Agent for me and in my name, place and stead, to vote as my proxy at any election

of the stockholders of THE RONALD MOTOR COMPANY

according to the number of votes I should be entitled to cast if then personally present.

In Witness Whereof, I have hereunto set my hand and seal this fourteenth day of April one thousand nine hundred and fifty-five.

Sealed and delivered in the presence of

_____

_____

R-64. AFFIDAVIT

116—Blank Affidavit.
JULIUS BLUMBERG, INC., LAW BLANK PUBLISHERS
71 BROADWAY and 1 RECTOR ST., NEW YORK

State of New York, } ss.
County of Lehigh

Oliver T. Smith being duly sworn, says that

Ronald R. Jonesly, formerly a resident of Madison, Lehigh County, New York, was an employee of the Family National Bank of Madison, New York, during the period from May 13, 1947 to August 17, 1949, that in his capacity as fiscal officer from May 13, 1947 to August 17, 1949 he was entrusted with large sums of money, that when he left the employ of the Family National Bank of Madison his records were completely in order and he left no personal debts outstanding.

Sworn to before me, this twelfth day of January 1954

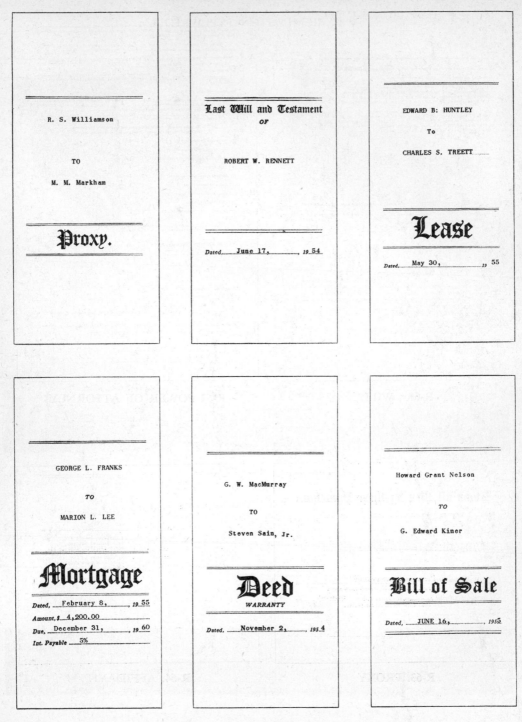

R. S. Williamson

TO

M. M. Markham

Proxy.

Last Will and Testament
OF

ROBERT W. RENNETT

Dated...........June 17,.................., 19.54

EDWARD B: HUNTLEY

To

CHARLES S. TREETT

Lease

Dated.....May 30,...........19 55

GEORGE L. FRANKS

TO

MARION L. LEE

Mortgage

Dated,.......February 8,......., 19 55
Amount, $...4,200.00.........................
Due,.....December 31,..........19 60
Int. Payable ....5%.....................

G. W. MacMurray

TO

Steven Sain, Jr.

Deed
WARRANTY

Dated,.......November 2,......., 195.4

Howard Grant Nelson

TO

G. Edward Kiner

Bill of Sale

Dated,........JUNE 16,.................., 1955

R-65. LEGAL TITLE PAGES

REMINGTON ELECTRIC   REMINGTON STANDARD

1. Paper Guide
2. Margin Set
3. Line Space Selector
4. Paper Release
5. Carriage Return

6. Carriage Release
7. Margin Release
8. Tabulator Set
9. Tabulator
10. Tabulator Clear

11. Variable Line Space
12. Line Finder
13. Ribbon Change
14. Ribbon Reverse
15. Motor Switch

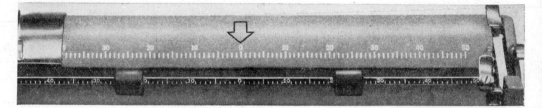

SETTING MARGINS

Move carriage to right or left as far as it will go. Hold down KMC key with right hand, while left hand moves carriage to position where margin stop is desired. Release carriage. Release KMC key. On machines with Remington's "Perfect Positioning Scale" above, set left edge of paper guide at white signal, margins at 30 and 30 for a 60-space line (zero is in exact center), 25-25 for a 50-space line, etc.

TABULATING

To set a tabulator stop, move carriage to desired point and depress the Tab Set key (A). Thereafter, to move carriage to that point, depress the Tabulator bar (B). To clear the machine of tab stops, depress Tab Clear key (C) while moving carriage from left to right. A single stop may be removed by tabulating to the stop, then pressing down the Clear key.

ROYAL ELECTRIC   ### ROYAL STANDARD

1. Paper Guide
2. Margin Set
3. Line Space Selector
4. Paper Release
5. Carriage Return

6. Carriage Release
7. Margin Release
8. Tabulator Set
9. Tabulator
10. Tabulator Clear

11. Variable Line Space
12. Line Finder
13. Ribbon Change
14. Ribbon Reverse
15. Motor Switch

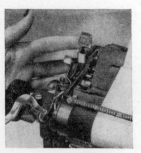

SETTING MARGINS

To set left margin, move carriage to point where the margin is desired, then flip the left margin lever forward and back again. To set right margin, position carriage where the right margin is desired, then flip the right margin forward and back.

TABULATING

To set a tabulator stop, move carriage to desired point and depress the Tab Set key (A). Thereafter, to move carriage to that point depress the Tabulator key (B). To clear the machine of tab stops, depress Tab Clear key (C) while moving carriage from left to right. A single stop may be removed by tabulating to the stop, then pressing down the Clear key.

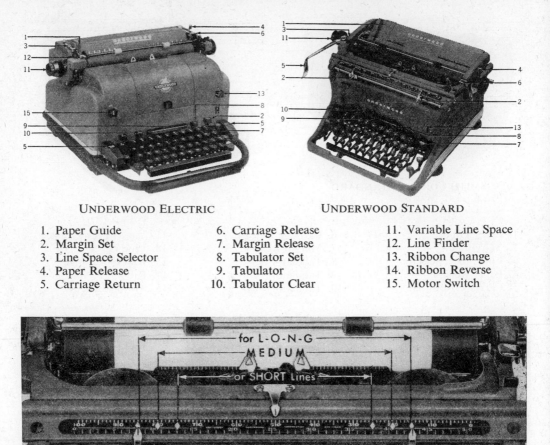

UNDERWOOD ELECTRIC   UNDERWOOD STANDARD

1. Paper Guide
2. Margin Set
3. Line Space Selector
4. Paper Release
5. Carriage Return

6. Carriage Release
7. Margin Release
8. Tabulator Set
9. Tabulator
10. Tabulator Clear

11. Variable Line Space
12. Line Finder
13. Ribbon Change
14. Ribbon Reverse
15. Motor Switch

SETTING MARGINS

The margin setting device on the Underwood Standard is located on the front scale, as shown above. Slide the left or right marginal stop to the desired position. Underwood's "See-Set" scales consist of a series of three diamonds on both right and left of the front scale — for short lines (inside diamonds), medium lines (middle diamonds), and long lines, (outside diamonds).

TABULATING

To set a tabulator stop, move carriage to desired point and depress Tab Set key (A). Thereafter, to move carriage to that point, depress the Tabulator bar (B). To clear the machine of tab stops, depress Tab Clear key (C) while moving carriage from left to right. A single stop may be removed by tabulating to the stop, then pressing down the Clear key.

R-69. SMITH-CORONA TYPEWRITER

R-70. IBM TYPEWRITER

SMITH-CORONA STANDARD

IBM ELECTRIC

1. Paper Guide	6. Carriage Release	11. Variable Line Space
2. Margin Set	7. Margin Release	12. Line Finder
3. Line Space Selector	8. Tabulator Set	13. Ribbon Change
4. Paper Release	9. Tabulator	14. Ribbon Reverse
5. Carriage Return	10. Tabulator Clear	15. Motor Switch

SETTING MARGINS—SMITH-CORONA

To set the right margin stop, move the carriage to the point where the margin stop is desired, flick the margin lever down and back. To set the left margin stop, move the carriage to the point desired and flick the margin lever up and back.

SETTING MARGINS—IBM ELECTRIC

Touch the carriage return key (for left margin) or move carriage to extreme right with carriage release lever (for right margin). Hold down margin set button. While button is down, move carriage to desired point. Release margin set button.

BRASS PLATEN FOR MAXIMUM COPIES

LABEL PLATEN FOR SMALL LABELS, CARDS

LIBRARY PLATEN FOR CARDS, LABELS

CARD PLATEN FOR GENERAL CARD WORK

10-KEY TABULATOR

This device is used for tabulating columns of figures with irregular left edge, such as in combining $10.15, $100.15, and $1,045.15. By depressing the proper tab key, the machine stops at the appropriate point for the amount to be typed.

FORMS FEEDING DEVICE

This Standard Register Dual Feed Device makes it possible to feed a wide form and a narrow form into the machine to be typed in one writing, and it keeps the multiple copies of the forms "in register."

AUTOMATIC TYPEWRITER

The "Auto-typist" makes it possible to type form letters automatically at speeds of over 100 words a minute. A perforated roll master is first cut, which then operates the typewriter.

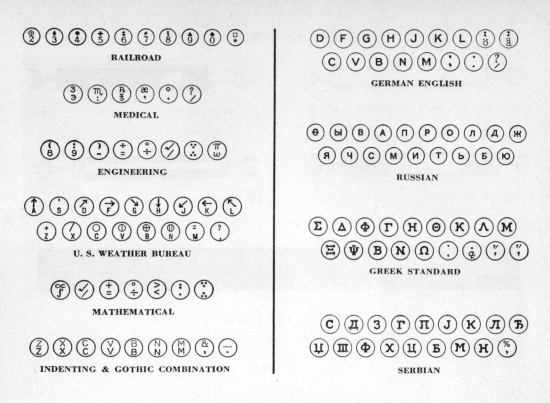

RAILROAD

MEDICAL

ENGINEERING

U. S. WEATHER BUREAU

MATHEMATICAL

INDENTING & GOTHIC COMBINATION

GERMAN ENGLISH

RUSSIAN

GREEK STANDARD

SERBIAN

R-72. VARIOUS SPECIAL KEYBOARDS

MODERN . . . . This is a sample
of 10 point Modern Type prepared on the
IBM Electric Executive Typewriter. The

REMINGTON TYPEWRITERS are available in a wide
range of type styles and keyboards to meet all
writing requirements. Remington Type is desig

ALPHABET KEYS HAVE FRACTIONS OR OTHER
SYMBOLS IN THE UPPER CASE OVER GOTHIC
CAPITAL LETTERS IN THE LOWER CASE.

REMINGTON TYPEWRITERS are available in a wide
range of type styles and keyboards to meet all
writing requirements. Remington Type is desig

THIS PART OF THE SPECIMEN IS WRITTEN IN THE INDENTING

R-73. VARIOUS TYPE STYLES

CHAIN FEEDING

Chain feeding can save much time not only in writing cards or short form letters, but also in addressing envelopes. To chain feed, carry the next piece to be typed to the machine and insert it before removing the completed piece. Then a single twirl of the platen knob removes one piece as the other is brought into typing position.

FEEDING CARBON PACK

An envelope or short piece of paper folded over the top of a pack of stationery and carbon sheets helps to feed a heavy pack into the machine evenly and saves the trouble of aligning the sheets after they are in the machine. Another method is to wrap a sheet of letter size paper completely around the platen and insert the carbon pack between the open flap of the paper and the platen, and feed through in the normal way.

"CROWDING" AND "SPREADING"

they had been

they have been

To "crowd," as in substituting *have* for *had*, first erase the incorrect word. Position the carriage where the first letter had been written. Space once. Hold the back spacer all the way down. Type the first letter. For each subsequent letter, space twice, hold down the back spacer and type the letter. To "spread," as in *had* for *have*, position the carriage where the first letter had been written. Space twice and hold down the back spacer. Type the first letter. For each subsequent letter, space twice, hold down the back spacer and type the letter.

they have been

they had been

SPECIAL CHARACTERS

Horizontal rule (underscore)................................ _____

Dotted rule (period)...................................... . . . .

Multiplication (small *x*)................................. 25 x 5

Minus (hyphen).. 15 – 5

Division (colon over hyphen)............................ 15 ÷ 5

Equal (two hyphens).................................... 10 – 5 = 5

Fraction (diagonal)..................................... 5/7

Degree (small *o*)...................................... 32⁰

Exclamation (Apostrophe and period)..................... !

Feet and inches (apostrophe, quotation).................. 5' 6"

In certain types of billing the words *at* and *cents* are designated by the symbols @ and ¢.
Depress the shift lock to type the underscore (6 key); release by depressing the shift key.

(Simplified)

1. *Line Spacing.* Use double spacing. Charge one error for every line wrongly spaced.
2. *Line Length.* Use a line length of around 60 to 75 spaces. One error for each line that is an extreme deviation.
3. *Paragraphing.* Use five-space indention for paragraphs. One error for each deviation.
4. *Punctuation and Spaces.* Punctuation and spaces are treated as part of the preceding word. One error if incorrectly made, inserted, or omitted, unless the preceding word has already been penalized. One error if incorrect spacing is used after a punctuation mark.
5. *The Dash.* Use two hyphens, without spacing before or after. One error if incorrectly made.
6. *Cut Characters.* Any word written so close to the top, bottom, or side of a sheet that a portion of any letter is cut off is counted one error.
7. *Word Division.* Any word wrongly divided at the end of a line is counted one error.
8. *Faulty Shifting.* Any capital letter typed so that only part of the letter appears is counted one error.
9. *Lightly Struck Letters.* If the outline of any letter is discernible, there is no error.
10. *Transposition.* Any transposition of letters within a word is counted one error. Words transposed are penalized one error for the transposition; an additional error is charged if there is a mistake within the transposed words.
11. *Rewritten Matter.* One error is charged for the rewriting, in addition to any errors that may appear in the first or second writing.
12. *Piling.* If part of a character overlaps another character, charge one error.
13. *Left-Hand Margin.* Except in paragraph indentions, if a line begins to the right or left of the normal margin, charge one error.
14. *Erasing.* The use of an eraser is not allowed.
15. *Last Word.* If the last word is not completed, but is otherwise correct, there is no error. If incorrect, charge one error.
16. *One Error per Word.* Only one error may be charged in any one word.
17. *X'ing.* Work in which material is *x*'d or letters are struck over will not be accepted.
18. *General Rule.* Every word omitted, inserted, misspelled, or in any manner changed from the printed copy, is charged one error.
19. *Gross Words.* In Typing Simplified, no computing is necessary to obtain the Gross Words on a 5-Minute Timed Writing. The figure at the far right of each printed line of copy represents the Gross Words a minute up to that point.
20. *Net Words.* If it is desired to adopt a ten-word penalty for each error, simply deduct 2 words a minute for each error from the Gross score on a 5-minute writing. On a 10-minute writing, this same penalty would mean a deduction of 1 word a minute per error.

INDEX

Numbers refer to lessons unless preceded by R, in which case the reference is to the indicated paragraph in the Reference Section. The reader is referred to the comprehensive Table of Contents at the beginning of *Typing Simplified* and to the Table of Contents of the Reference Section on page viii for much of the information ordinarily given in an index. Only the first occurrence of each type of office-style production work is indexed. Other lessons offering the same type of work may easily be found in the Table of Contents.